IMAGES
of America

TOWNS OF LINCOLN COUNTY

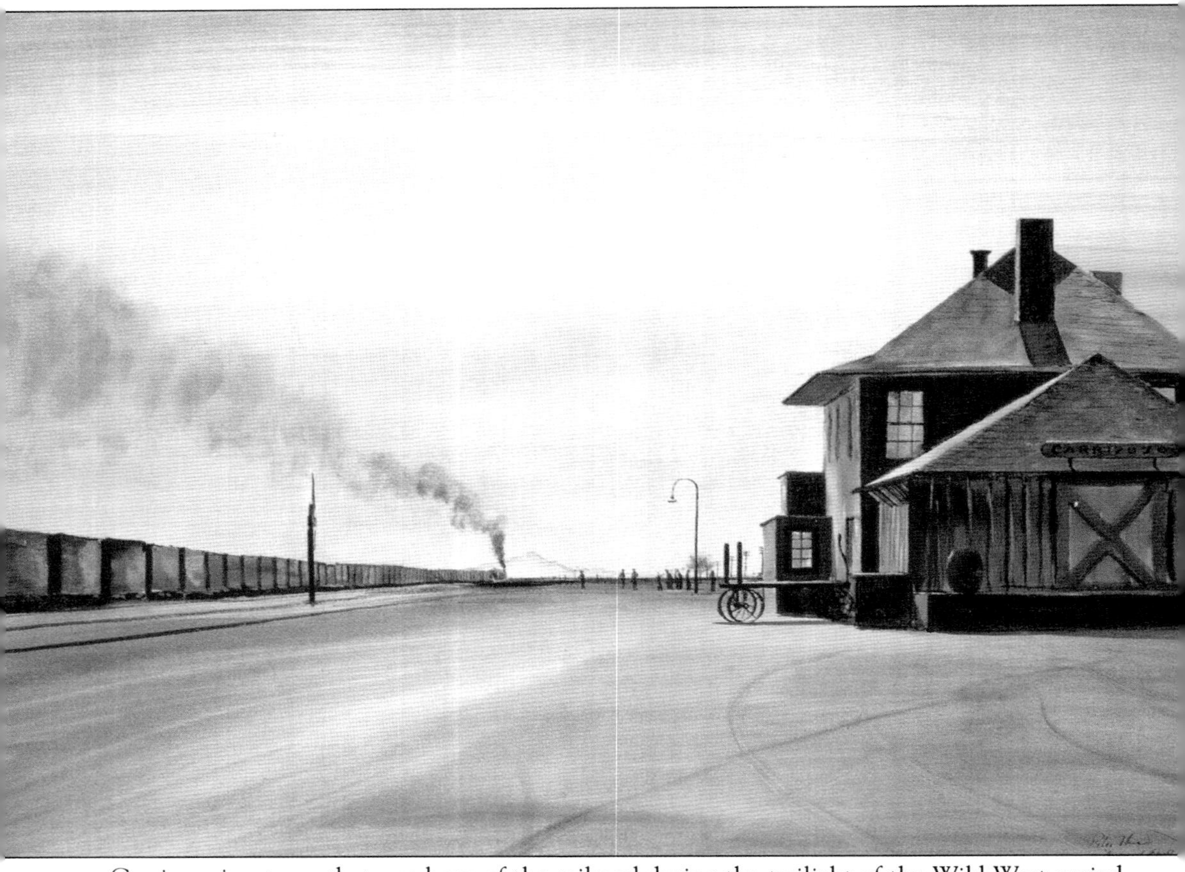

Carrizozo is a town that was born of the railroad during the twilight of the Wild West period. Located in the far western half of the county, Carrizozo became the county seat of Lincoln in 1913. The painting above, *Westbound Freight*, was created in 1940 by renowned Hondo Valley painter Peter Hurd. (Courtesy Michael Hurd and the Roswell Museum and Art Center.)

On the Cover: Fox Cave is a popular tourist stop and curio shop that opened up back in the 1940s on Highway 70. Before travelers stopped there on their way to or from Ruidoso Downs, Fox Cave was a hideout for Billy the Kid, or so legends say. It has recently been reopened as Fox Cave and Gem Mine, which also houses the Ruidoso River Museum. (Courtesy Historical Society for Southeast New Mexico #912.)

IMAGES
of America

TOWNS OF LINCOLN COUNTY

John LeMay

ARCADIA
PUBLISHING

ISBN 978-0-7385-7908-5

Published by Arcadia Publishing
Charleston, South Carolina

Printed in the United States of America

Library of Congress Control Number: 2009943322

For all general information contact Arcadia Publishing at:
Telephone 843-853-2070
Fax 843-853-0044
E-mail sales@arcadiapublishing.com
For customer service and orders:
Toll-Free 1-888-313-2665

Visit us on the Internet at www.arcadiapublishing.com

For my grandparents:
Lola and J. W. Patterson
Art and Clarena LeMay

Contents

ACKNOWLEDGMENTS

For writing this, my third title in the Arcadia Images of America series, I had more help in gathering images than in the two previous volumes. So if space is cramped here in the acknowledgements, please forgive me. First off, I thank my editor Jared Jackson for encouraging me to write this volume. And as always, I again thank the indefatigable Elvis E. Fleming for proofreading this work and the Historical Society for Southeast New Mexico (HSSNM) for providing most of the photographs. I also thank Karen Mills of the Lincoln County Historical Society, the Lincoln State Monument and the Anderson-Freeman Museum, Beatrice Sanchez at the Hubbard Museum of the American West, Lyn Kidder, Herb Brunell, Eleanor Bonnell, Virginia Watson-Jones, Neil Riebe, James Owens, Frederick Nolan, Bob Boze Bell, Robert McCubbin, Dean Wilkey and Stephen Hussman of New Mexico State University Library Archives and Special Collections, and Johnson Stearns.

As this is my last book for Arcadia Publishing, I would also like to say that this book was meant as an overview of Lincoln County but is not meant to be the definitive volume on any one of the towns therein. For instance, there already exists the wonderful *Ruidoso and Ruidoso Downs* from Herb Brunell and Lynn Kidder, and to anyone else who wishes to write a volume solely on Fort Stanton, Carrizozo, Capitan, White Oaks, or any of the other towns pictured in this book, the interest is certainly there. Arcadia Publishing will be more than happy to hear from you, and I and many others will be more than happy to read it.

INTRODUCTION

When driving west from Roswell to Lincoln County, the change is not always immediate. When first crossing the county line from Chaves County to Lincoln County, the landscape is dotted with prairie grass, yucca cacti, and sagebrush, for the most part the same. But after several miles, the change is evident. The climate, as if by magic, turns crisp and cool with a unique scent in the air, and the landscape quickly changes from that of the desert to the green undulating hills of a Peter Hurd painting.

One then enters the Hondo Valley, a land of ranches, giant cottonwoods, and rolling hills, making for a truly unforgettable landscape. It was here that painter Peter Hurd did most of his landmark work and inspired other artists such as Sydney Redfield and Kim Wiggins.

Traveling northwest from the Hondo Valley, one will arrive in the town of Lincoln itself, which used to be the county seat before switching to Carrizozo. Although Lincoln is no longer the county seat, it is still one of the most well-known settlements in New Mexico due to its Wild West past.

Just as the city of Roswell will always be known for flying saucer crashes, Lincoln and the county it is situated in will forever be the home of the Lincoln County War, fought in the later half of the 1870s over land and cattle. The war had such an impact on Lincoln that the small village still exists today as a New Mexico State Monument, with some calling the town a "living museum."

The story of the Lincoln County War itself has been told and retold time and time again in various books and films. And it is no wonder; the story has a cinematic flair of epic proportions with romance, gun battles, property destruction, betrayal, and ultimately, tragedy.

If one is to look through any book on Southern New Mexico, they will find a common thread in the form of the Lincoln County War, or if not the war itself then at least its star player, Billy the Kid. Ask almost anyone in Fort Sumner, Lincoln County, or Roswell about the Kid and they will claim to have had a relative that either rode with, hid, shot at, or was shot themselves by Billy the Kid. The young desperado was born in the slums of New York City or so the legend says. In reality, Billy the Kid's past can only be speculated upon, and two-thirds of his short life is widely unknown. The Kid has since become the focus of the Lincoln County War story for many, and accounts often begin with his story. But trouble had been brewing in Lincoln long before the Kid arrived on the scene.

Lincoln, at the time known as Las Placitas, owes much of its settlement to the military encampment of Fort Stanton. Back in the mid-1800s, even though the New Mexico Territory was property of the U.S. Government, it was not yet a state. In New Mexico at the time, the population was sparse, lawlessness abounded, and Native American raids were still in abundance there, while in more settled territories of the West, they had finally begun to cease. In the New Mexico Territory, Lincoln County occupied one-fourth of the territory itself, thus making it the largest county in the United States.

Fort Stanton was established along the Rio Bonito in 1855 as a military fort, which served the purpose of protecting nearby settlers from Mescalero Apaches, and sometimes vice versa by protecting the Native Americans from angry settlers. When the Mescalero Apache Indian Reservation was formally established in 1873, it became the fort's job to supply food and supplies to the Indians. Before the creation of the reservation, an honorably discharged major, Lawrence G. Murphy, who was stationed at Fort Stanton, decided to open up a general store, L. G. Murphy and Company, in 1866. This, it could be said, is where the trouble all started, as Major Murphy began his ascent to power. Even though the story of the Lincoln County War is painted in shades of grey and neither side was perfect in their morals, Murphy and his clan were clearly the villains.

Joining Murphy in business was a young Irishman who had also been stationed at the fort, James J. Dolan. Murphy took a liking to young Dolan, with many saying Dolan could be considered Murphy's adopted son. Dolan began as a clerk in the store, but with his stealthy negotiating skills he soon rose to the status of full partner. The store was a great success, so much so that in their dealings with the Native Americans Murphy and Dolan gained the backing of the Mescalero Apache, which made government officials decidedly nervous. Rumors circulated that L. G. Murphy and Company's contract as Indian agents was in fact fraudulent, and the company was backed by a higher political power known in New Mexico at the time as the Santa Fe Ring. Although its existence could not be proven at the time, the ring was supposedly made up of a powerful group of New Mexico lawyers and politicians headed by Thomas B. Catron, for a time a U.S. district attorney. Some even said that then governor Samuel B. Axtell was a member of the ring, and thus this group secretly ruled New Mexico in an intriguing example of Old West conspiracy.

Allegations that L. G. Murphy and Company was in league with the ring, and the fact that young Dolan had threatened a certain Captain Randlett with his life, resulted in their expulsion from Fort Stanton, with Captain Randlett calling their business a "den of infamy" in 1873.

Dolan and Murphy easily relocated their business to Placitas, now called Lincoln, where they already had a small branch established. The small adobe building proved too small for their needs, so Murphy built a much larger two-story structure, which easily made it the largest building in Lincoln at the time, and it still is to this day very day. "The House," as the business was unofficially called, soon gained a monopoly on all of Lincoln. Along with Murphy and Dolan's financial power, they also gained power in politics by installing their henchmen into various county offices.

Because of L. G. Murphy and Company's political power and monopolization of the area economy, which included lucrative government beef contracts, they were even able to force those that did not do as they pleased out of the area all together. They would then take the said person's land and rent it out to a new settler, even if the former person had legal rights to the land.

It was even said that Murphy and Company sold stolen cattle culled from the herds of New Mexico's richest cattle baron, John Simpson Chisum of Roswell. By this point, the conflict was set, and all it would take to explode into action was the arrival of several newcomers, among them a lawyer and his wife, a young English cattleman, and an even younger desperado destined to become Billy the Kid.

One

Lincoln and the Bloody Range War

Although the Lincoln County War had been brewing for a long time, it did not fully erupt until the killing of John H. Tunstall, a young Englishman with a ranch in Lincoln County who just happened to be in competition with L. G. Murphy and Company. It is no coincidence that a sheriff's posse from Lincoln murdered Tunstall in cold blood. One of the witnesses to this crime, and later an avenger to it, was William H. Bonney, alias Billy the Kid.

Tunstall and lawyer Alexander McSween had just opened up a new store in Lincoln. Although there were a few other general mercantiles in Lincoln, none of them could compete with L. G. Murphy and Company, none except for Tunstall and McSween's new store. Also backing the duo was cattle baron John Chisum, at odds with Murphy and Company for years since they occasionally stole his cattle and competed for government beef contracts.

Tunstall's brutal murder would be followed by several intense gun battles for the next year between the two sides. J. J. Dolan, who had since taken over for L. G. Murphy, and his followers had the law on their side (including backing from attorney general Thomas B. Catron). But McSween and Chisum also had their own makeshift posse called the Regulators, which were led by Tunstall's previous foreman, Dick Brewer. Among the Regulators members was Billy the Kid, Josiah "Doc" Scurlock, and Charley Bowdre. Over the next few months, battles were fought on the streets of Lincoln, Blazer's Mill, and culminated in a five-day siege at McSween's home in Lincoln where the lawyer met his untimely end.

Finally, Lincoln had even garnered Pres. Rutherford B. Hayes' attention. Hayes removed the current New Mexico governor Samuel B. Axtell from office and replaced him with Lew Wallace. With threats of martial law issued by President Hayes, the people of Lincoln began to simmer down, and afterwards Governor Wallace offered amnesty to anyone who would testify to the events of the so-called war. Although lawlessness would still be rampant, the war was over.

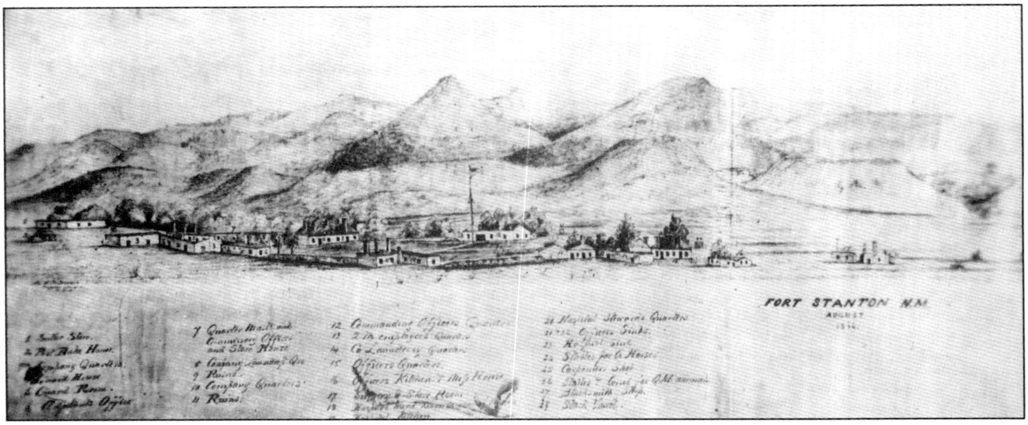

Above is a detailed drawing of Fort Stanton as it appeared c. 1866. After being deactivated as a military post in 1896, it was reopened three years later as a marine hospital, specifically for the treatment of tuberculosis, which led to several additions to the fort turned hospital. During the World War II years, Fort Stanton served as an internment camp for both Germans and Japanese Americans. In August 2007, Fort Stanton was finally recognized as a New Mexico State monument. Below is a view of Fort Stanton from the east in the 1950s. For a comprehensive history of Fort Stanton, see *Fort Stanton: An Illustrated History* by Linda Sanchez. (Above, courtesy HSSNM #1542; below, courtesy HSSNM #3213.)

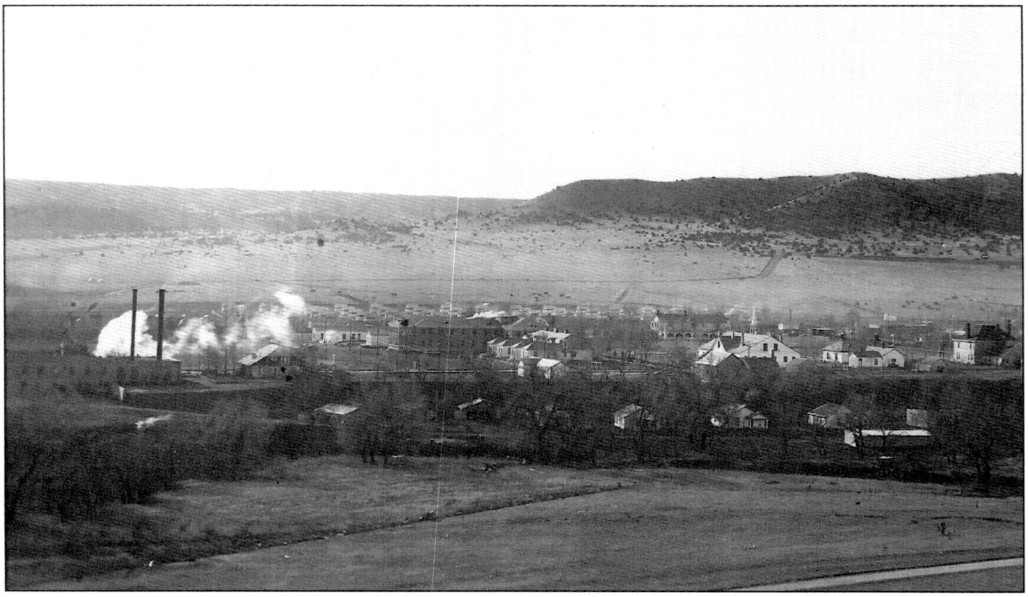

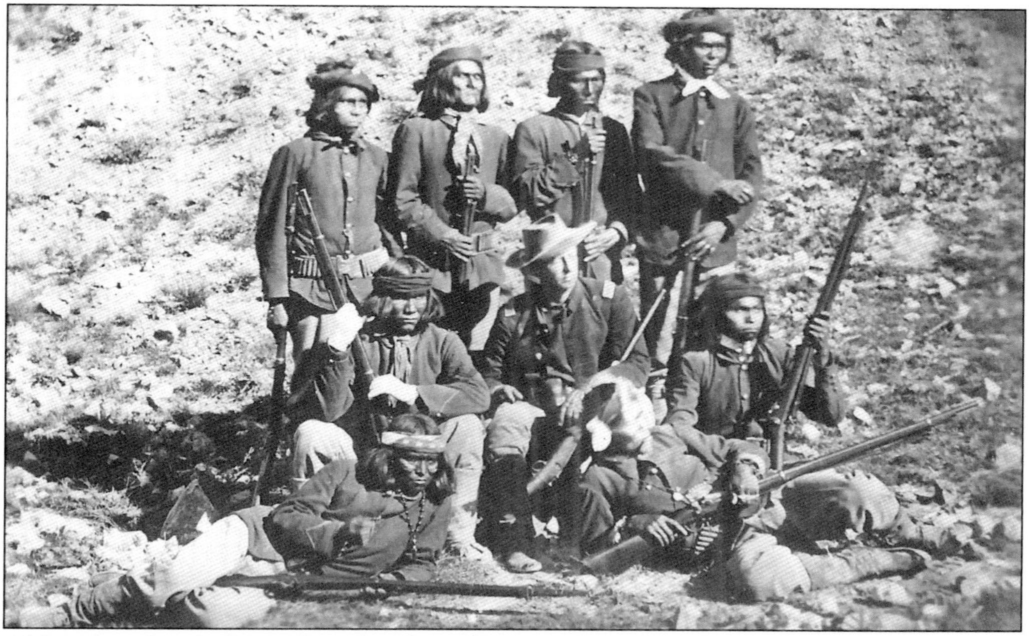

Although today the Mescalero Apache Indian Reservation is located in Mescalero in Otero County, it used to be located in the vicinity of Fort Stanton. Notice the Fort Stanton buildings in the background of the image below with the teepees. The reservation was established at Fort Stanton in 1873 by Pres. Ulysses S. Grant and later moved to its present location outside of Lincoln County in 1883. Above is a group of Indian Scouts from the Mescalero Apache Indian Reservation. (Above, courtesy HSSNM, Larkham Album #9 1998-2; below, courtesy HSSNM Larkham Album #8 4049-6.)

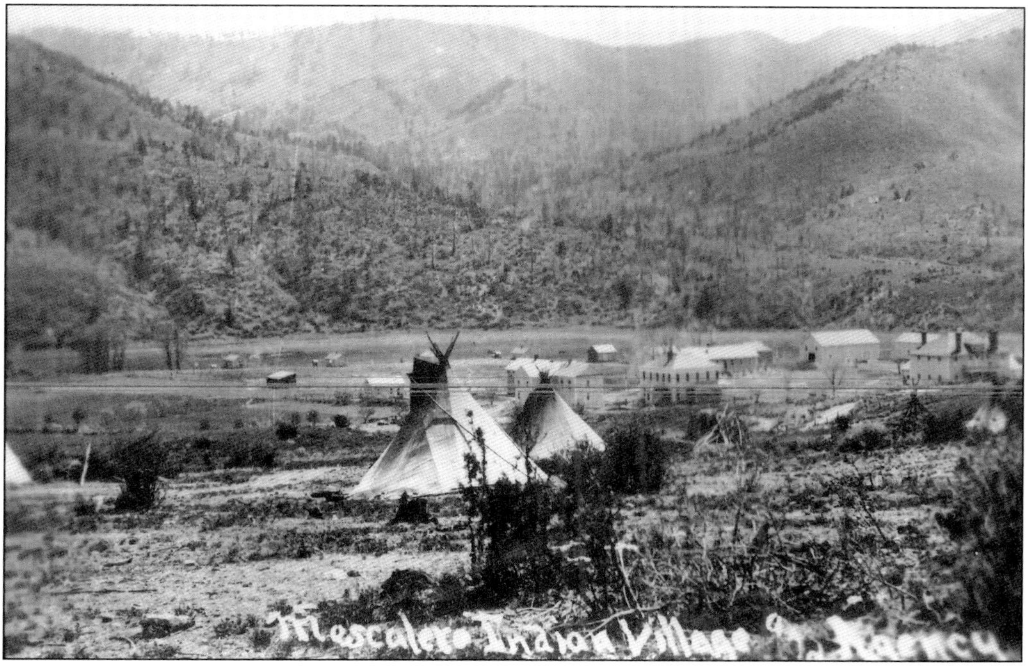

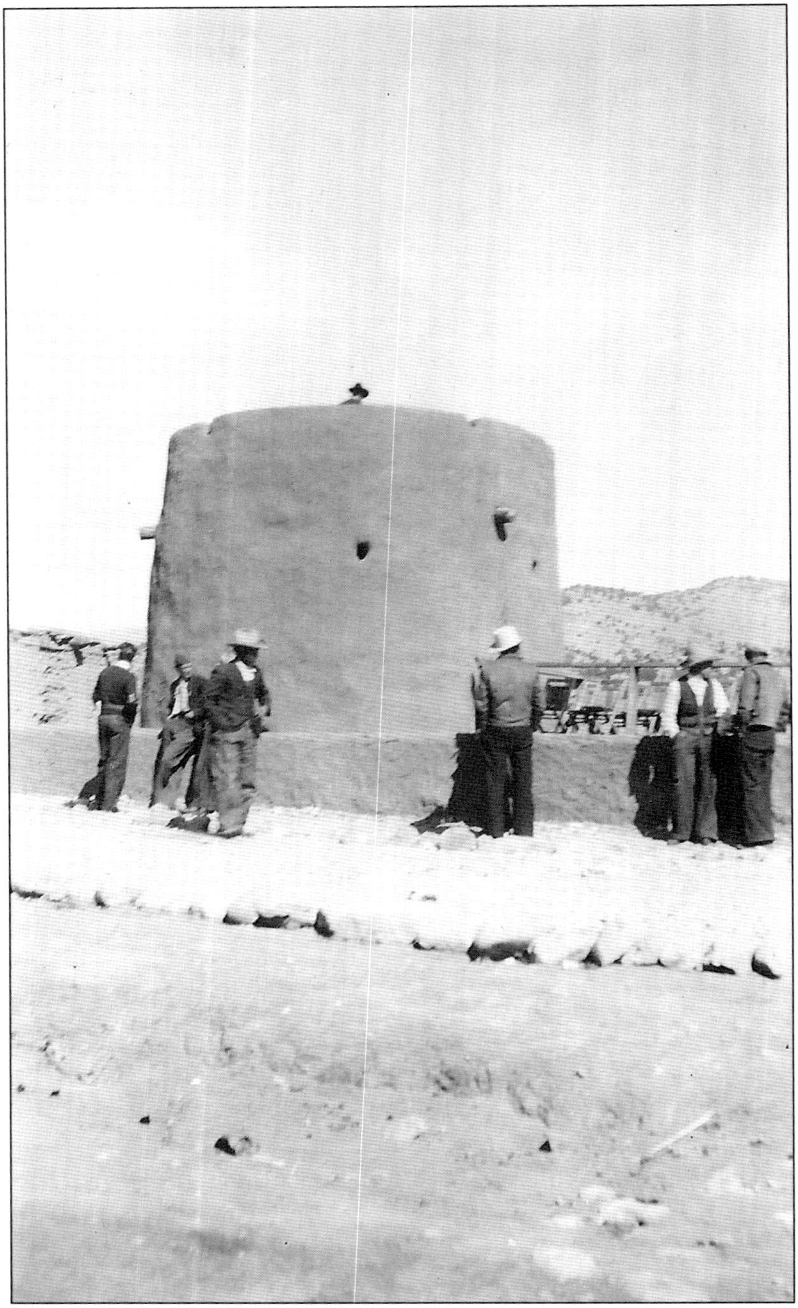

One of the oldest structures in Lincoln, dating back to its settlement in the early 1850s, is El Torreon. El Torreon translates into English as the fort. The purpose of the fort was to serve as a lookout point for the early Spanish settlers to spot approaching Mescalero Apache Indians. In the event of a raid against the settlers, El Torreon, with its thick stonewalls, became a fortress for them to hole up and defend themselves. During the Lincoln County War, it was used by some of J. J. Dolan's sharpshooters. The photograph above shows El Torreon and a few onlookers after a restoration that took place in the mid-1930s. (Courtesy HSSNM #389.)

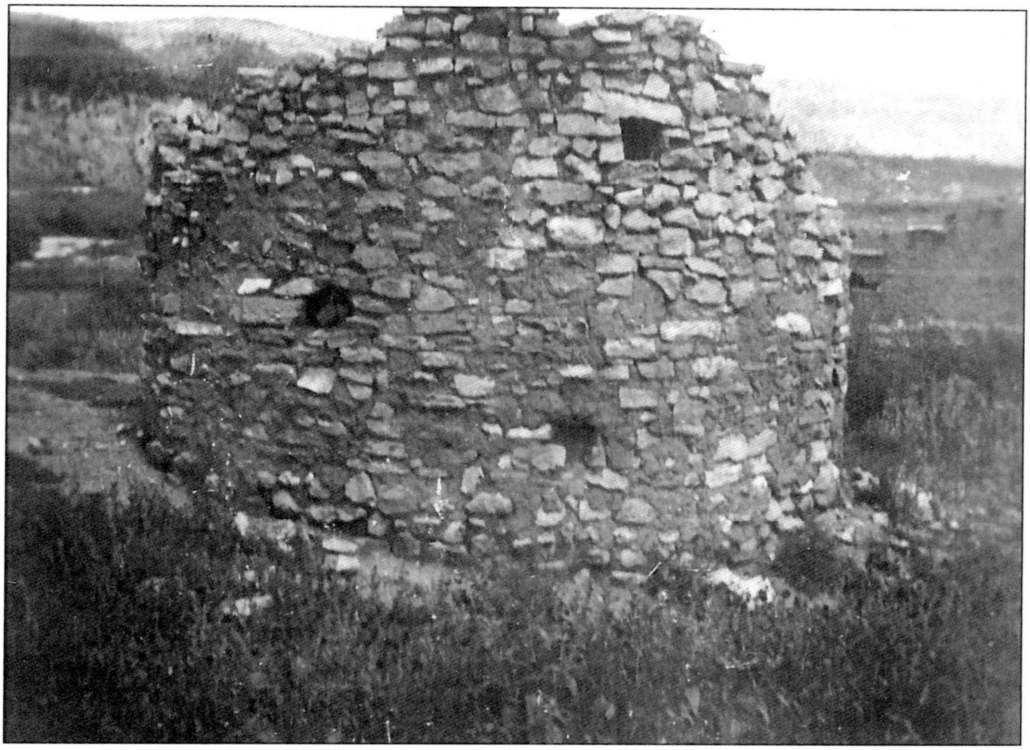

The above photograph shows El Torreon before its 1930s restoration. Around 1935, the Chaves County Archeological and Historical Society, today known as the Historical Society for Southeast New Mexico, came to Lincoln from Roswell to restore the old, decaying structure. Heading up the project was Maj. Maurice G. Fulton, one of the leading Lincoln County War historians, and Amelia Bolton Church. "The restoration at El Torreon was a vital part of the rebuilding of Lincoln as an historical attraction," wrote historian Elvis E. Fleming in *Roundup on the Pecos*. El Torreon can be seen again with several Lincoln residents in the *c.* 1939 postcard below. (Above, courtesy HSSNM #1275; below, courtesy HSSNM #3510.)

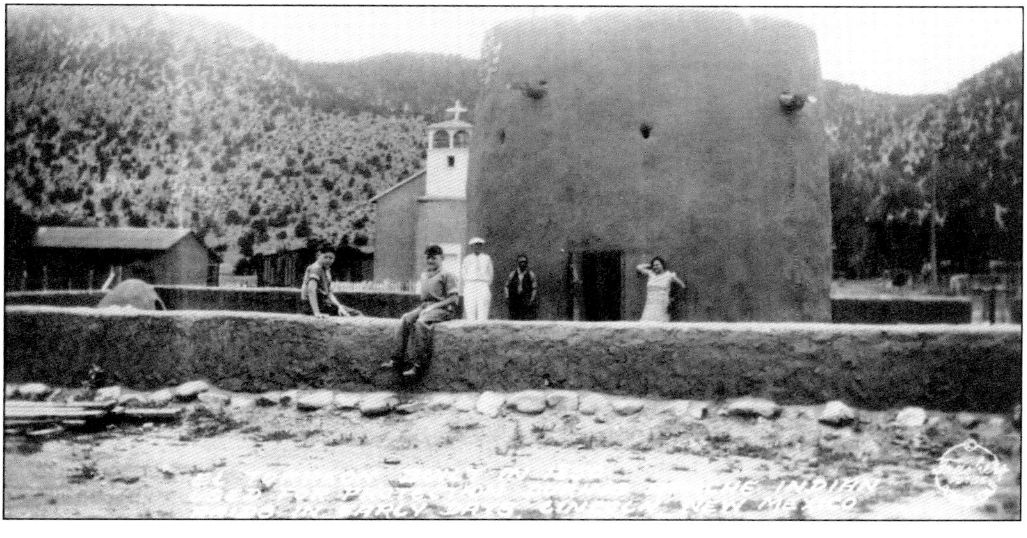

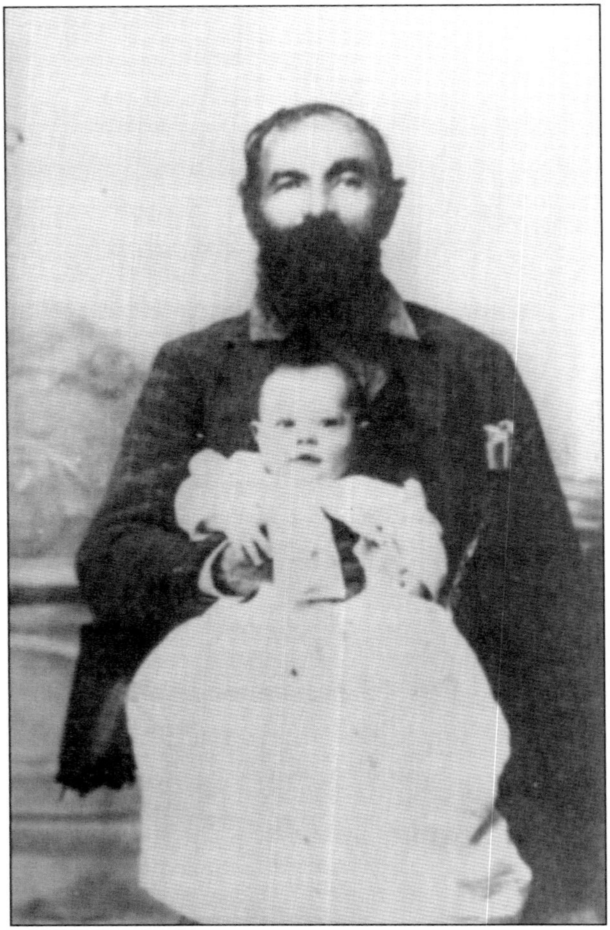

One would not guess it from the serene photograph below, but a lot of blood was shed in Lincoln during the later half of the 19th century. Lincoln was formerly known as Las Placitas Del Rio Bonito before the name was changed to Lincoln. The occasion was the creation of Lincoln County in 1869, which was at the time the largest in New Mexico and the whole United States. The county was almost named Baca County, in honor of Capt. Saturnino Baca, pictured left with his daughter, Charlotte, but Baca refused and said it should be named after the slain President Lincoln. Placitas was chosen as the county seat because of its close proximity to Fort Stanton, while others such as Tularosa, San Patricio, and Presidio de la Luz were deemed too far away. (Left, courtesy Robert McCubbin; below, courtesy HSSNM #590.)

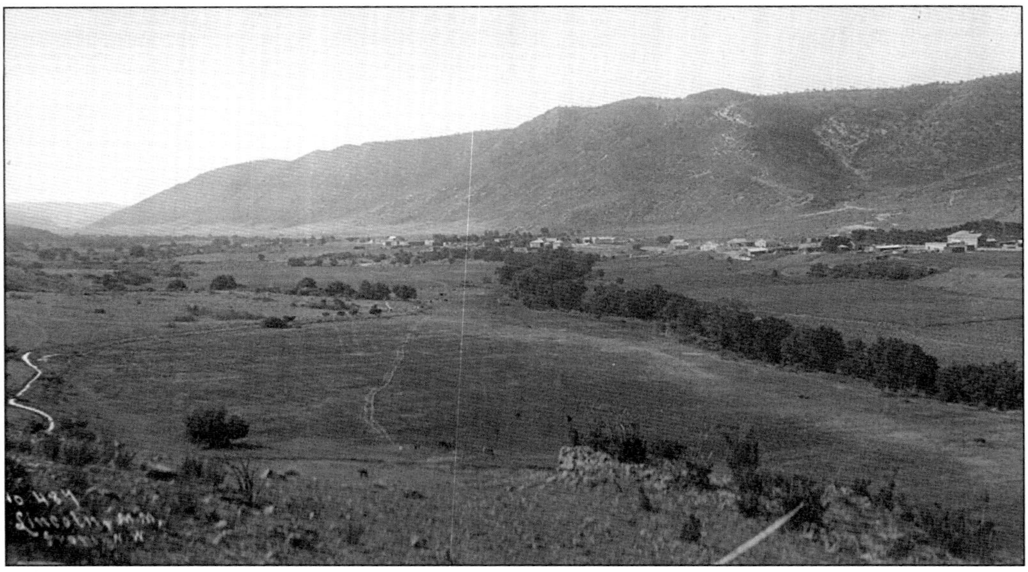

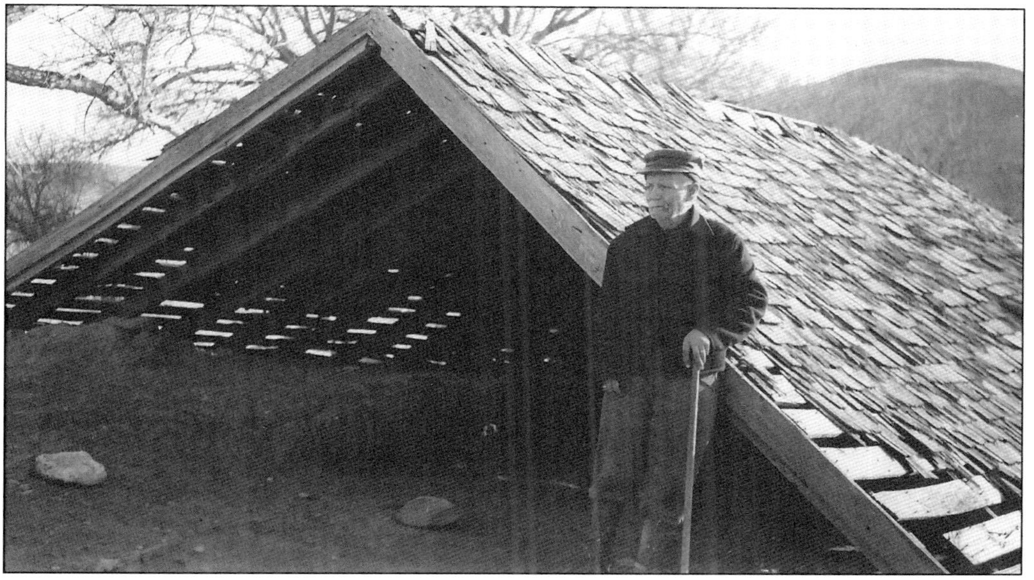

Before the Lincoln County War officially commenced, the first killing in relation to the animosity of the people of Lincoln towards Lawrence G. Murphy was that of Robert Casey. Casey, whose mill and a relative, Ad Casey, are pictured above, was murdered in the streets of Lincoln after a heated political convention in which he berated Murphy in 1875. More famous is the execution of Casey's killer, William Wilson, in the case of the famous double hanging. Wilson was to be hung from the gallows until dead. After hanging for nine and a half minutes, the body was cut down and put into a casket, until it was evident that Wilson was not yet dead. Wilson was then hung again for 20 minutes and then placed in his coffin for good. Below is the Casey home. (Above, courtesy HSSNM #1444E; below, courtesy HSSNM #1444F.)

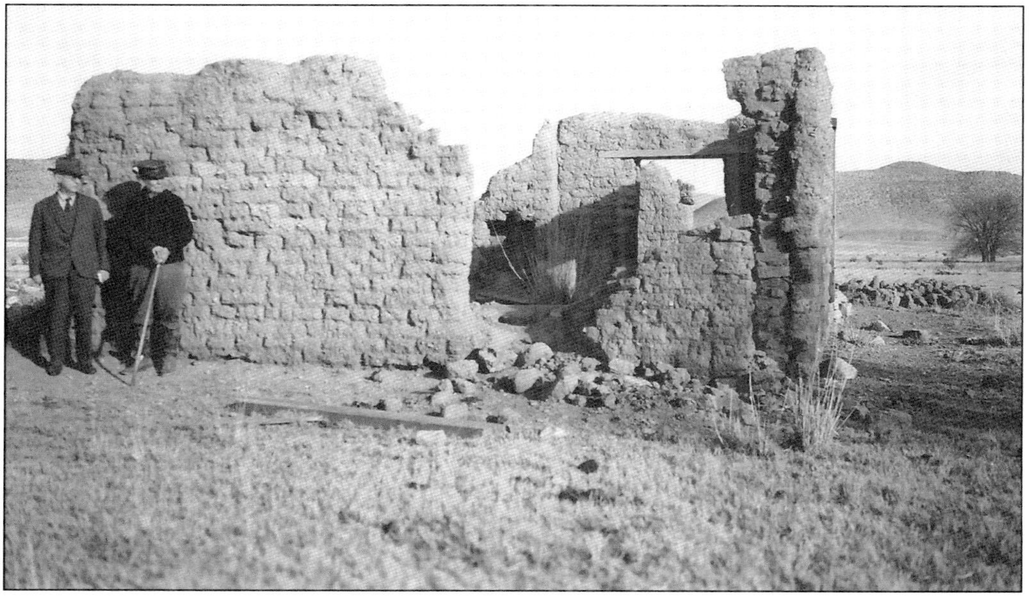

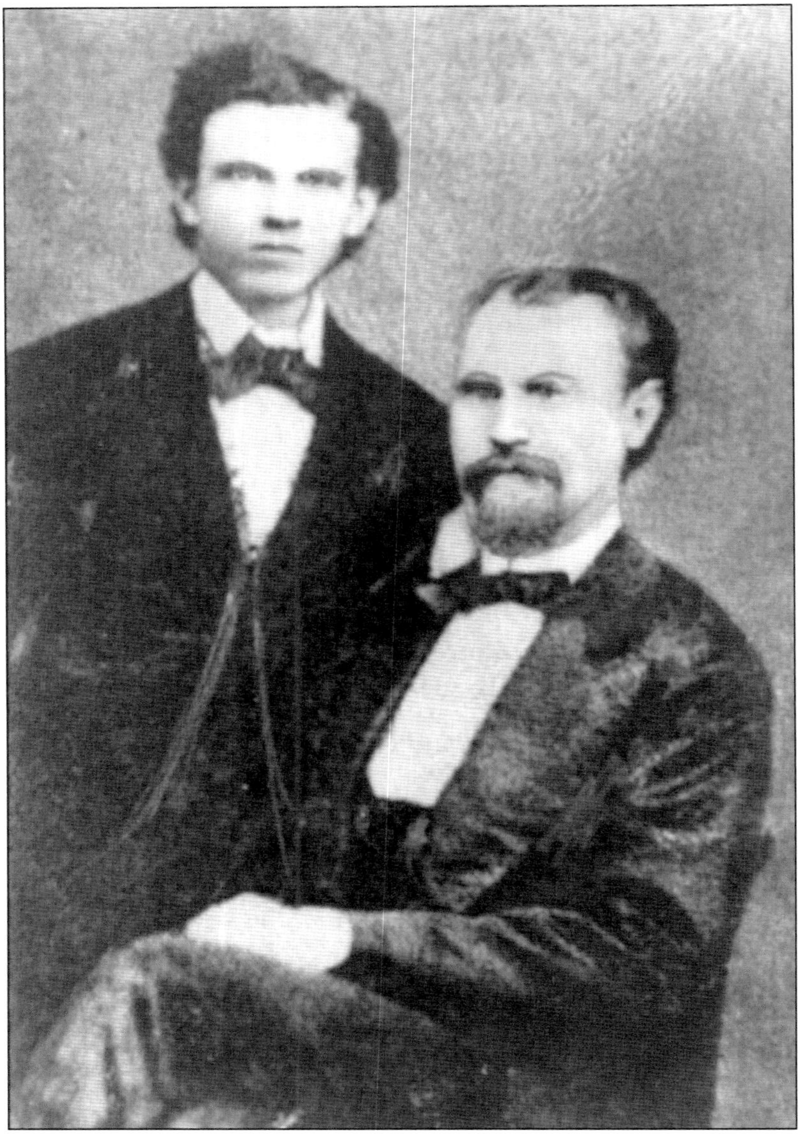

The masterminds behind L. G. Murphy and Company pictured are James J. Dolan, standing on left, and Maj. Lawrence G. Murphy, sitting on the right. Ironically enough, Murphy had studied for the priesthood in his native Ireland before coming to America and joining the army. For a time he was a lieutenant under Col. Kit Carson in the First New Mexico Cavalry, and then later, while under Carson during the 1863 Navajo campaign, he was promoted to major at Fort Stanton. After being honorably discharged at Fort Stanton, Emil Fritz and Murphy began the Murphy and Fritz Company, a post trading business at the fort. When Fritz died, Murphy changed the name of the business to L. G. Murphy and Company. Eventually James J. Dolan, a young Irishman also discharged from Fort Stanton, began working as a clerk at L. G. Murphy and Company. By the time of the duo's expulsion from Fort Stanton, young James was a full partner. When the business moved to Lincoln, Murphy would eventually turn the firm over to Dolan, who renamed it J. J. Dolan and Company, even though most still referred to it as the Murphy store. (Courtesy Robert McCubbin.)

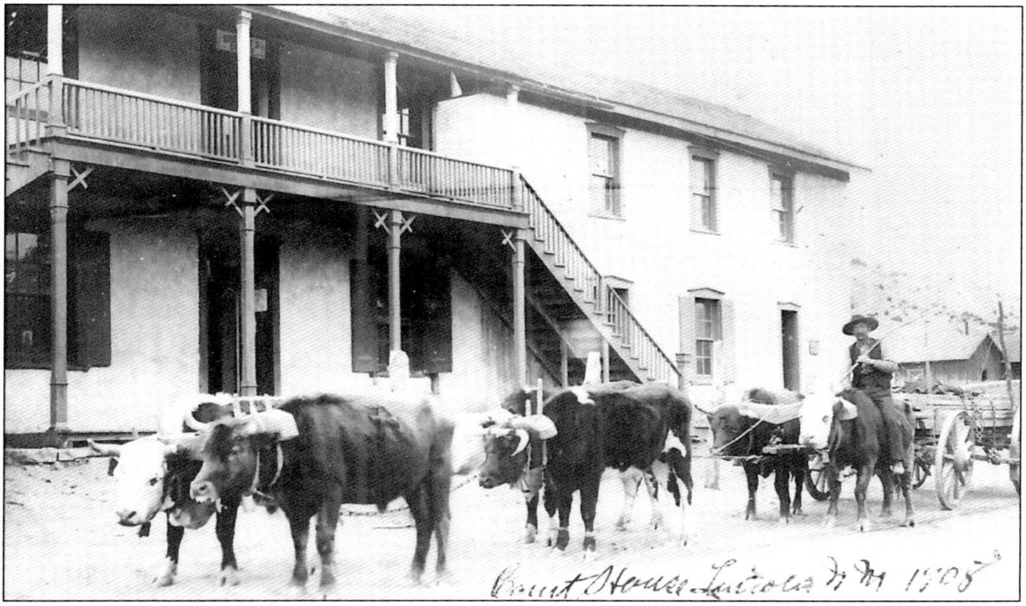

The photograph above shows the last oxen train in Lincoln around 1908 in front of the courthouse, which was originally built as L. G. Murphy's store. "The House," as it was called during L.G. Murphy and Company's reign, was a large, two-story structure and the most impressive building in the whole county outside of Fort Stanton itself. It consisted of two floors; on the first was the store itself as well as various offices, a saloon, and even a gambling hall. The second floor served as living quarters. L. G. Murphy and Company became J. J. Dolan and Company in March 1877 as the Lincoln County War troubles had just begun to heat up. Murphy, a heavy drinker, had recently suffered a breakdown and thus isolated himself from the war troubles. (Above, courtesy HSSNM, Larkham Album 3 #495; below, courtesy HSSNM, Larkham Album 3 #484.)

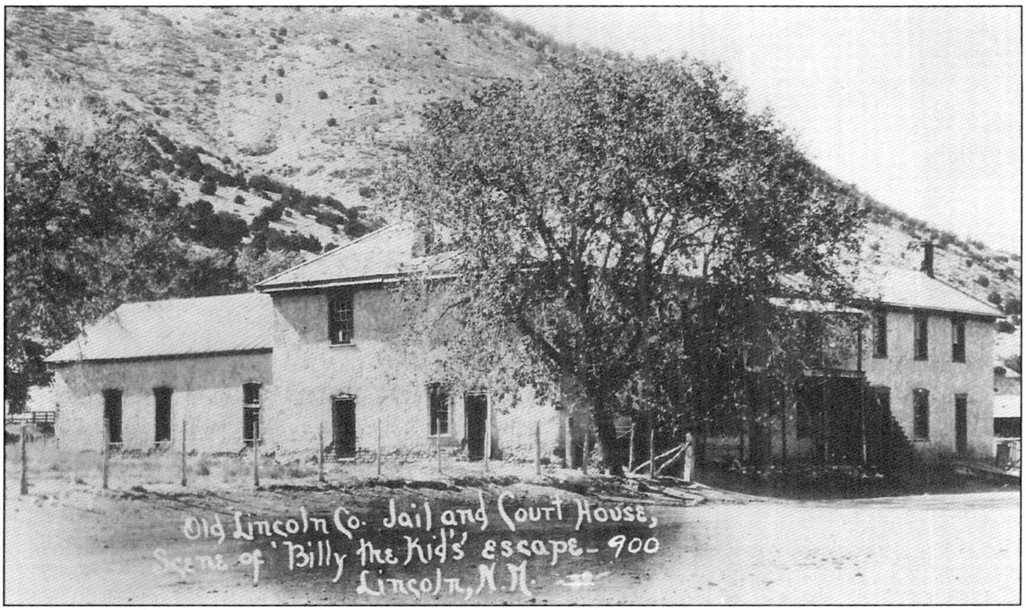

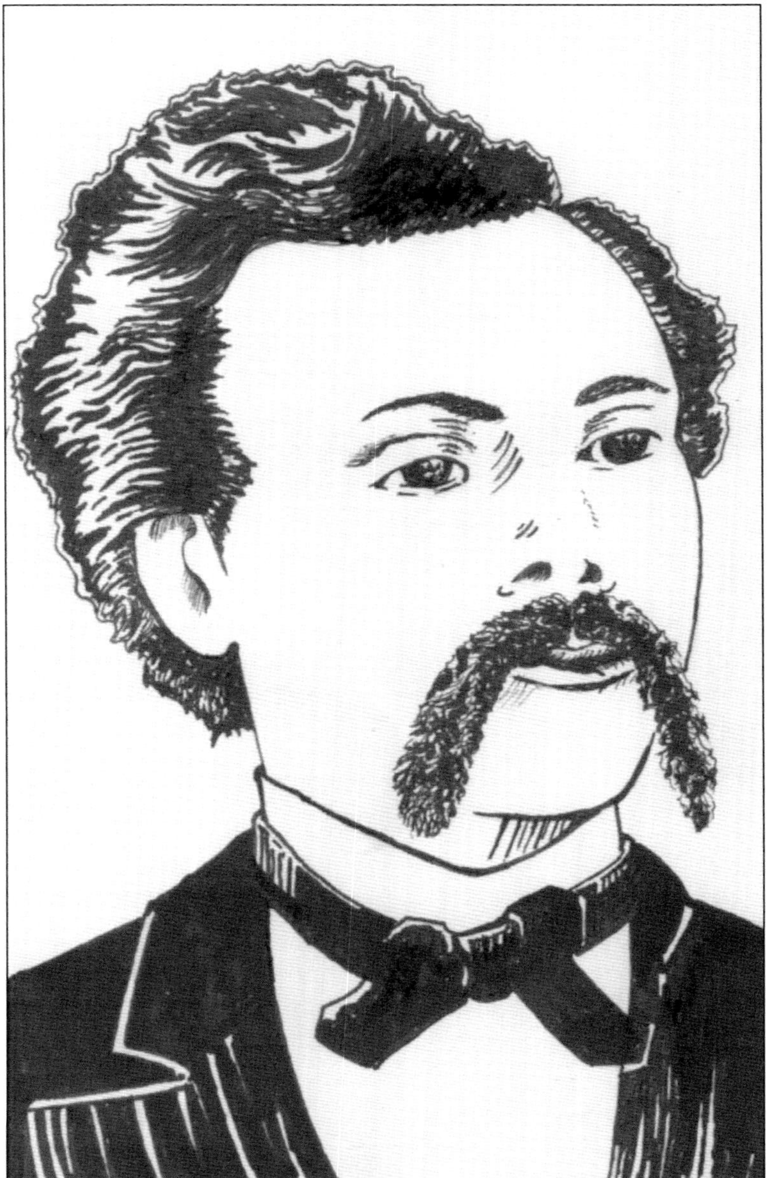

Alexander McSween, above, and his young bride, Susan, were en route to Santa Fe when they had a chance meeting with Miguel Antonio Otero, a future governor of New Mexico, at camp Punta de Agua. McSween was born to Scottish parents on Prince Edward Island and planned on become a protestant minister before he migrated to the sates to become a lawyer. When Otero learned McSween was looking for a place to practice, he told him he should go to Lincoln and off the McSweens went, arriving there in 1875. It was not long before McSween caught on to the tyranny of the Murphy clan and aligned himself with a young Englishman in his early 20s, John H. Tunstall. Tunstall arrived in Lincoln in November 1876, and it did not take him long to stir up trouble. In less than a year and a half, the Murphy-Dolan party murdered him. The object of their ire: Tunstall opened his own store called J. H. Tunstall and Company to compete with Murphy's. (Courtesy Neil Riebe.)

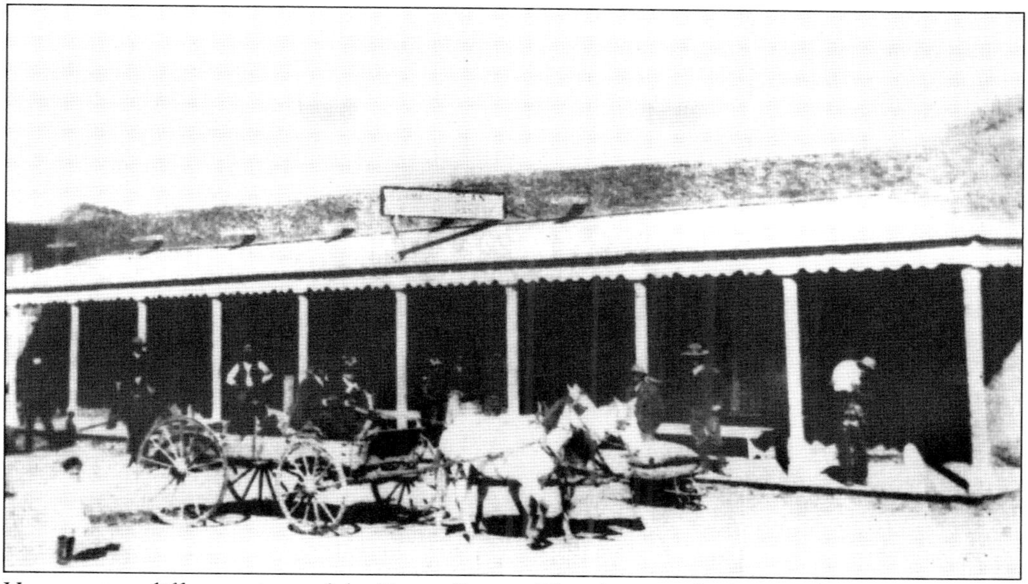

Here are two different views of the Tunstall store. The photograph above is from the late 1800s, and below is a more contemporary view from the 20th century. The store was a great success with the people of Lincoln who were eager to get out from under the Dolan firm's heavy thumb (and prices) when it first opened. Anticipating tough times, Tunstall and McSween had the store built with thick, bulletproof adobe walls and window shutters with steel plates that were placed in between the wood planks. The decision was a wise one as J. J. Dolan and Company quickly became at odds with their new competitor. The store was later taken over by the Pennfield family and still stands in Lincoln today as a museum. (Above, courtesy Robert McCubbin; below, courtesy Lincoln State Monument and the Anderson-Freeman Museum.)

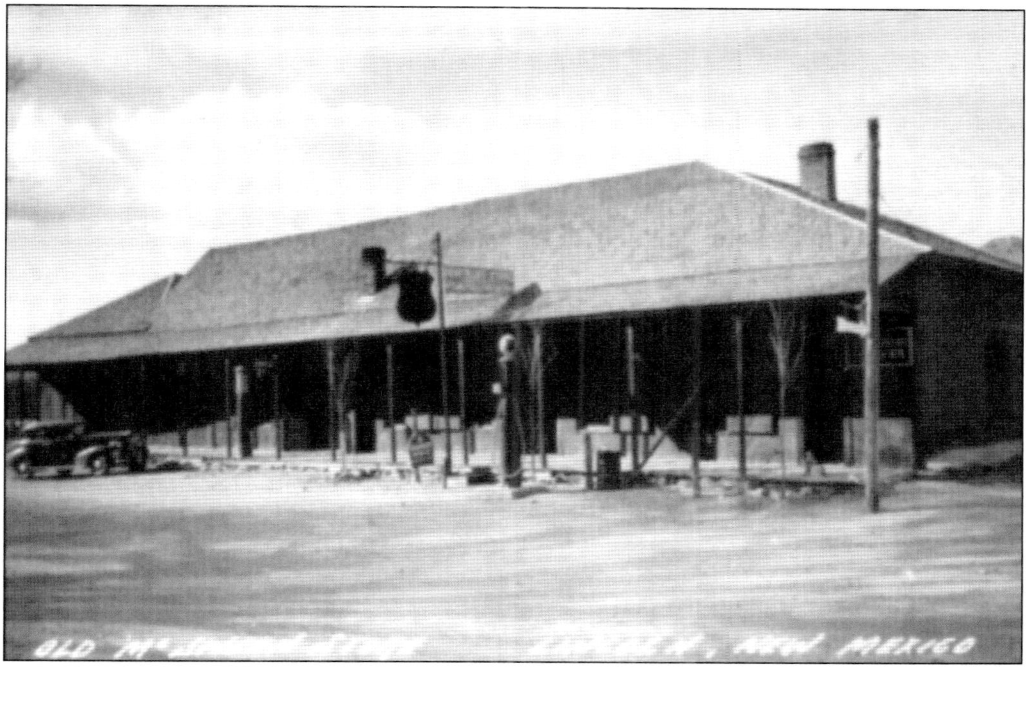

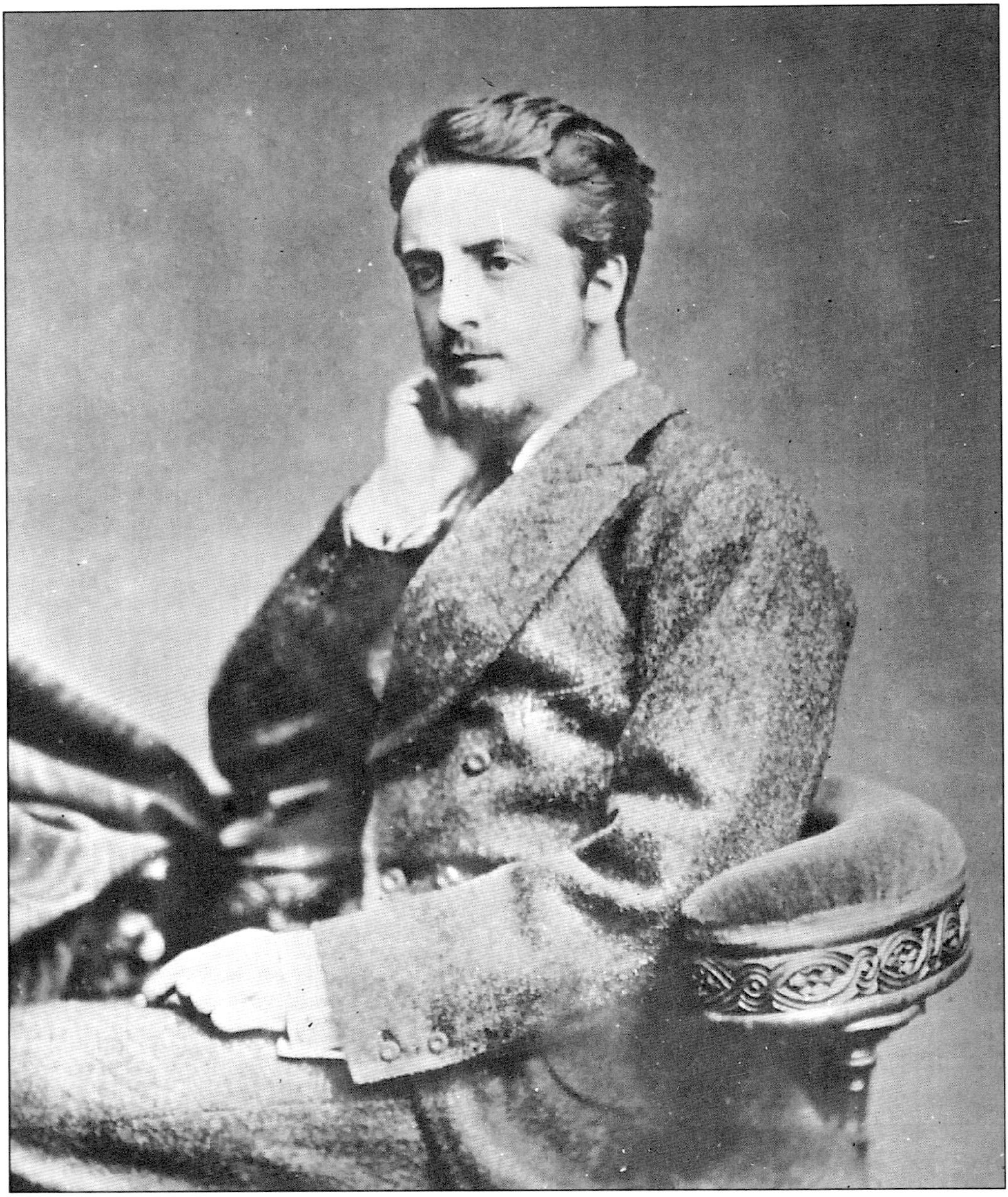

Although John Tunstall, above, is often portrayed as an older man in films based on the Lincoln County War, such as *Young Guns*, Tunstall was in fact not much older than Billy the Kid. The events leading up to Tunstall's death are somewhat complicated, but in short, even though animosity had always existed between Tunstall and the Dolan party, the proverbial straw that broke the camel's back was the matter of some uncollected life insurance. Emil Fritz, Lawrence Murphy's former partner, had passed away with McSween handling the life insurance, which he believed should go to Fritz's heirs. J. J. Dolan believed it should go to J. J. Dolan and Company. Dolan then took legal action against McSween, trying to possess some of his cattle, which eventually led a posse to Tunstall's ranch to obtain said cattle. Tunstall decided to go to Lincoln with a small herd of horses in hopes of settling the complicated legal matter. (Courtesy Fredrick Nolan.)

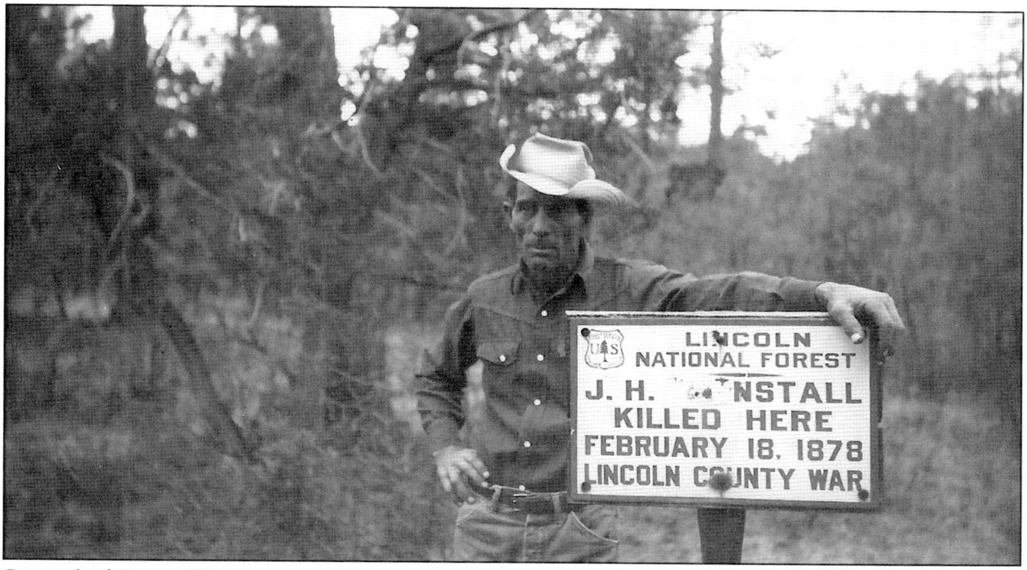

Several of Tunstall's men were with him on his way to Lincoln, among them William H. Bonney and Dick Brewer. Unbeknownst to them, a deputy sheriff's posse under the leadership of J. Billy Mathews consisting of nearly 20 men, among them outlaw Jesse Evans, was headed to intercept them. What happened when the two crossed paths is heavily debated, but it seems some of Tunstall's men had gone off to chase some wild turkeys. Tunstall approached the posse with peaceful intentions and was shot by Buck Morton and then again by Jesse Evans, who also killed Tunstall's horse. When Tunstall's men arrived at the fray, they decided not to pursue, being wildly outnumbered. At the marker (above) commemorating Tunstall's death is prominent Hondo area rancher Ralph Bonnell and again to the right with his son, David, in 1957. (Above, courtesy HSSNM #4044D; right, courtesy HSSNM #4709.)

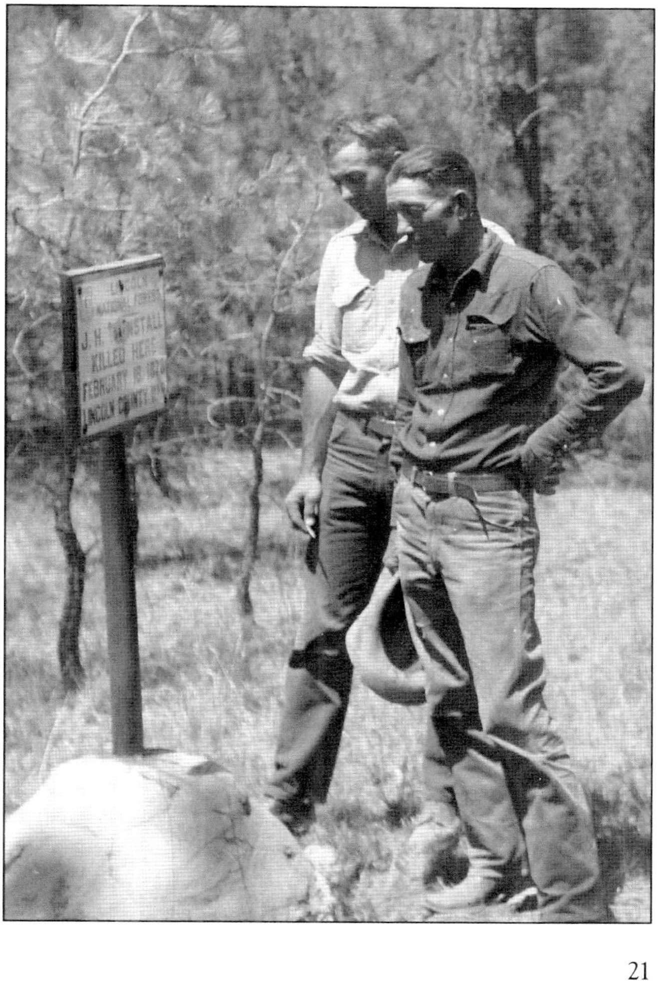

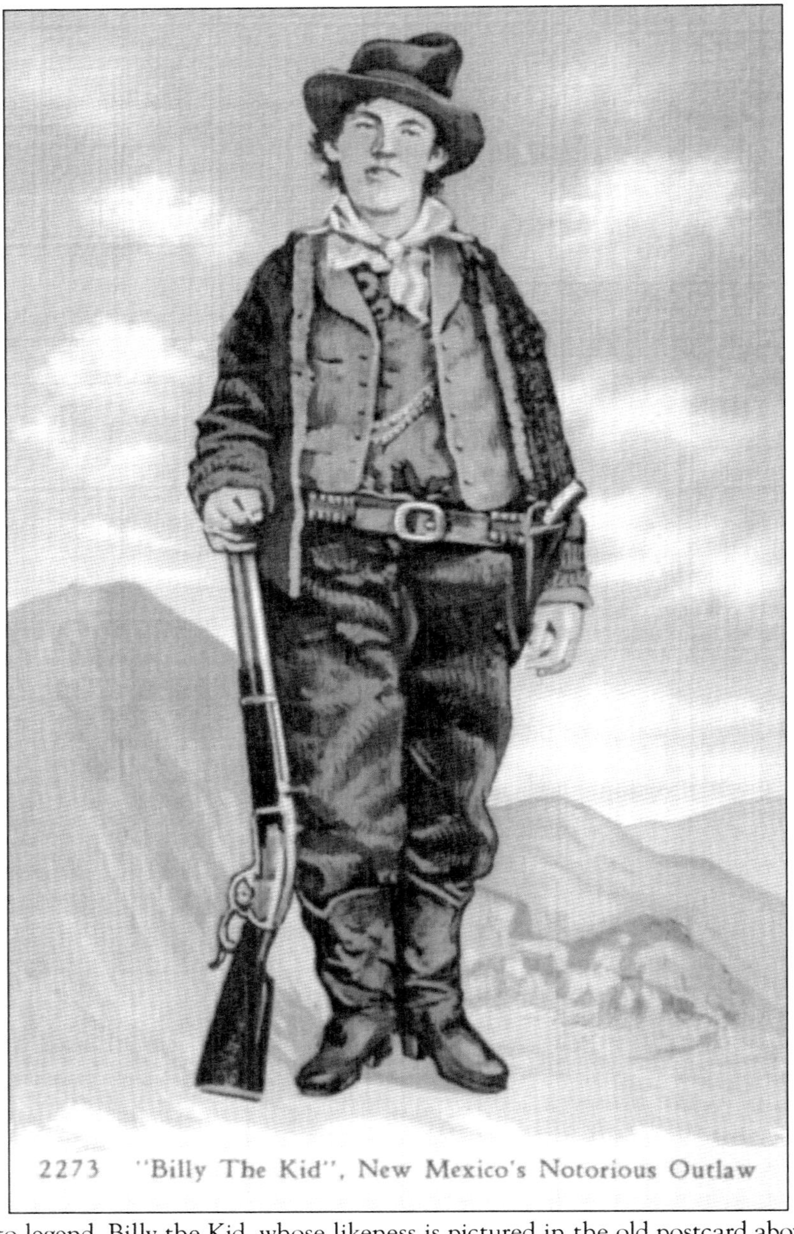

Contrary to legend, Billy the Kid, whose likeness is pictured in the old postcard above, did not kill 21 men (one for each year of his life) and where he was born is still uncertain. Historians do know he was born William Henry McCarty in November 1859 to Catherine and Michael McCarty (killed in the Civil War). Catherine was remarried to Henry Antrim and moved to Silver City with her two young sons and died in 1874. The Kid's first crime was committed at age 15 when he helped steal some Chinese laundry, wherein he was arrested and easily escaped. He killed his first man in self-defense in Arizona at age 17, after which he headed for New Mexico and fell in with outlaw Jesse Evans and his gang. By November 1877, he was making an honest living as William H. Bonney under the employment of John Tunstall, and the rest, as they say, is history. (Courtesy HSSNM #914.)

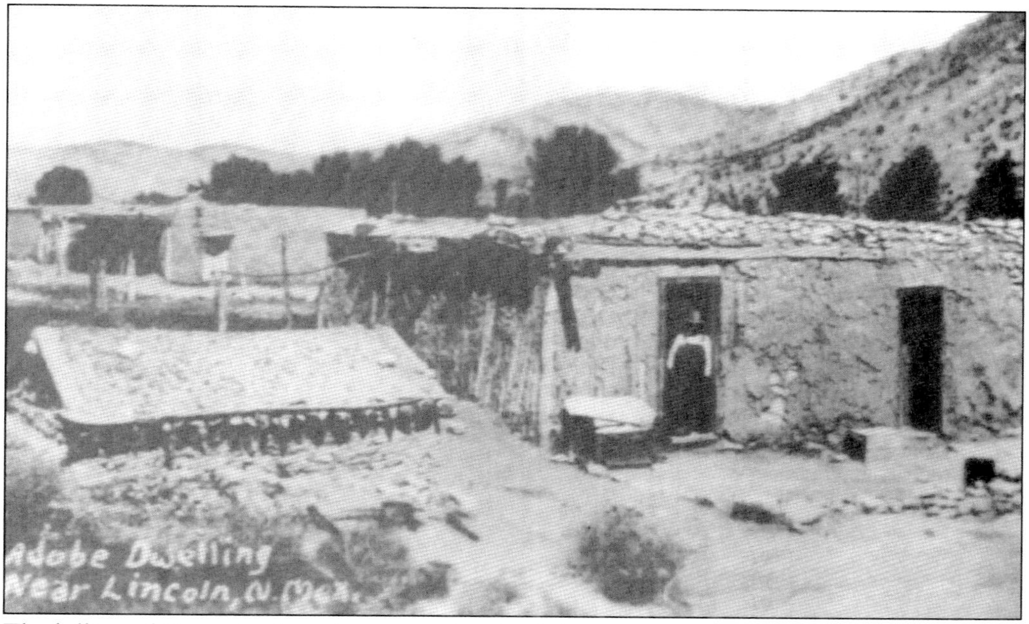

The killing of Tunstall affected everyone involved, but none more vengefully than William H. Bonney, aka Billy the Kid, who vowed to track down and avenge all of Tunstall's killers. What John Tunstall thought of Billy Bonney can only be speculated, but Bonney himself greatly admired the Englishman, in part because he had given Bonney a horse, a saddle, and some new guns. Some said this was the first present the Kid had ever received. The Kid was particularly well liked by the Mexican American settlers in the region, who lived in adobe homes like the one shown above. The Kid was also popular at dances, such as the ones held in the San Juan Church pictured below, with the Mexican girls. However, he never attended a dance at San Juan, as it was not built until after his death. (Above, courtesy Lincoln State Monument and the Anderson-Freeman Museum; below, courtesy HSSNM #1155.)

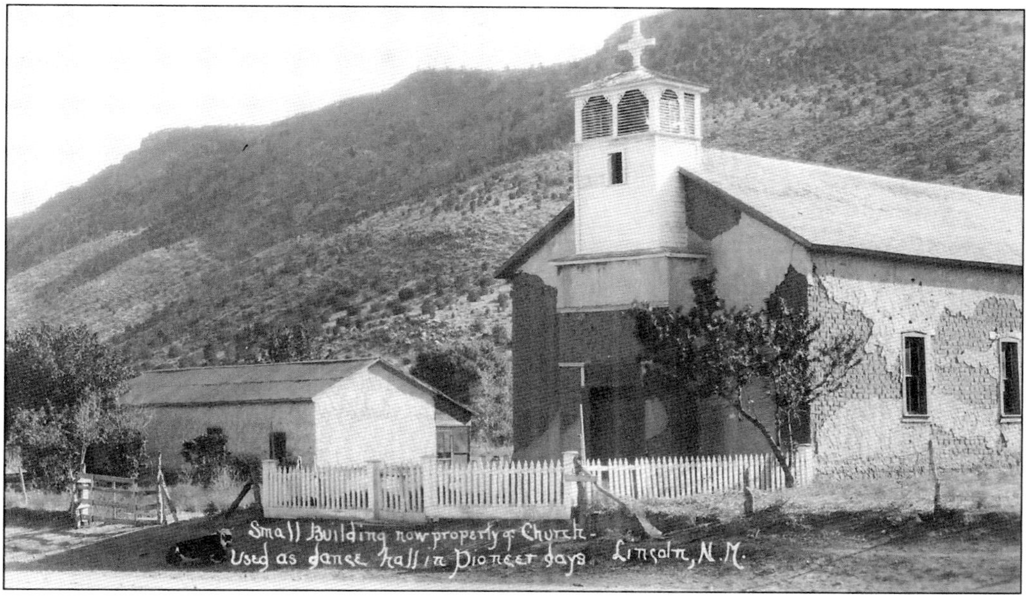

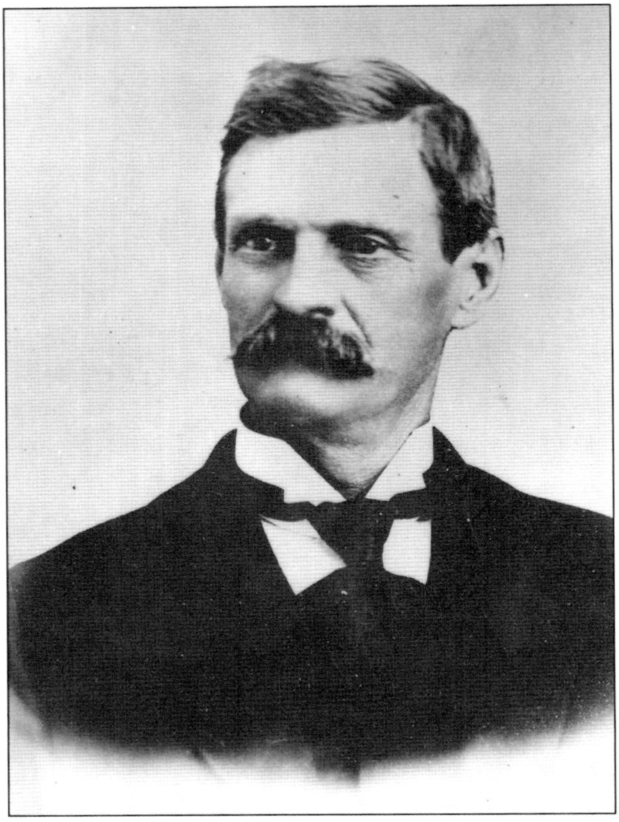

Some of the Murphy men are pictured on this page. An important player in the fray was sheriff William Brady, who was under J. J. Dolan Company's thumb. Shown here is his deputy sheriff, J. "Billy" Mathews, who headed the posse to intercept Tunstall, although it is unlikely that Mathews had intentions of killing Tunstall. Tunstall's killing can be attributed to the outlaws Jesse Evans and Buck Morton, who jumped the gun and shot the young Englishman. Mathews, on the other hand, had kept diplomatic relations to some extent with the McSween faction. Pictured below is George W. Peppin, who would succeed Brady as sheriff after Brady's murder. It was no secret that Peppin was sympathetic to the Dolan faction, and when Governor Axtell appointed him sheriff, it made many speculate that the governor was also on their side. (Left, courtesy HSSNM #1564; below, courtesy Robert McCubbin.)

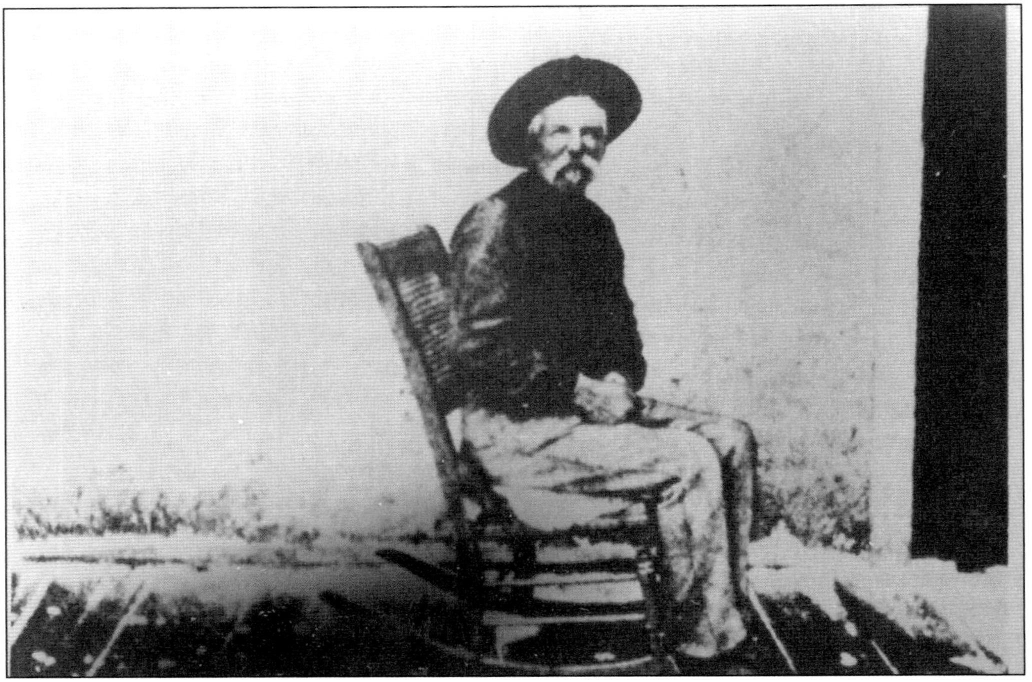

With the law working against them, the McSween party formed their own official posse called the Regulators. They were sworn in by justice of the peace John B. Wilson and given arrest warrants for those responsible for Tunstall's death. The head of the Regulators was Dick Brewer, right, and with him about 10 others including Billy the Kid, Josiah "Doc" Scurlock, Charley Bowdre, and Frank Macnab (a cattle detective.) Later on they would be joined by the Coe cousins, Frank and George. George Coe and his wife are pictured below at the Lincoln County courthouse in the 1920s. Eventually Governor Axtell had Wilson's title revoked, therefore rendering the Regulators to the status of vigilantes rather than an official constable's posse. (Right, courtesy Frederick Nolan; below, courtesy HSSNM #5499.)

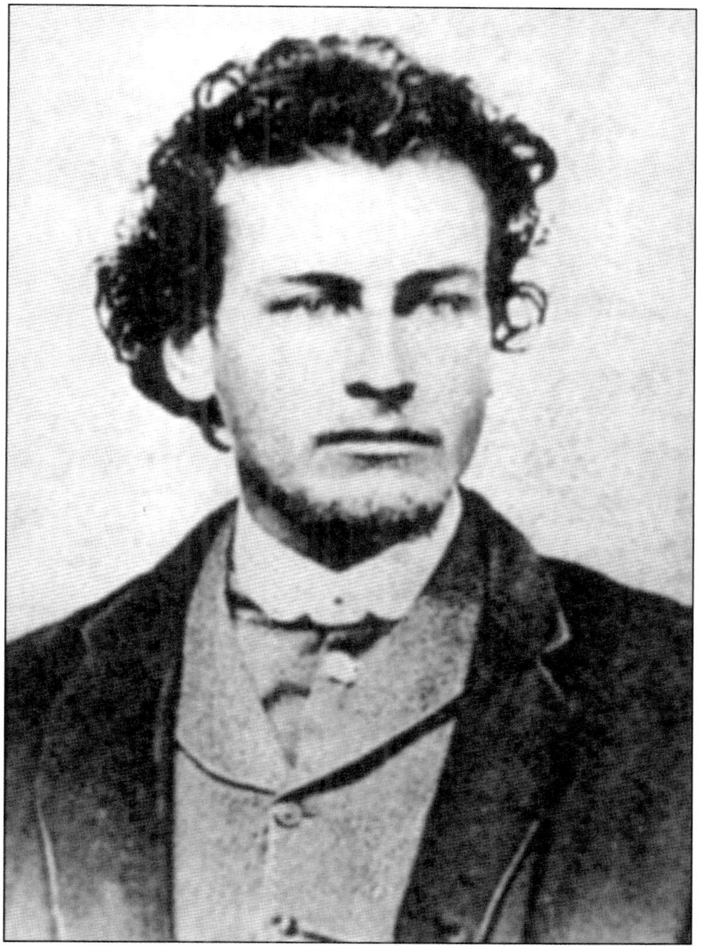

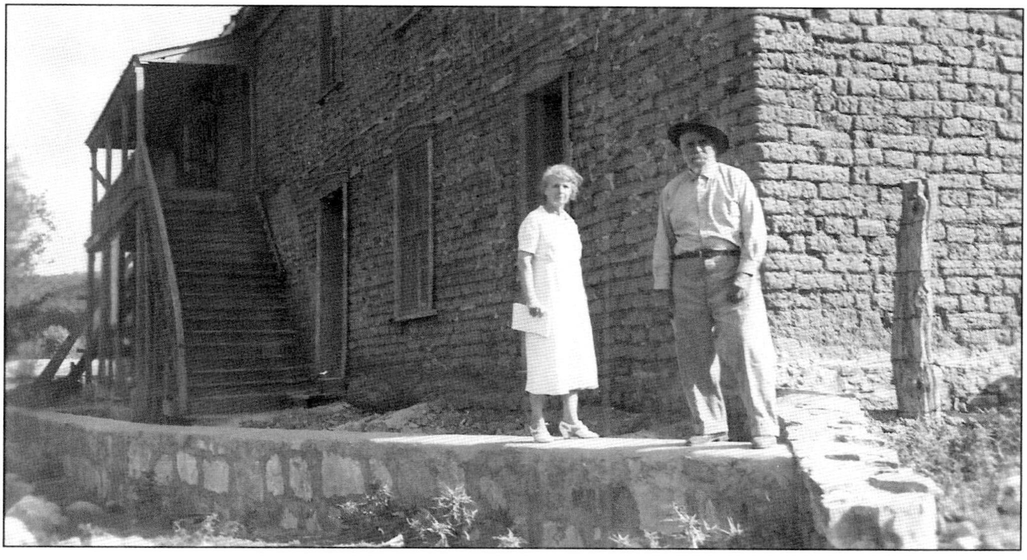

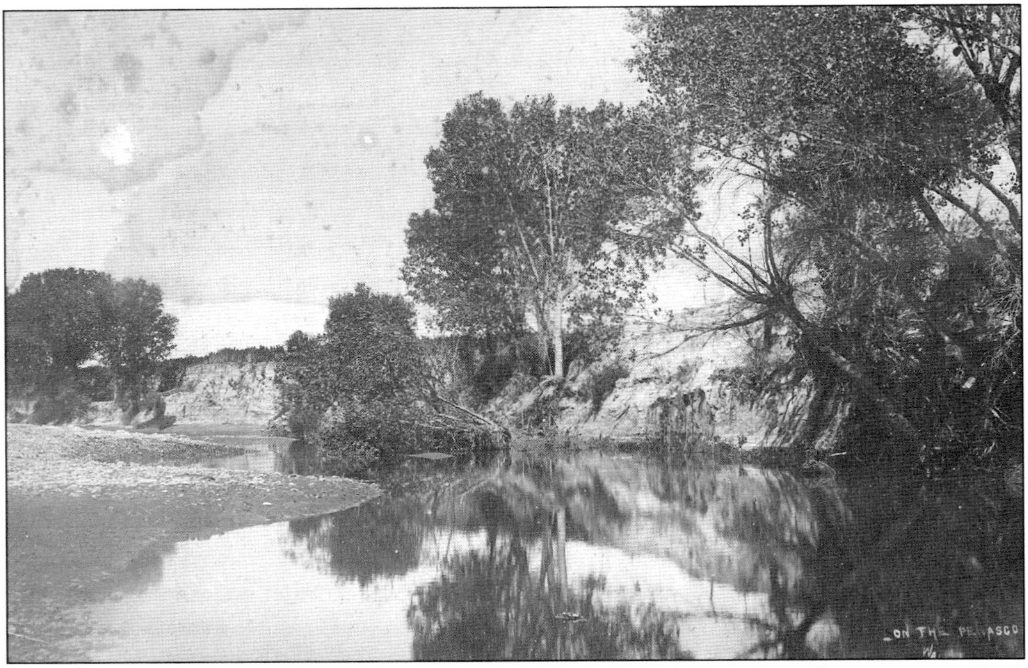

In March 1878, the Regulators caught up to some of Tunstall's killers when they ran across Dick Floyd, Frank Baker, Buck Morton, and others at the Peñasco River, pictured above. Giving chase on horseback and firing many shots for several miles, the Regulators captured Morton and Baker and brought them to John Chisum's ranch, below. Afterwards they took the prisoners through Roswell so that Morton could mail a letter there. In his letter, Morton stated he did not believe he would get back to Lincoln alive. At Agua Negra Spring, Morton and Baker were both shot. The Regulators claimed the two took posse member William McCloskey's gun, shot him, and fled. Others say Billy the Kid killed McCloskey himself (suspecting him of being a turncoat) and then the posse killed Morton and Baker in cold blood. (Above, courtesy HSSNM #411; below, courtesy HSSNM #1564-62.)

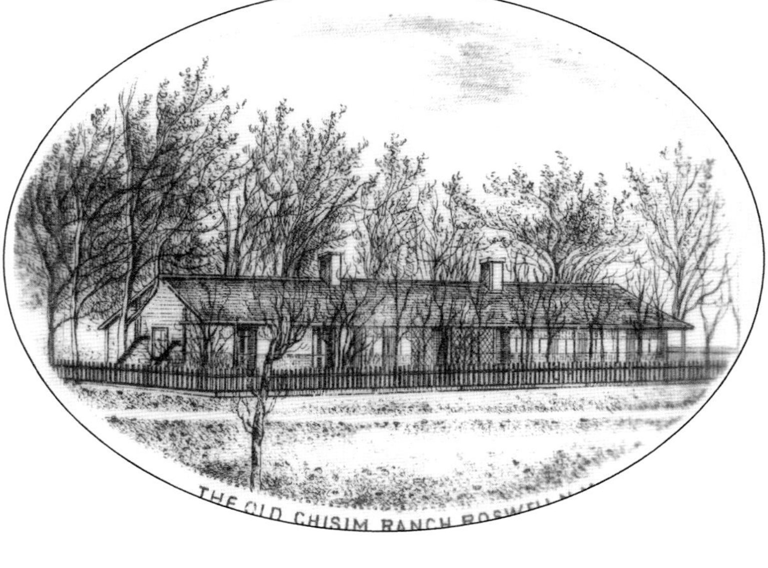

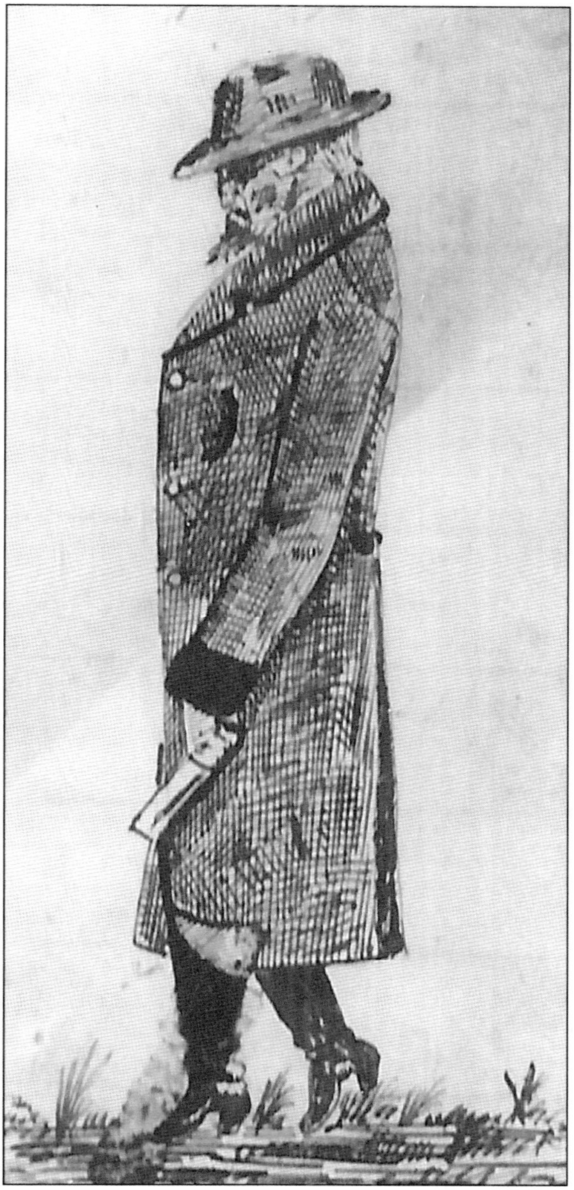

Ash Upson played the role of war correspondent during the Lincoln County troubles. He was an important player, sympathetic to the McSween faction. Called the "quintessential drunken Western journalist" by Tom Sheridan in his work, *The Bitter River: A Brief Historical Survey of the Middle Pecos River*, Upson was the postmaster at Roswell for a time, which gave him considerable leverage with both sides, so much leverage that he once threatened to leave town if a regiment of soldiers did not come in to keep the peace in Roswell, and he briefly got his way. McSween had a private mail service set up between he and Upson so that the Murphy-Dolan faction could not intercept his mail. Upson also ghostwrote his friend Pat Garrett's book, *An Authentic Life of Billy the Kid, the Noted Desperado of the Southwest*. Consequently Upson stayed with the Kid and his mother in Silver City, New Mexico, briefly before the war. Upson's likeness, as drawn by his niece, is pictured above. (Courtesy HSSNM #1564.)

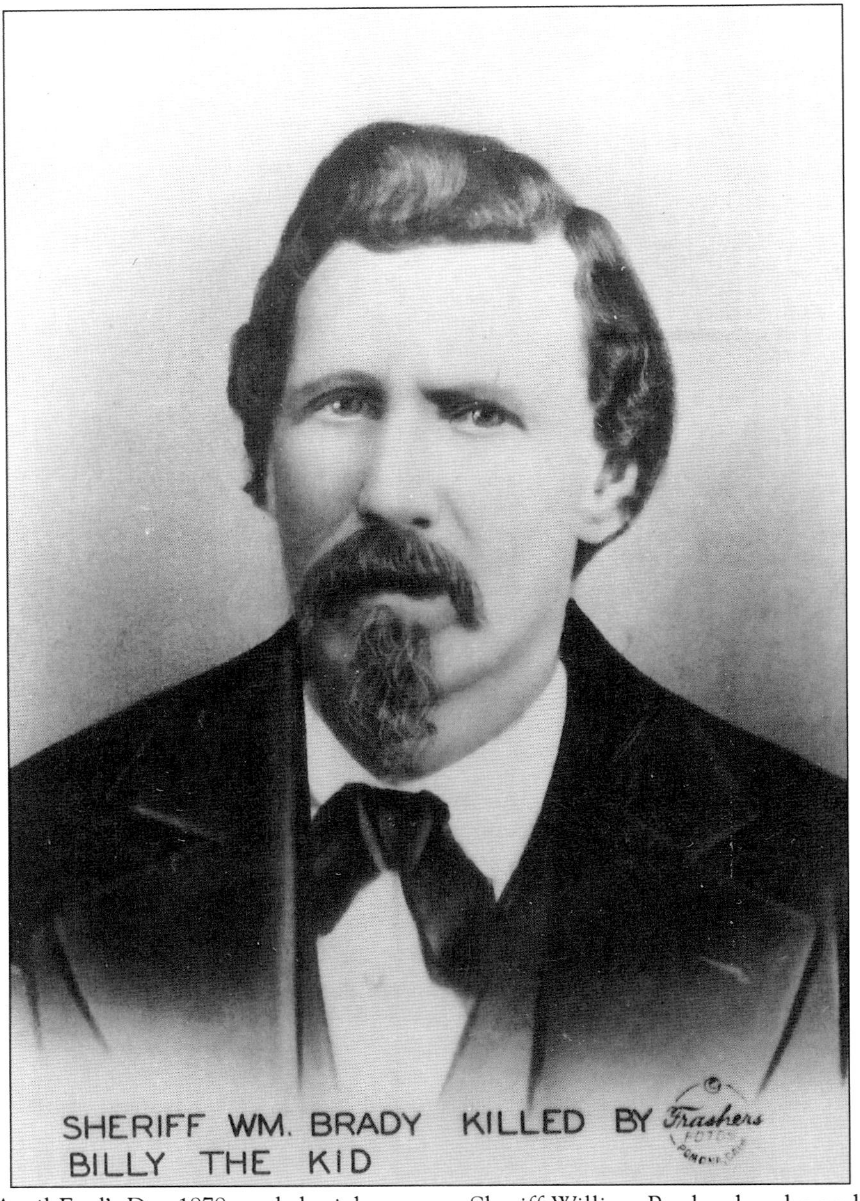

It was April Fool's Day 1878, and the joke was on Sheriff William Brady when he and deputy sheriffs J. Billy Mathews, George Peppin, John Long, and George Hindman walked unsuspectingly down the street in Lincoln into a cavalcade of bullets. Sheriff Brady and Hindman were mortally wounded amidst the ambush of lead, while Long fled to El Torreon and Mathews and Peppin to the Cisneros house. The source of the gunfire was the Regulators, who just happened to be in town and in the Tunstall store. As luck would have it for them, Brady and his men had walked into an unexpected ambush. Braving gunfire (unsuccessfully, as he was hit in the hip by Mathews), Billy the Kid ran out into the street to retrieve his Winchester from Brady's body. Brady had apparently taken the rifle from the Kid back in February, and he wanted it back. All of the Regulators escaped the deputy sheriff's return fire, but Jim French, unable to mount his horse, hid under the Tunstall floorboards. (Courtesy Frederick Nolan.)

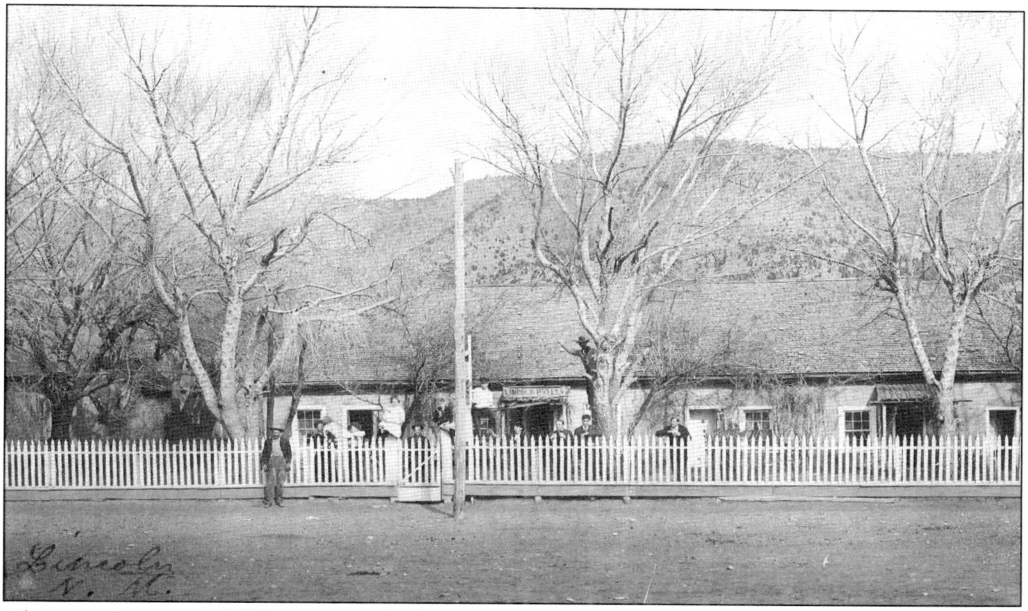

Above is the original Wortley Hotel where Sheriff Brady ate his last meal before being shot. In fact, many other fighters in the war received their last meals from the hotel. Today the Wortley, formerly owned by Pat Garrett, still operates as it did back in the Old West with rooms minus telephone and television. The hotel proudly proclaims: "No guests gunned down in over 100 years." (Courtesy HSSNM #4069.)

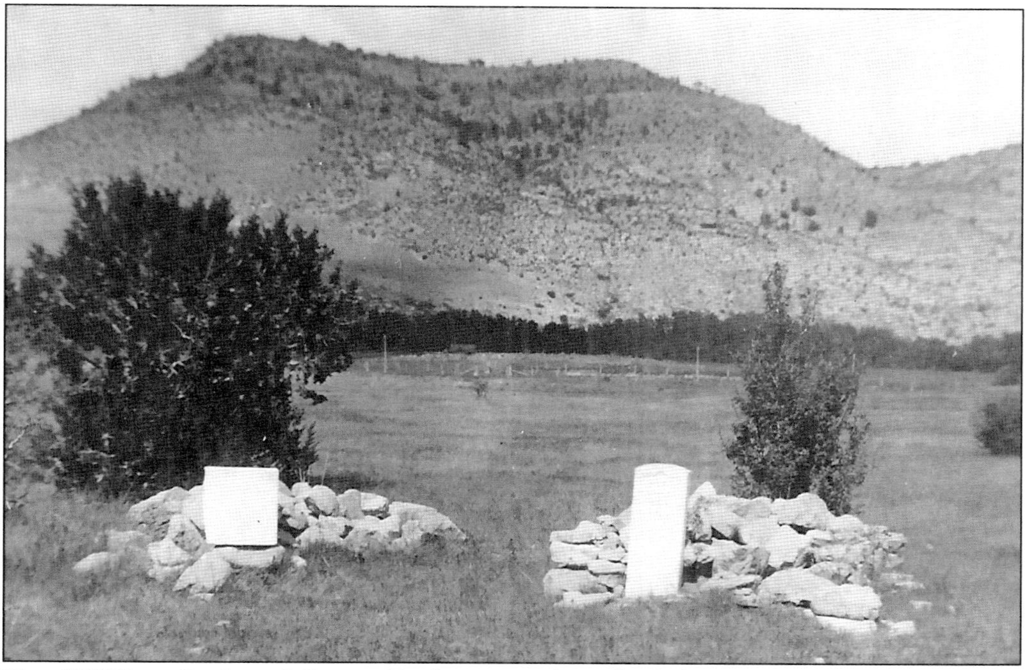

Sheriff William Brady and George Hindman were buried side by side on Brady's ranch east of Lincoln. Brady's tombstone is likely the one on the right. Hindman's headstone was eventually stolen and has yet to be returned. (Courtesy HSSNM #1543A.)

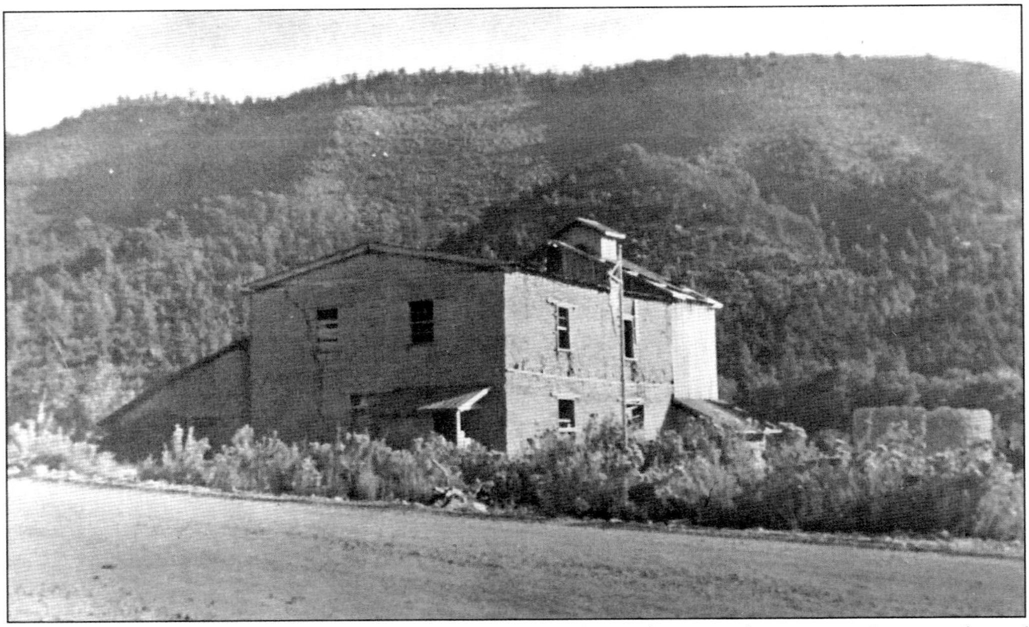

While eating a meal at Blazer's Mill, above, the Regulators happened upon another member of the posse that had killed Tunstall. "Here's Buckshot Roberts!" one of the Regulators cried upon seeing Andrew L. Roberts, called Buckshot because of his many scars from past gun battles. Somewhat disgraced by the coldblooded killing of Sheriff Brady, of which he was not involved, Dick Brewer tried to arrest Roberts peacefully, sending the newest Regulator, Frank Coe, out to talk to Roberts. Impatient with the negotiations, Charlie Bowdre and two others went to make an arrest, and when Roberts refused, Bowdre shot him in the stomach. Roberts then managed to barricade himself in the study of Dr. William Blazer, the ruins of which are shown below. Luckily for Roberts, there were 1,000 rounds of ammunition and several guns in the room. (Above, courtesy HSSNM #2080; below, courtesy HSSNM #3262.)

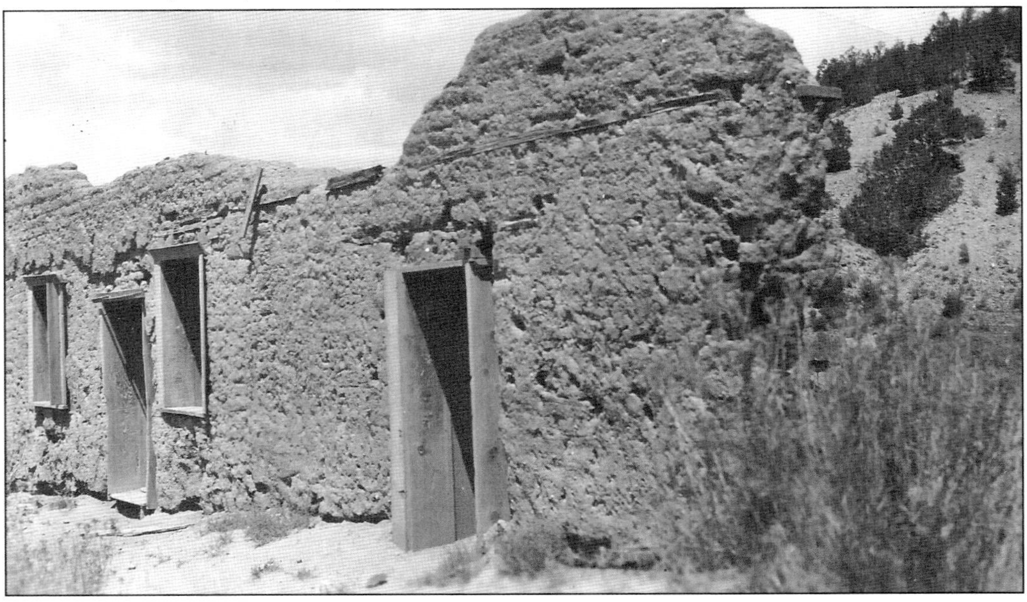

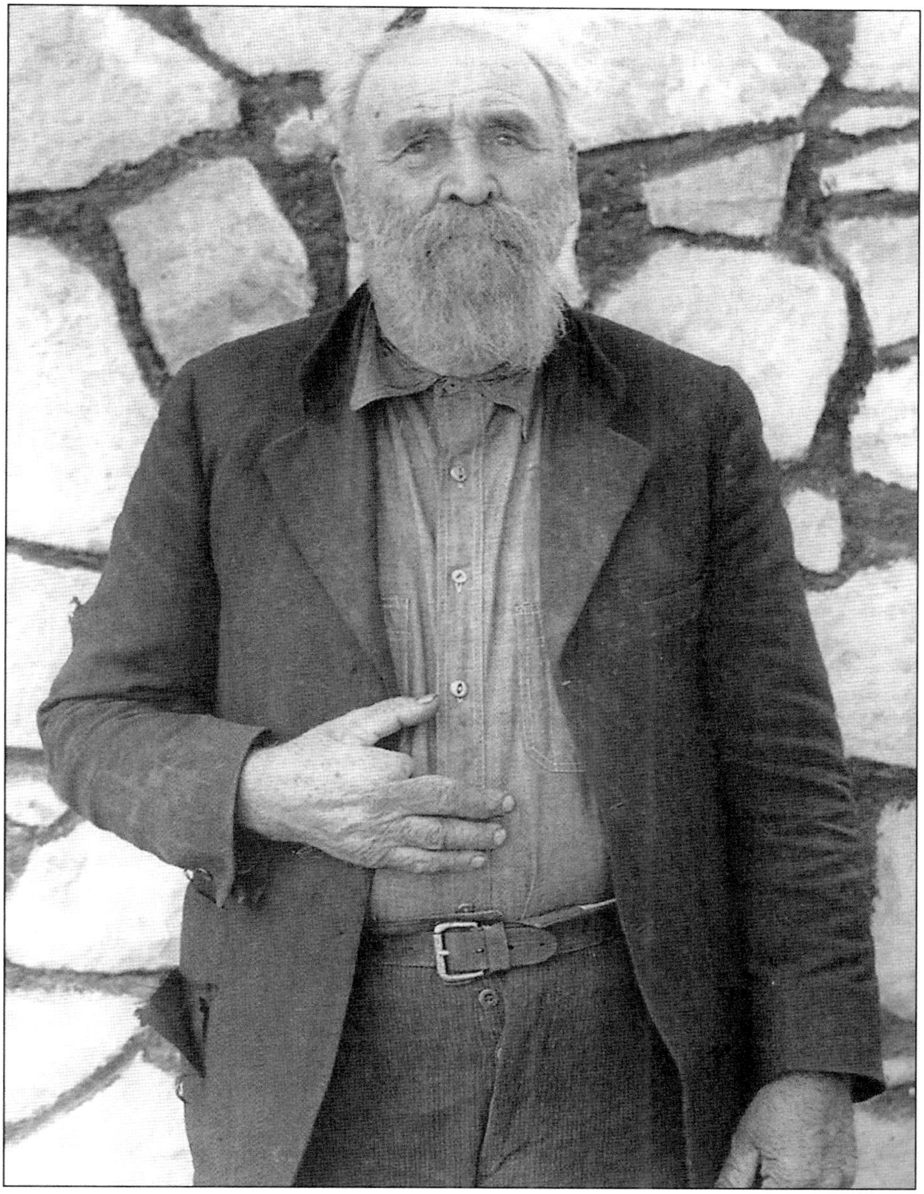

George Coe displays his trigger finger, or lack thereof, in this photograph taken at White Sands National Monument by George A. Grant in 1934. Coe had his trigger finger shot off by Andrew "Buckshot" Roberts at Blazers Mill on April 4, 1878. Also wounded in the fight were John Middleton, who took a shot in the chest; Charlie Bowdre had his gunbelt blown off; Doc Scurlock was hit in the leg; and Billy the Kid's arm was grazed. Dick Brewer decided to take another position in the fight and hid behind some logs. Roberts saw Brewer peeking his head above the logs and shot him square in the forehead, causing instant death. With their leader now dead, the Regulators decided to regroup at the Coe Ranch near the Ruidoso. Roberts died the next day from the shot inflicted by Bowdre and was buried next to his enemy Dick Brewer. Actually, an alternate story says, to avoid digging two graves, the men were buried (in separate caskets) right on top of one another. (Courtesy Robert McCubbin.)

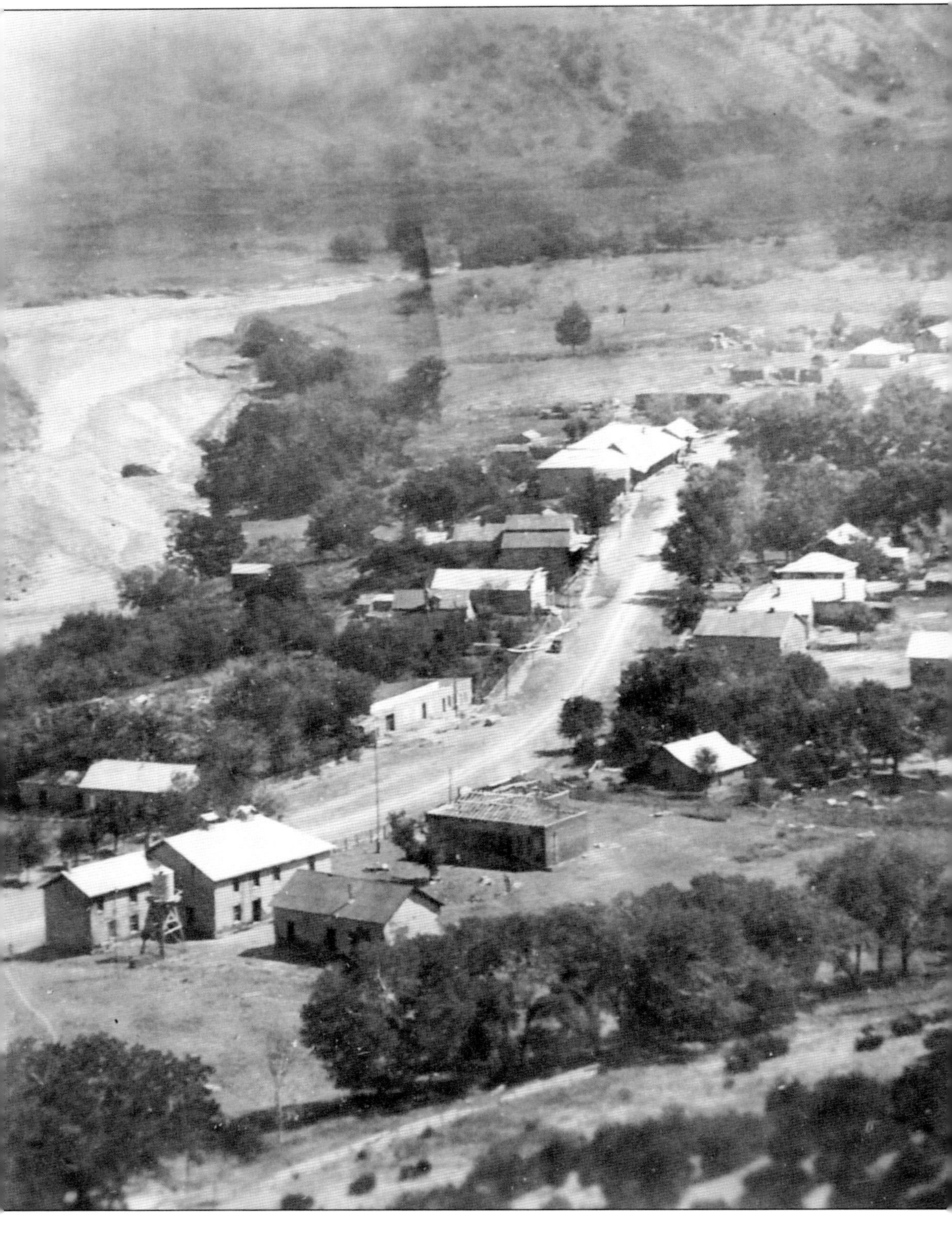

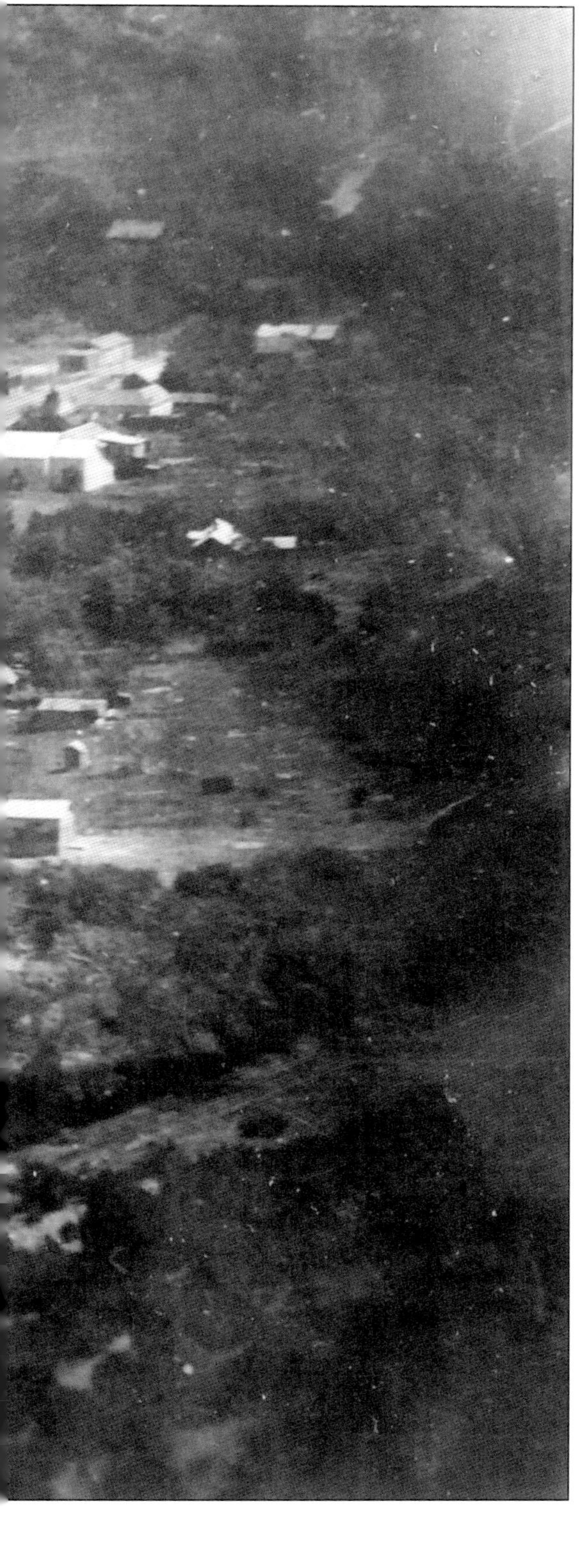

Things came to a head in Lincoln during what is today called the Five Day Battle, a siege lasting nearly a week between the Murphy and McSween factions in what would be their final showdown. McSween's men and the Regulators, including Billy the Kid, holed up in the McSween home for five days, exchanging gunfire with the Murphy party. Eventually some panicked families in Lincoln called in the big guns at Fort Stanton. On July 19, Col. Nathan Dudley and his men arrived in Lincoln and sided with Dolan, pointing a cannon at the McSween home. Eventually fire was set to the house, causing the Regulators to flee. While Billy the Kid miraculously escaped to fight another day, Alexander McSween was shot five times while exiting the burning house. (Courtesy HSSNM #1546.)

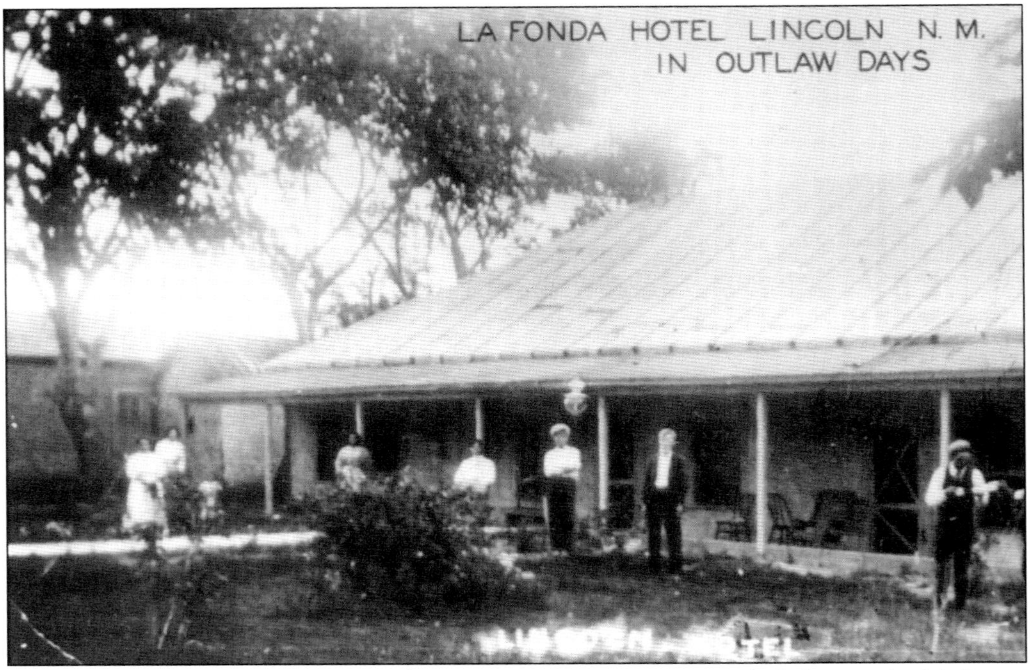

During the Five Day Battle in 1878, the McSween men were not just holed up in the McSween house. A regiment of 20 to 30 men, led by Regulator Martin Chaves, positioned themselves in the Montano Store, and Charlie Bowdre, Doc Scurlock, "Dirty Steve" Stevens, and John Middleton, among others, hid out at the Ellis Store, which is labeled as the La Fonda Hotel above. The Ellis Store is one of the oldest homes in Lincoln, dating back to 1861, and still operates to this day. During the shooting at the Five Day Battle, an Ellis family member, Ben, was hit by a stray bullet in the neck while tending his horses. (Above, courtesy HSSNM #5160C; below, courtesy Lincoln State Monument and the Anderson-Freeman Museum.)

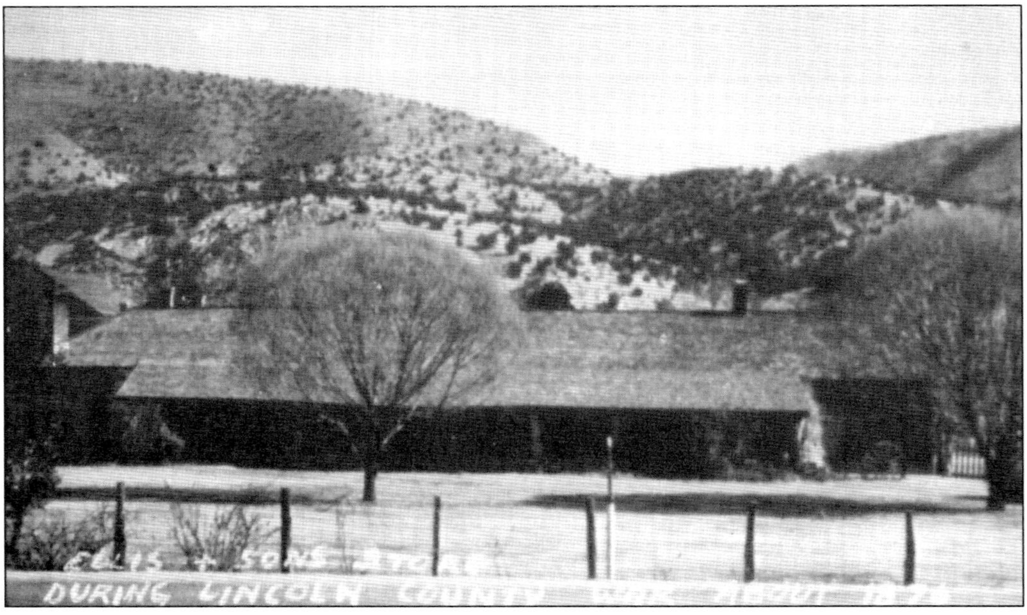

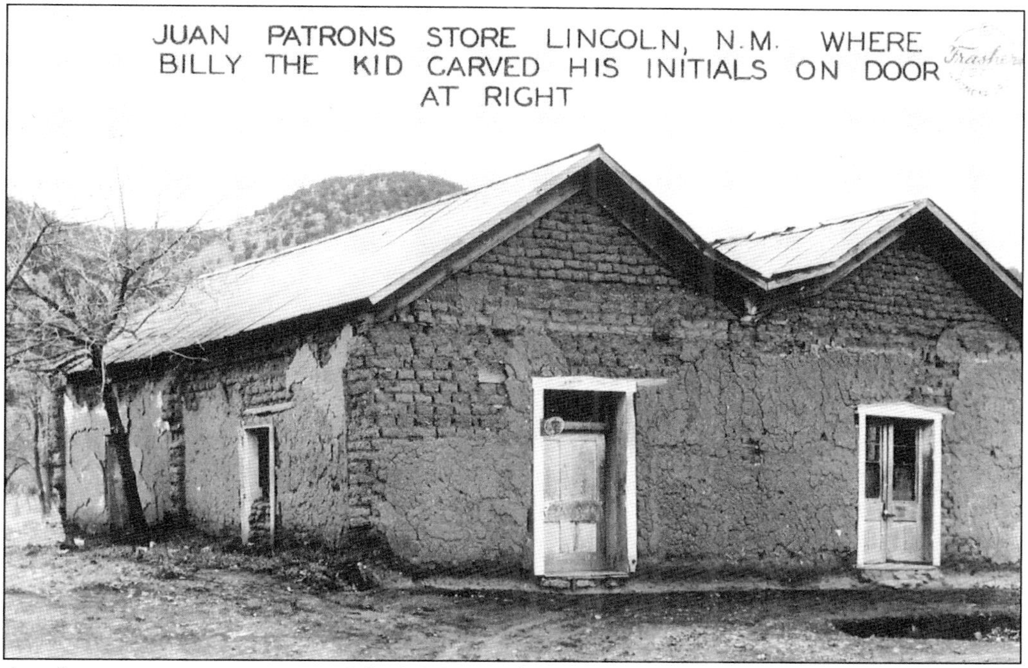

Another important supporter of the McSween faction was Juan B. Patron and his family. The family store and residence where Billy the Kid is believed to have carved "Kid" into the door is shown above. In 1877, Juan Patron became the youngest speaker of the house of representatives in the New Mexico territorial legislature at the time. He and his family operated the store, built sometime prior to 1868, in Lincoln from 1871 to 1880. Another undated photograph of Lincoln during the "outlaw days" is shown below. (Both courtesy HSSNM #5160D and #5160A.)

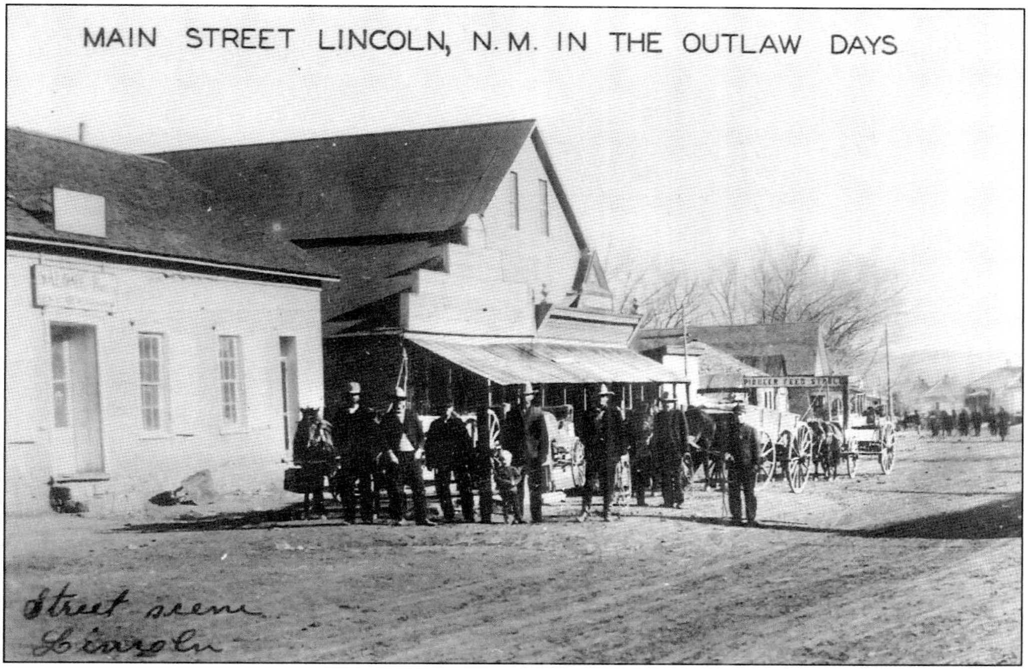

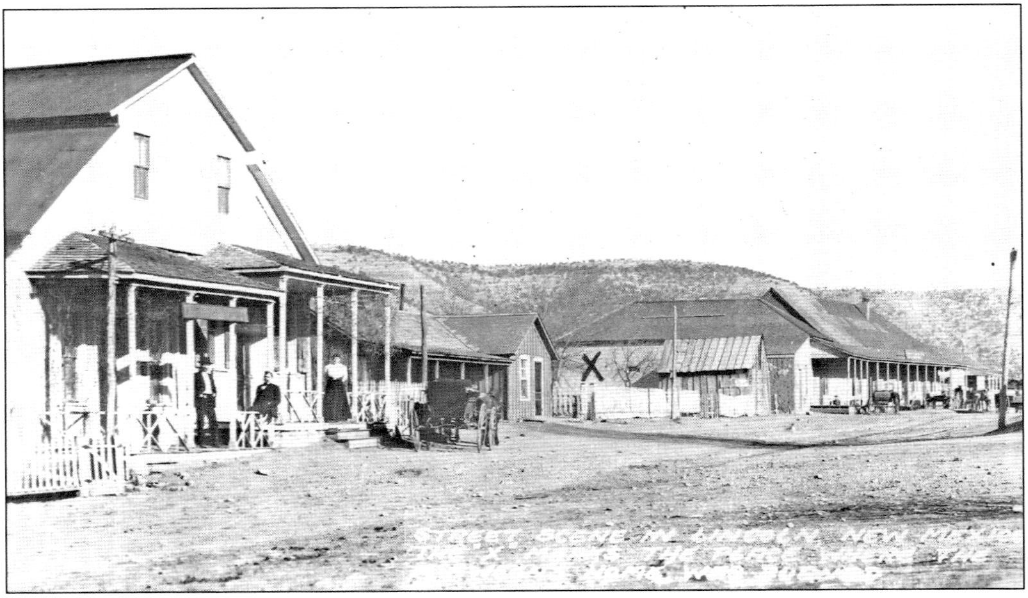

The spot where the old McSween home once stood, before it was burned down in the fire during the Five Day Battle of 1878, is marked by the "x" in the photograph above. It should be noted that today researchers now doubt that may be the exact spot where it stood. (Courtesy HSSNM #3509.)

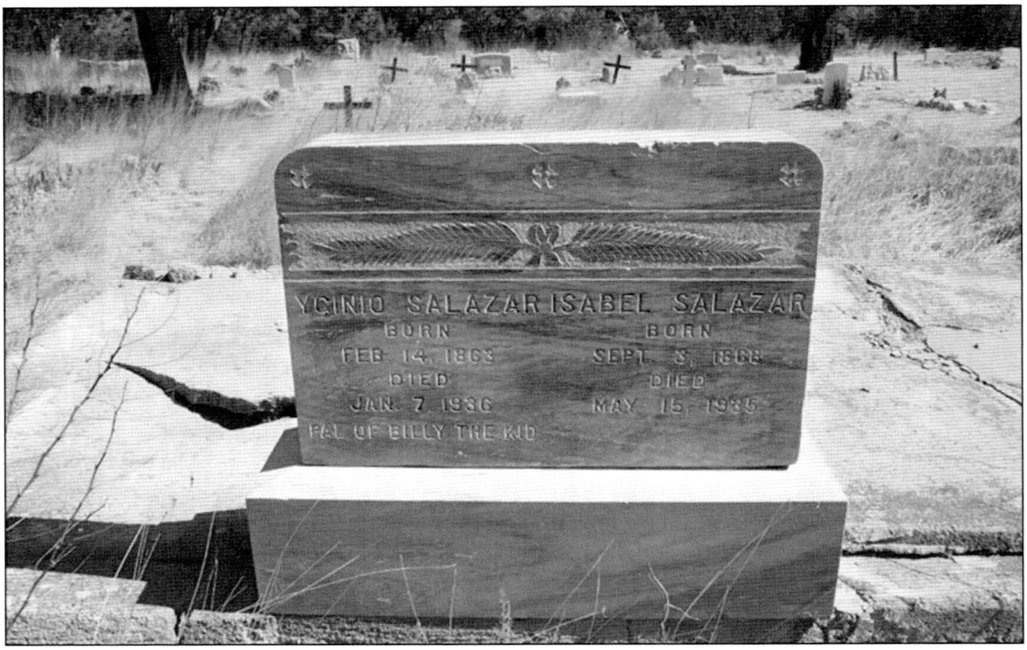

Yginio Salazar was one of the survivors of the burning McSween house. Salazar, who had been shot twice in the fight, played dead outside of the house. Reportedly a man checking the bodies kicked Salazar and then prepared to shoot him before Milo Pierce interjected, saying it was better not to waste a bullet on a dead man. After all was quiet, Salazar crawled away to safety. (Courtesy James Owens.)

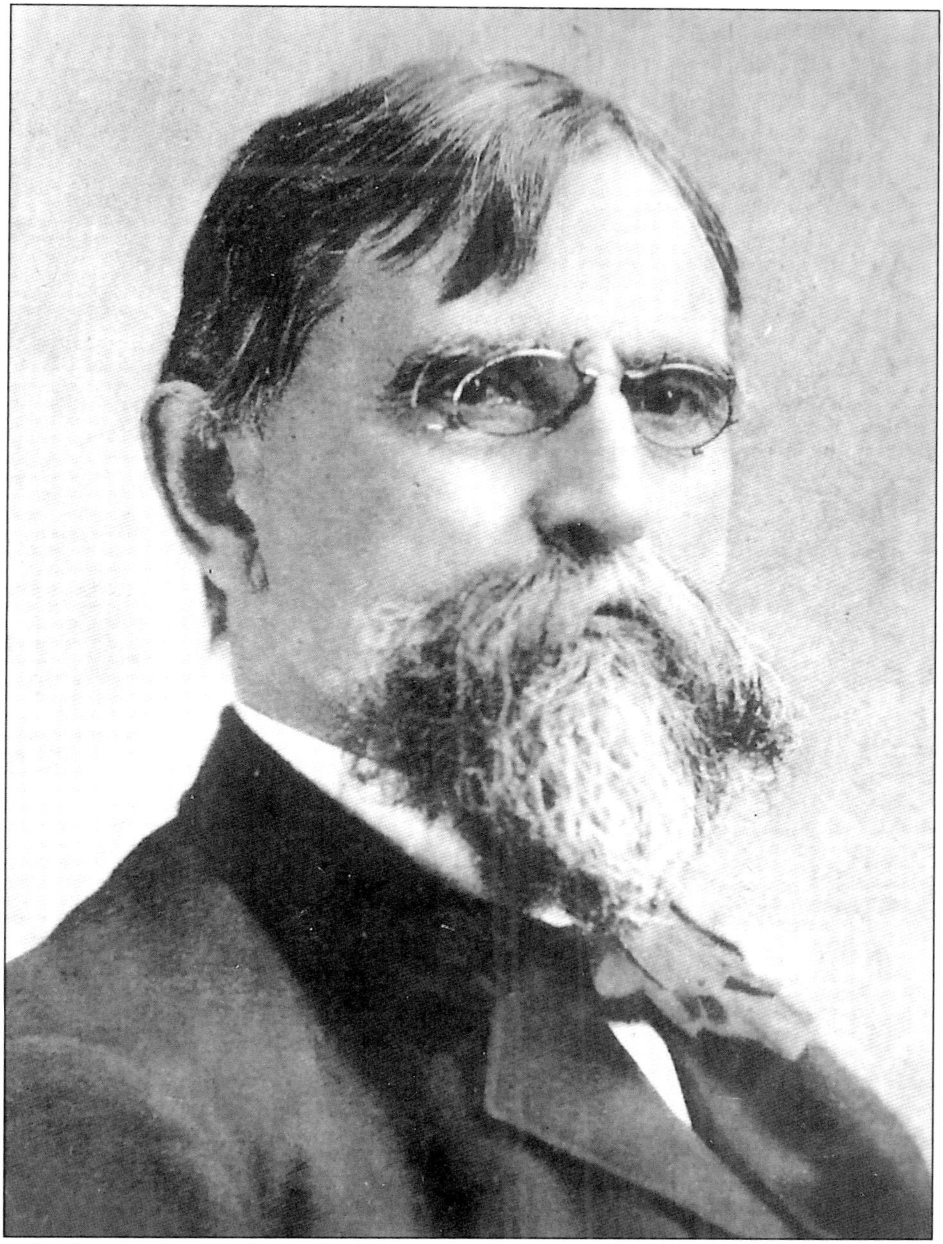

After the Five Day Battle, the violence in Lincoln was so out of hand, it attracted the attention of Pres. Rutherford B. Hayes. Hayes removed Gov. Samuel B. Axtell from office and replaced him with Gen. Lew Wallace, above, who made it his personal mission to clean up New Mexico Territory. Wallace offered amnesty to anyone who would testify to the events in Lincoln and had a secret meeting with Billy the Kid at the Squire Wilson home in Lincoln. The Kid turned himself in to the law in order to testify about Alexander McSween's killing and other events in the war. Although there were still two notable killings in the Lincoln County War's aftermath, for the most part peace was beginning to return to the Hondo Valley. (Courtesy HSSNM Larkham Album 8 #2949.)

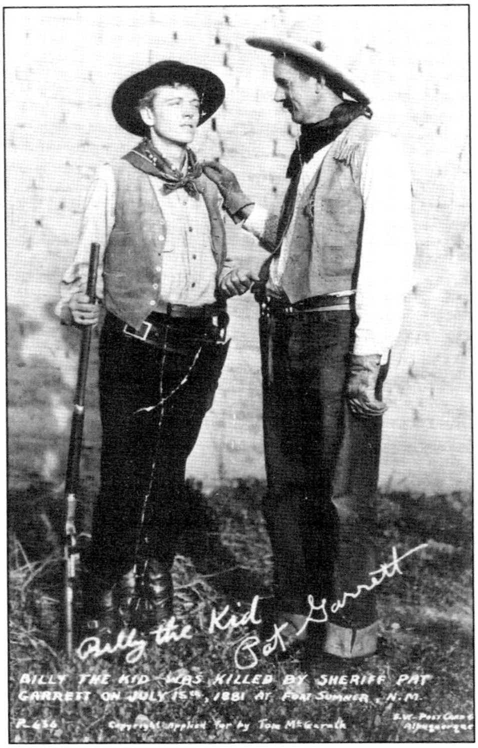

Disgusted and tired of the court proceedings pertaining to Col. Nathan Dudley's involvement in the destruction of the Alexander McSween home (Dudley would be found not guilty), Billy the Kid slipped out of his shackles in Lincoln and rode to Fort Sumner on June 17, 1879. Thus began the Kid's career as a real outlaw, getting into gunfights, rustling cattle, gambling, and hiding out on the trail. The Kid became such a problem that Pat Garrett, riding his horse in the postcard below, was made sheriff to deal with him. Billy the Kid and Pat Garrett, portrayed by actors at left, had ironically been gambling buddies in Fort Sumner and were often seen together. The duo has been featured on many postcards such as these and is a classic case of friends turned enemies. (Left, courtesy HSSNM #5203; below, author's collection.)

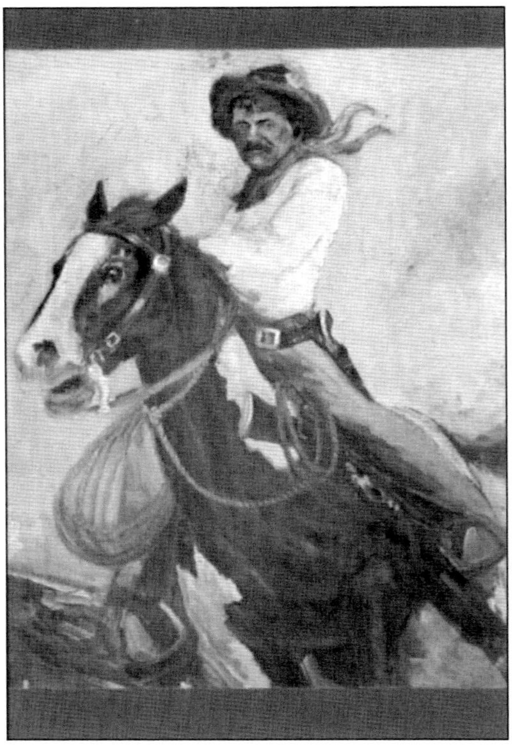

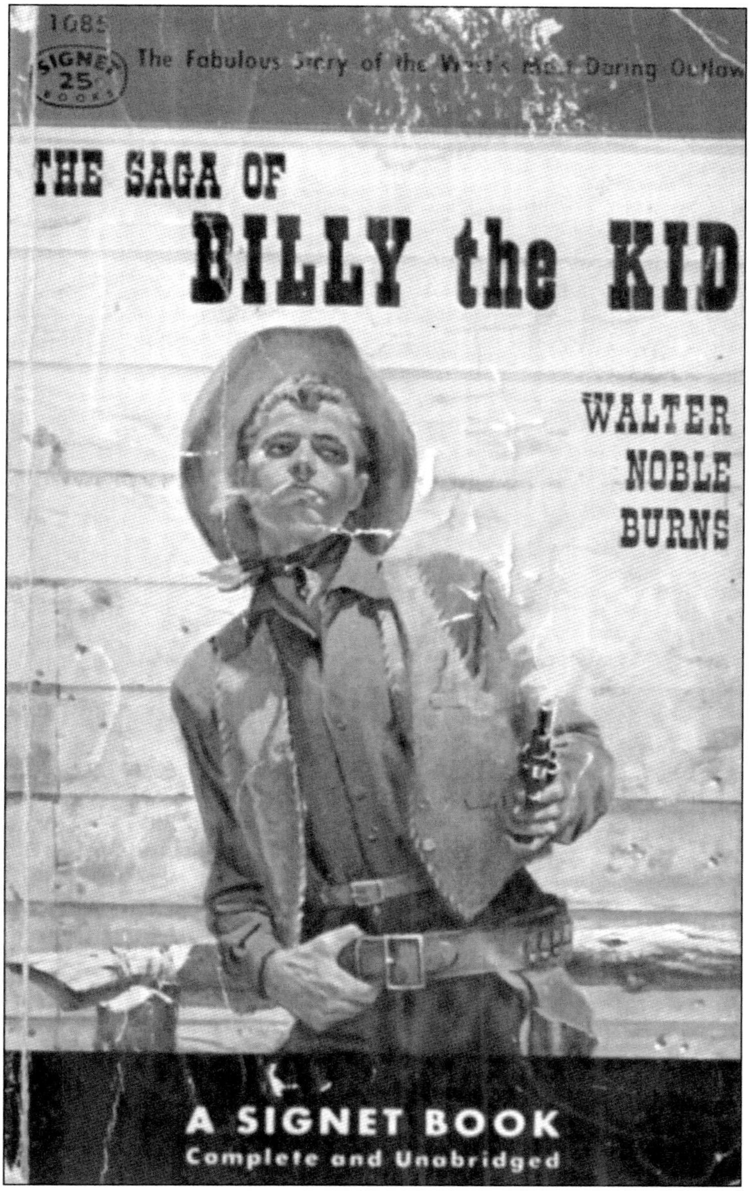

Billy the Kid's exploits after the end of the Lincoln County War, as an outlaw on the run rustling cattle and avoiding Sheriff Pat Garrett's posse, are among his most famous adventures. Many of the Kid's compadres would meet their ends in several gun battles in the winter of 1880. Tom O'Folliard was shot in a bloody battle in the snow-covered town of Fort Sumner on December 19, 1880. Only four days later, on the day before Christmas Eve, Sheriff Garrett shot Charlie Bowdre to death and finally captured Billy the Kid at Stinking Springs. In the months to come, Billy would be sentenced to hang for his crimes and was jailed in Lincoln at the old Murphy store, which had been converted into the Lincoln County courthouse. It was around this time that Billy the Kid became a famous outlaw. *The Saga of Billy the Kid* by Walter Noble Burns, a Signet Books reprint of which is pictured above, shows a James Dean–inspired rendition of the Kid. The book was extremely successful when it was first printed. (Author's collection.)

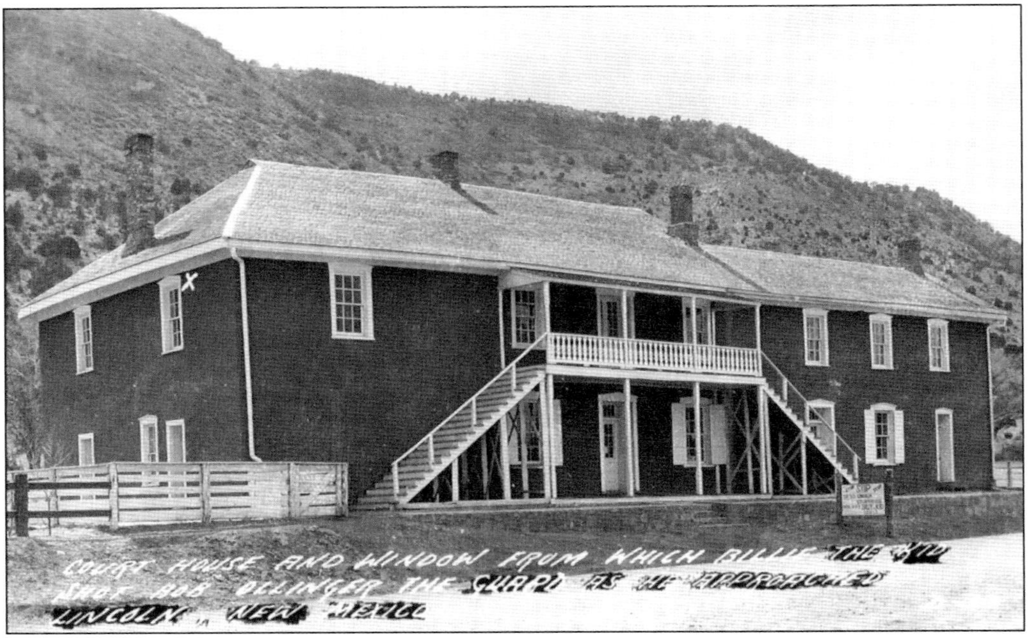

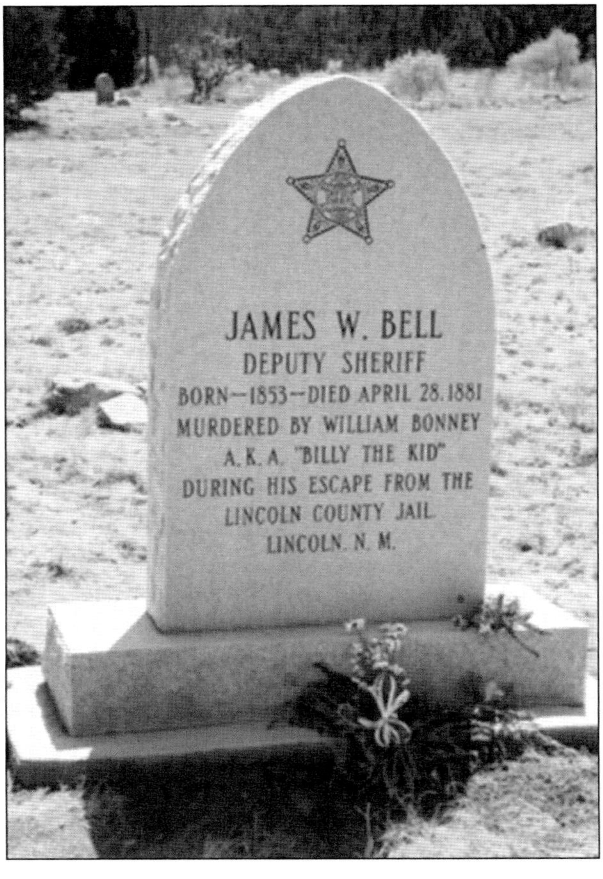

The "x" marks the spot where Billy the Kid shot deputy "Pecos" Bob Olinger from the second-story window of the Lincoln County courthouse pictured above. Olinger had constantly taunted the Kid since his arrival there. Earlier that day, while being escorted upstairs after a visit to the outhouse by deputy sheriff J. W. Bell, the Kid turned on Bell with a pistol (where he got it is still unknown) and ordered him to stay where he was. Bell, whose grave is pictured at left, turned to run away and the Kid shot him, leaving him to stagger outside into the arms of Godfrey Gaus, where he died. Olinger rushed from outside the Wortley Hotel to the courthouse to see what the commotion was. "Hello, Bob," the Kid called to him from the window and shot him dead. (Above, courtesy HSSNM #4044B; left, courtesy James Owens.)

After his escape from the courthouse, Billy the Kid fled to the ranch of Jose Pablo Cordova, shown at right, where Cordova, a judge in Lincoln County at one time, cut off his leg irons. The story goes that the Kid had to seek refuge in a tree all night because of Cordova's dogs until the next morning, when Francisco Cordova called them off. (Courtesy HSSNM #2152.)

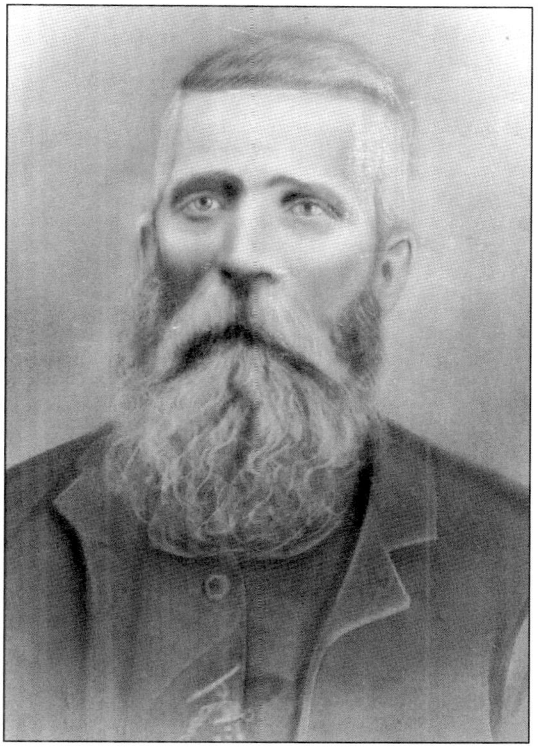

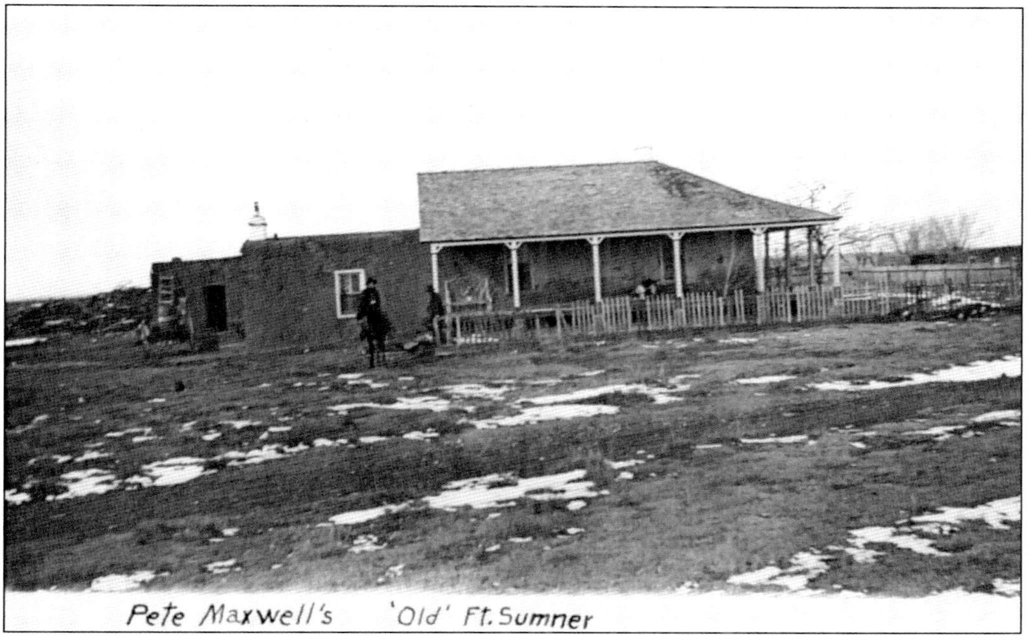

Billy the Kid eventually returned to his old stomping grounds at Fort Sumner to see one of his many Mexican sweethearts. It is in the house above that Pat Garrett finally shot and killed him. This photograph shows the Pete Maxwell home, formerly the officer's quarters in Fort Sumner, from the side in its later years. (Courtesy HSSNM #1416.)

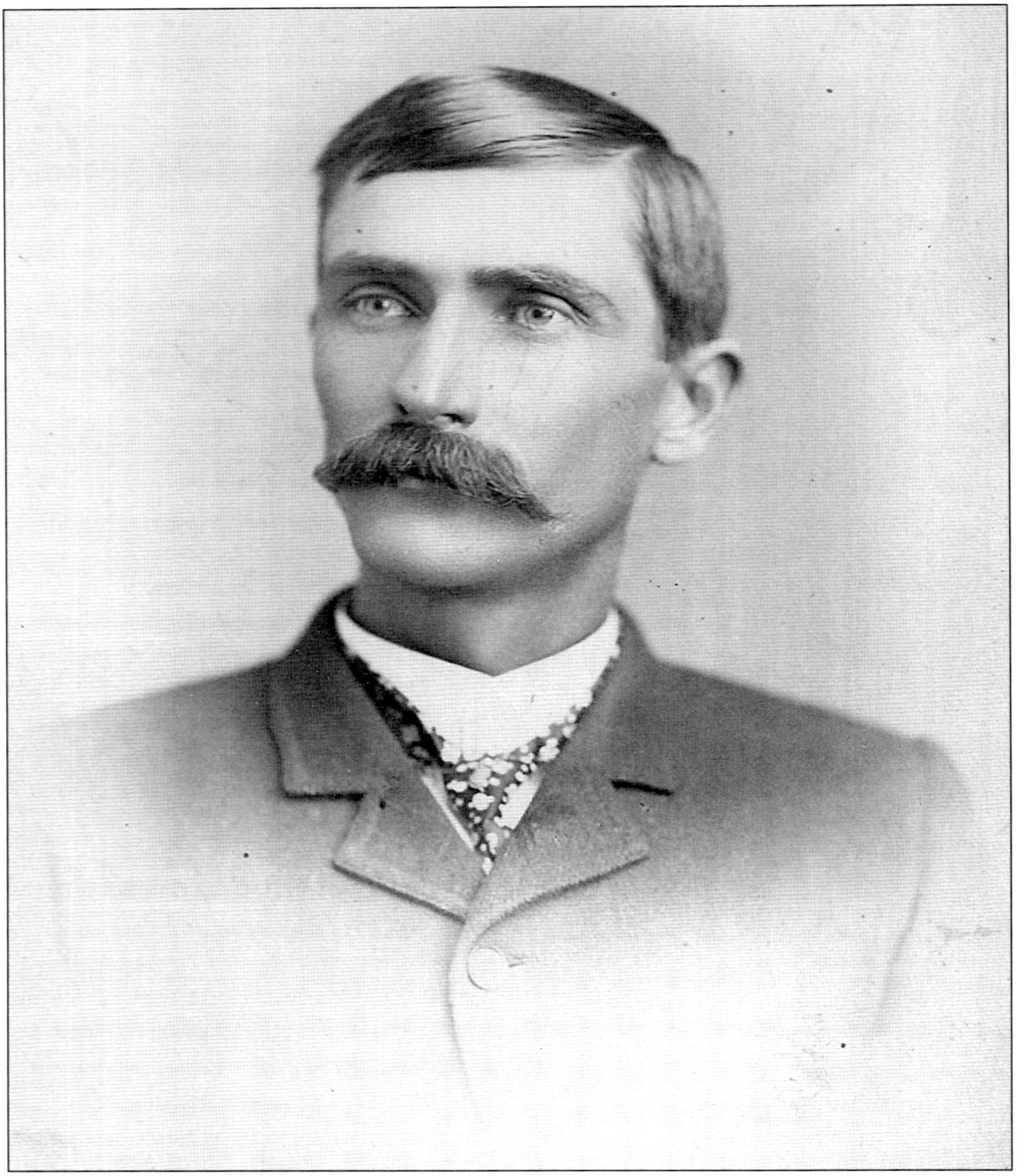

The photograph above, taken in Las Vegas, New Mexico, shows a young Patrick Floyd Garrett. Garrett, a remarkably tall man, was called "one long-legged son of a bitch" by many of the outlaws he apprehended. He was born in June 1850 in Chambers County, Alabama. Garrett's life exploits, which included run-ins and business deals with none other than Pres. Theodore Roosevelt, could fill many pages, but in short Garrett will always be known as the man who shot Billy the Kid. Actually Garrett may have killed more men than the Kid himself, the first being a fellow buffalo hunter in 1877 in self-defense. Eventually Garrett gave up the buffalo hunting profession and came to Fort Sumner, where he became Billy the Kid's gambling buddy and later the sheriff that hunted him down. By July 1881, Garrett was again in Fort Sumner, hot on the trail of the Kid, where he would eventually kill him. Garrett himself would be killed under somewhat mysterious circumstances outside of Las Cruces in 1908. (Courtesy HSSNM #1925.)

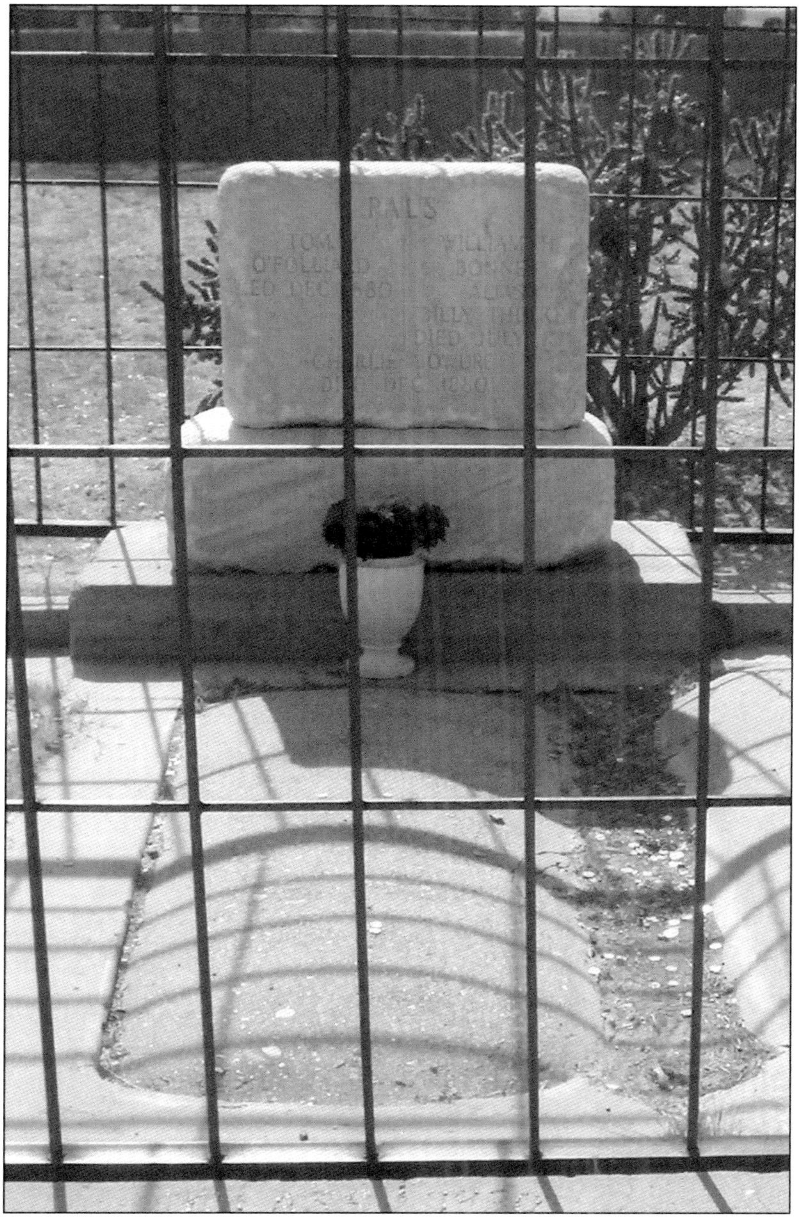

"Quien es?" were Billy the Kid's last words as he wandered past deputies John Poe and Tip McKinney into Pete Maxwell's house. The Kid had gone out to cut some meat hanging near Maxwell's home for a midnight snack when he saw the two men outside and decided to go into the house and investigate. As he walked into Maxwell's bedroom, he was shot dead in the dark by Pat Garrett, who just happened to be in the right place at the right time. Billy the Kid had the most interesting life after death of any outlaw of the Old West. His Fort Sumner headstone, now behind bars above, has been stolen and recovered twice. Not only that, no more than three men surfaced in the 20th century who were rumored to be a surviving Billy the Kid, among them Brushy Bill Roberts of Hico, Texas; John Miller of Ramah, New Mexico; and a fellow who dropped dead outside of Lordsburg, New Mexico, called Walkalong Smith. (Author's collection.)

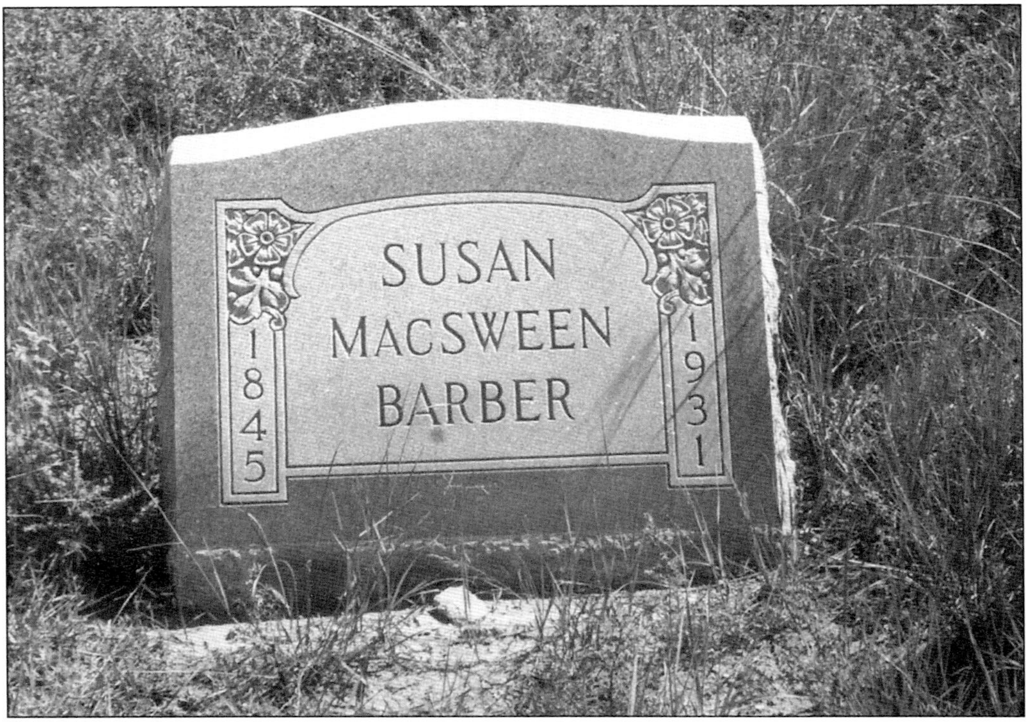

After the war, Susan McSween started her own successful ranch near the Three Rivers area and became known as the Cattle Queen of New Mexico. Susan McSween briefly married George Barber in 1891 and divorced him by 1894. Eventually she moved her ranch to White Oaks and even had a partnership in a silver mine there. Susan McSween Barber was one of the last survivors of the Lincoln County War and died in White Oaks in 1931 at age 86. Her grave in the Cedarvale Cemetery in White Oaks can be seen above. Grave markers for her first husband, Alexander McSween, and his business partner, John Tunstall, can be seen below, although the markers are not where the two men are actually buried. (Above, courtesy HSSNM #2141B; below, courtesy James Owens.)

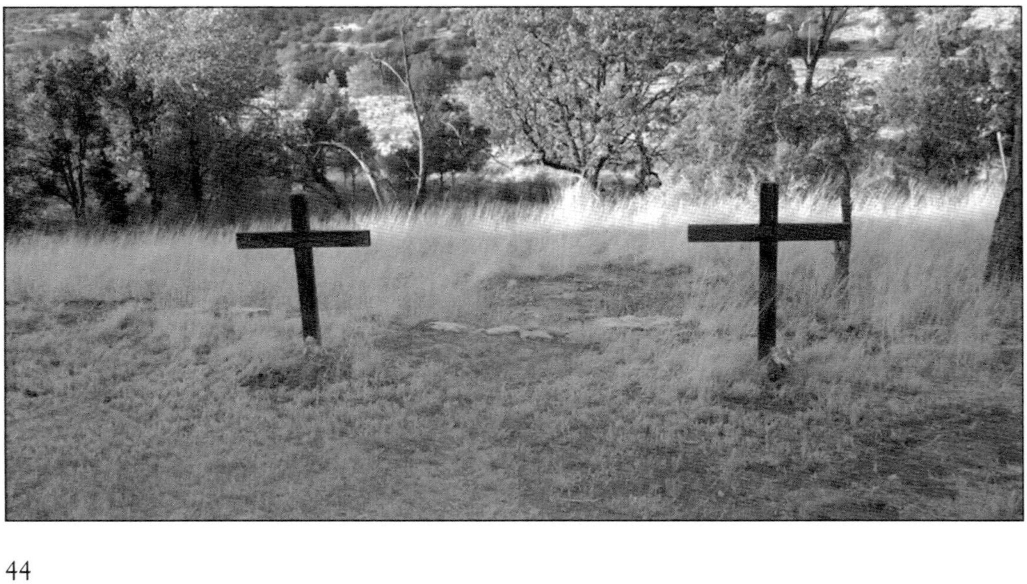

Lawrence G. Murphy passed away not long after the five-day siege in Lincoln. Murphy succumbed to cancer on October 20, 1878. Murphy had been drinking heavily in Santa Fe before he was taken to St. Vincent's hospital, where he died. He was buried at the Masonic and Odd Fellows Cemetery but later moved to the Santa Fe National Cemetery where the grave marker at right was erected. (Courtesy James Owens.)

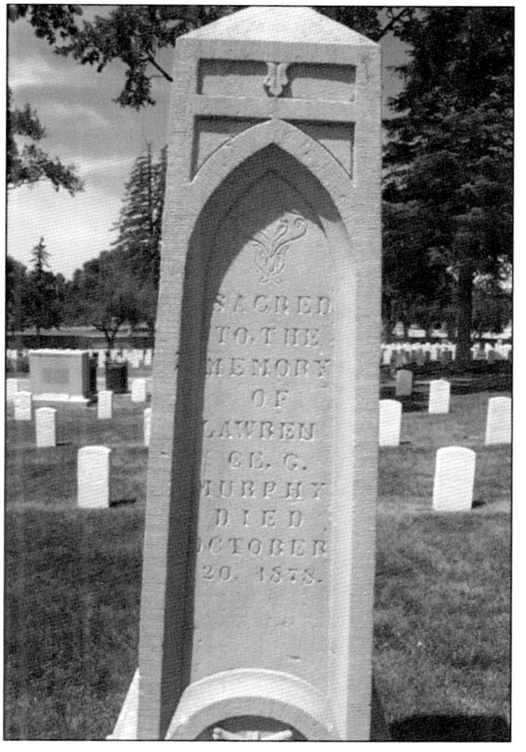

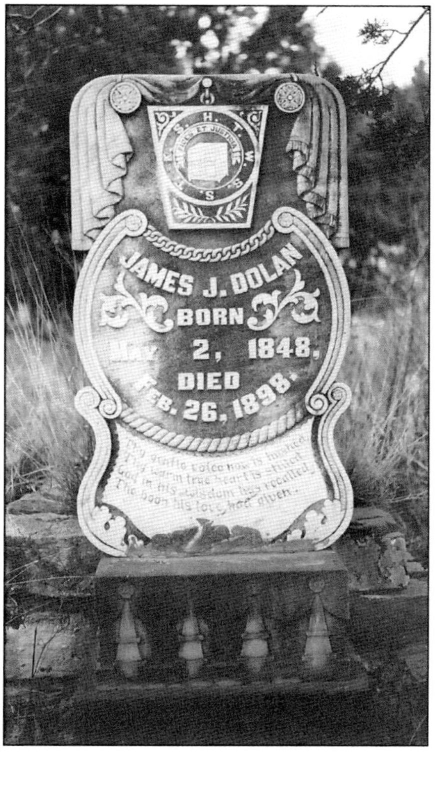

James J. Dolan would live for some time after the Lincoln County War and was acquitted for his crimes. He married Caroline Fritz in Hondo in 1879, and the couple had four children, two of whom would die very young. Ironically Dolan would end up owning both the old Tunstall store and ranch. Dolan died of a cerebral hemorrhage in 1898 at the Tunstall ranch. (Courtesy HSSNM #1445A.)

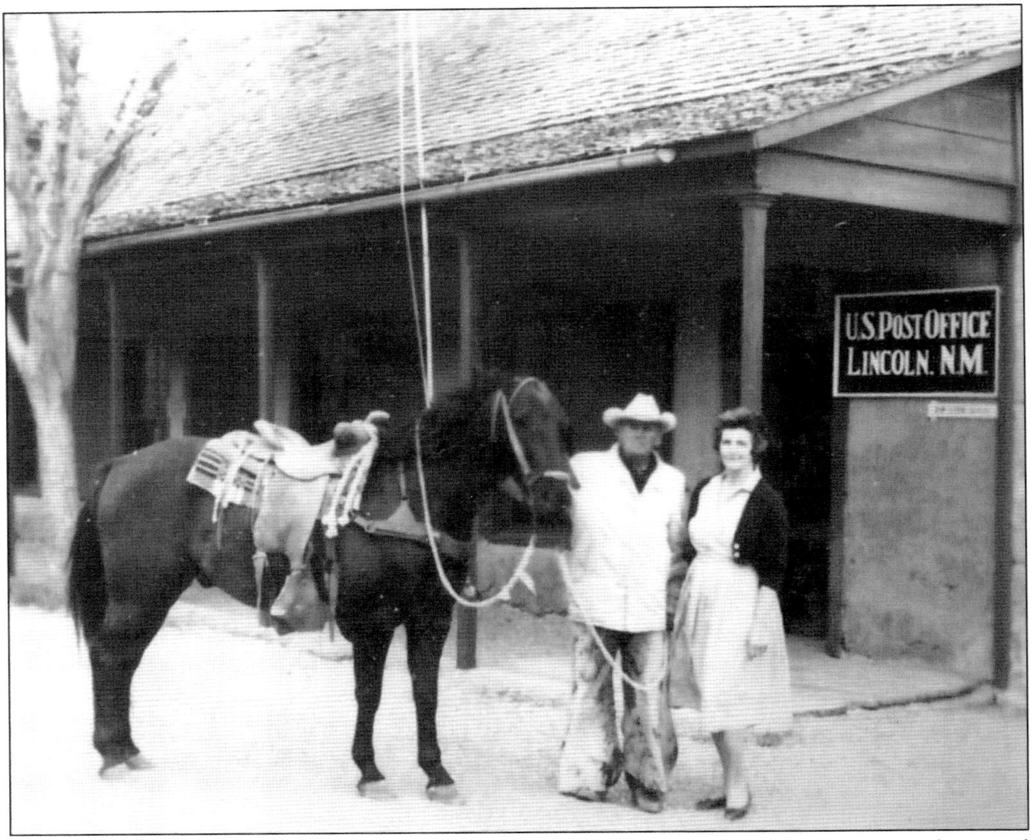

Life would go on in Lincoln after the war was over. Ironically, today the war that almost destroyed the town is now the one thing that sustains it. The Tunstall Store eventually became the Pennfield Store and also housed a post office. Above is the postmistress of the time in this fairly recent but undated photograph. The interior mail room can be seen below. (Above, courtesy HSSNM Larkham Album 8 #2967; below, courtesy HSSNM Larkham Album 1 #74.)

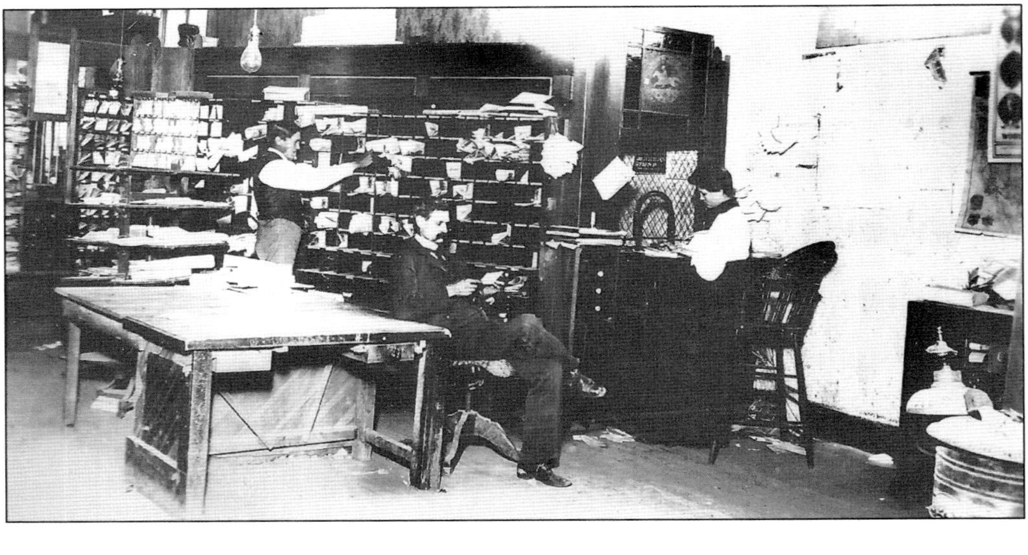

Although La Paloma Bar, constructed in 1890 by Rocco Emilio, was not built until after the Lincoln County War, it too has a colorful history. Rosario Emilio, Rocco's son and owner of the bar, was convicted of murder and sentenced to hang. Rosario escaped the noose, fleeing town, never to be recaptured. In the 1980s, then owner Roman Maes used a burro to haul an old cross to the top of a hill near Lincoln, which can be seen to this day. Maes said he had good luck after placing it there. In 1989, after the Maes's deaths, the saloon and museum was closed down. (Right, courtesy HSSNM #2276C; below, courtesy HSNM #4073.)

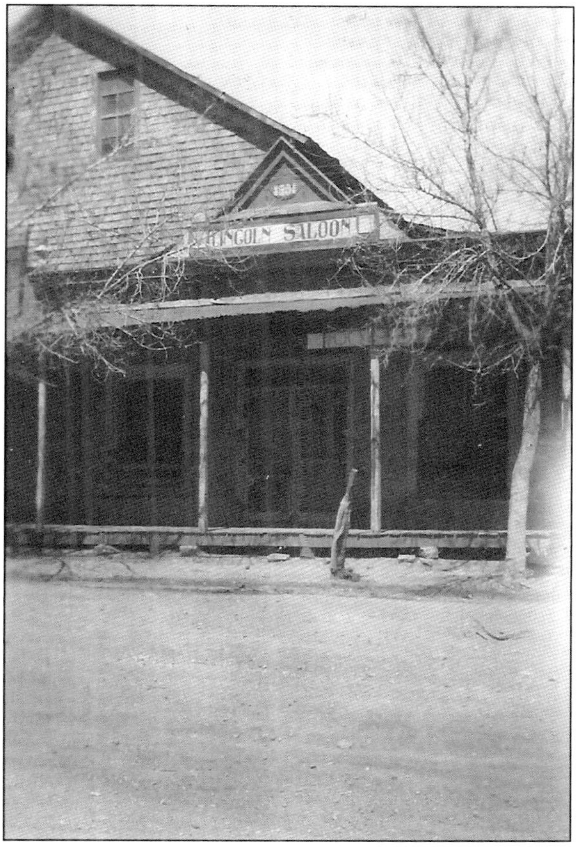

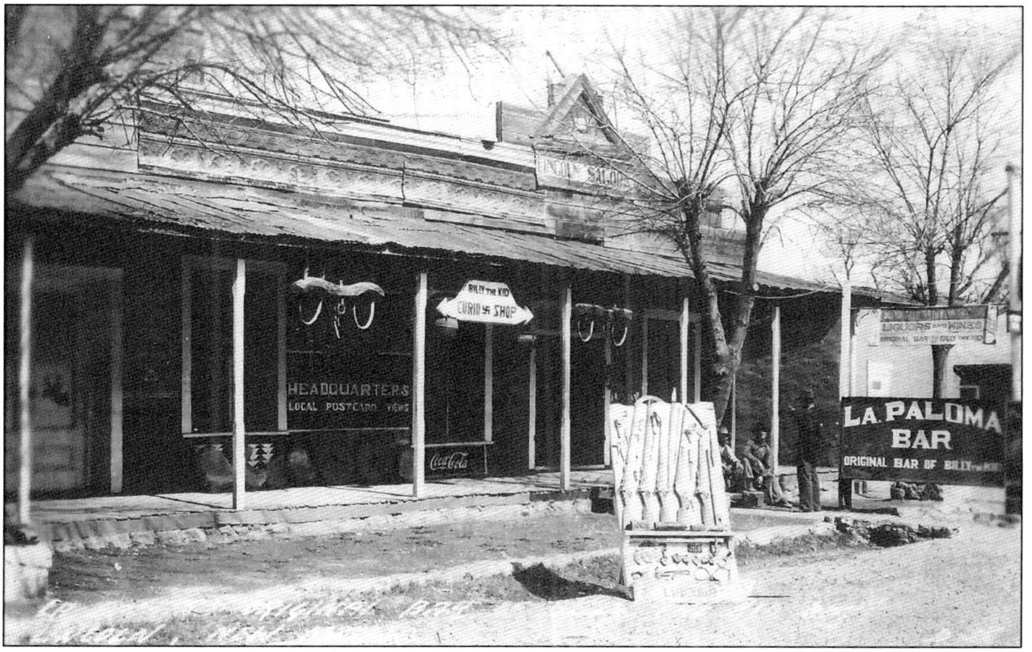

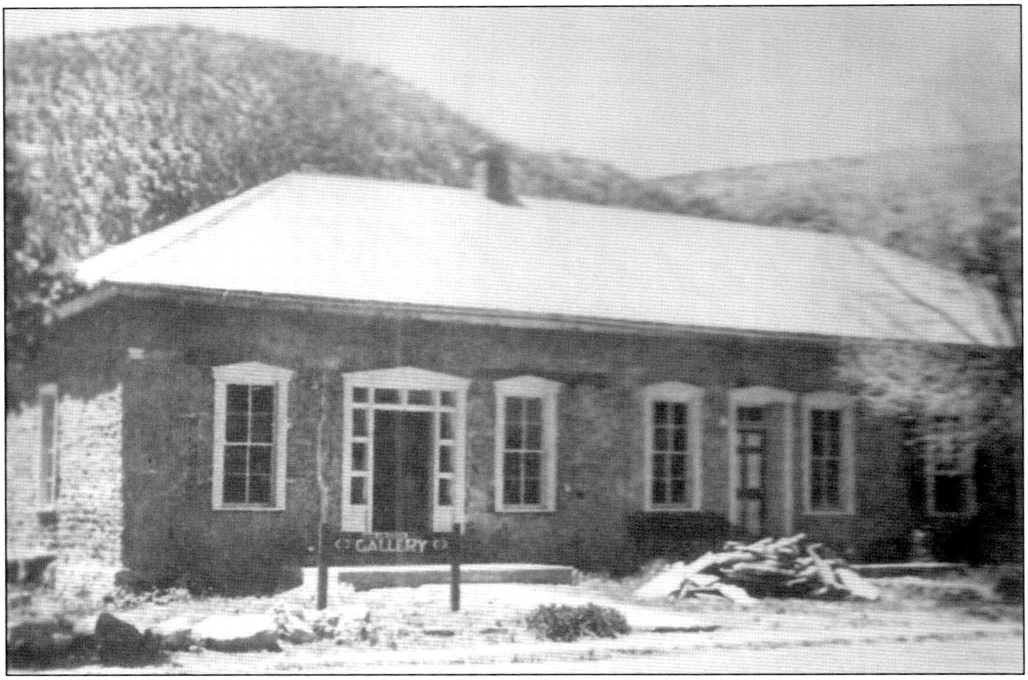

This structure still serves Lincoln today as an art gallery. (Courtesy HSSNM Larkham Album 8 #4016.)

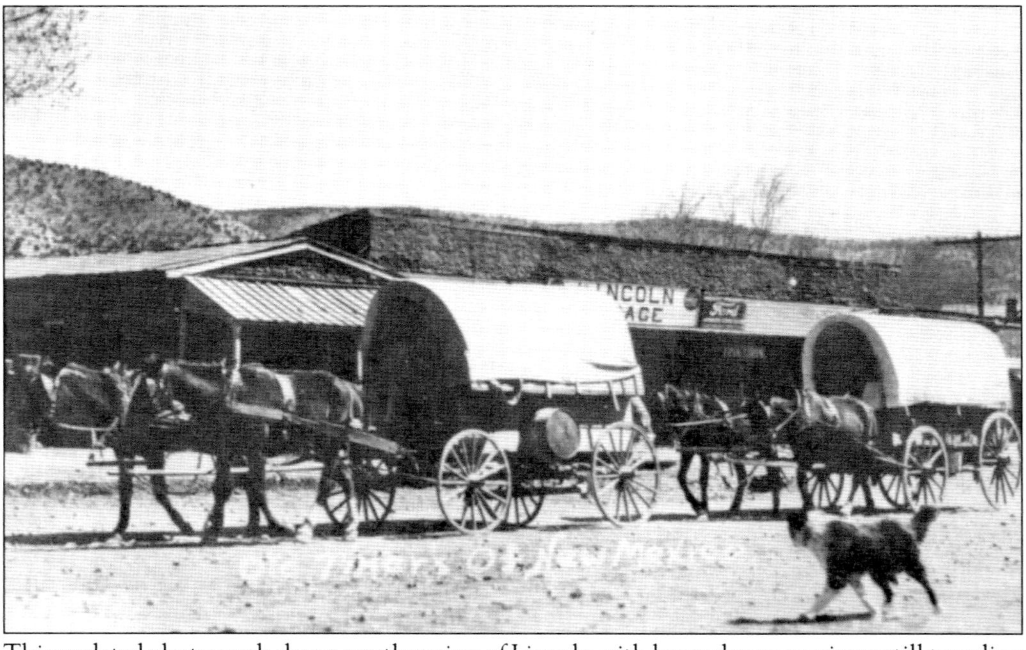

This undated photograph shows another view of Lincoln with horse drawn carriages still traveling its streets. (Courtesy Lincoln State Monument and the Anderson-Freeman Museum.)

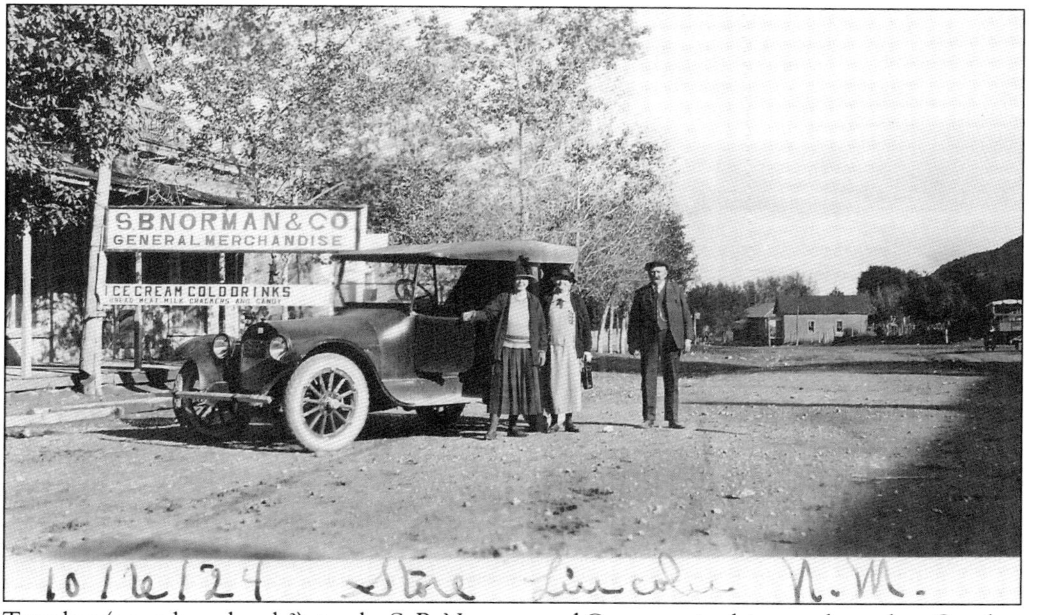

Travelers (or perhaps locals?) stop by S. B. Norman and Company in this snapshot taken October 16, 1924. (Courtesy HSSNM #2800B.)

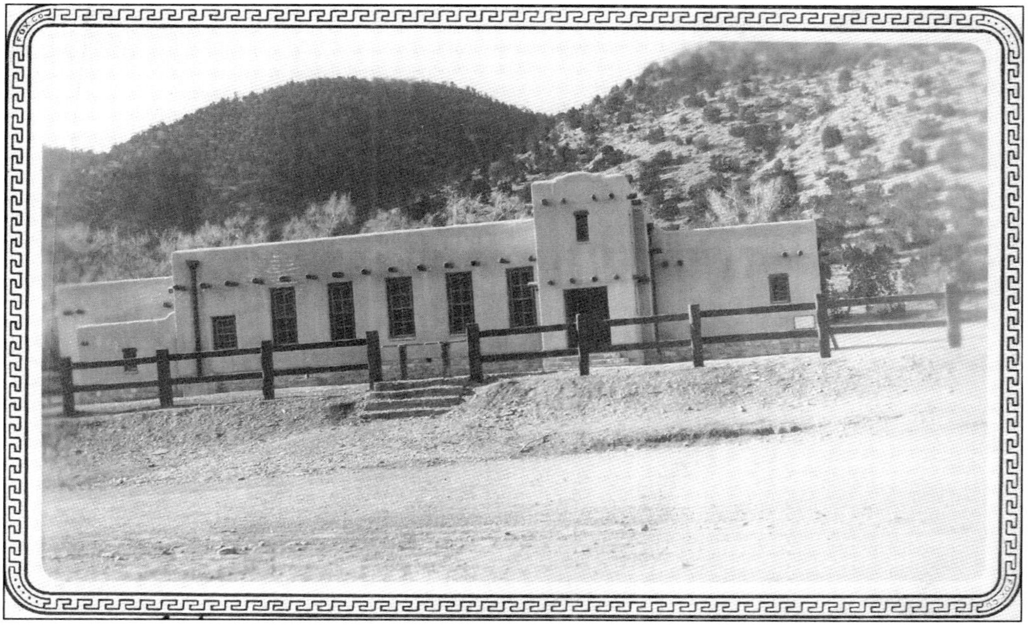

One of the newest structures in Lincoln is this WPA-built schoolhouse, erected in 1936. Before it was built, the site housed an older schoolhouse built in 1926 and the county garden, which from 1881 to 1913 had a pond and shade trees on its well-kept grounds. (Courtesy HSSNM #3505.)

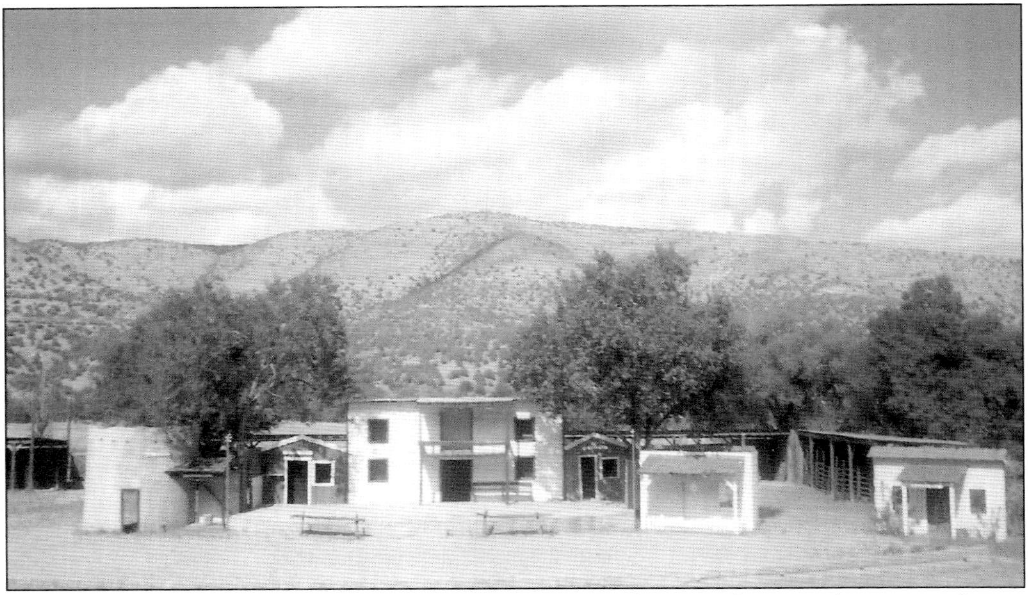

While Las Vegas, Nevada, may have a miniature replica of New York city within its city limits, Lincoln has its own miniature replica of itself: the Pageant Grounds. Built between 1953 and 1954 for the folk pageant *The Last Escape of Billy the Kid*, the pageant grounds are still being used to this day, and *The Last Escape of Billy the Kid* is one of the few remaining folk pageants still performed in America. In 2010, the pageant's 70th anniversary will be marked, and it is now part of Old Lincoln Days held the first Friday, Saturday, and Sunday in August. (Above, Author's collection; below, courtesy HSSNM #6295.)

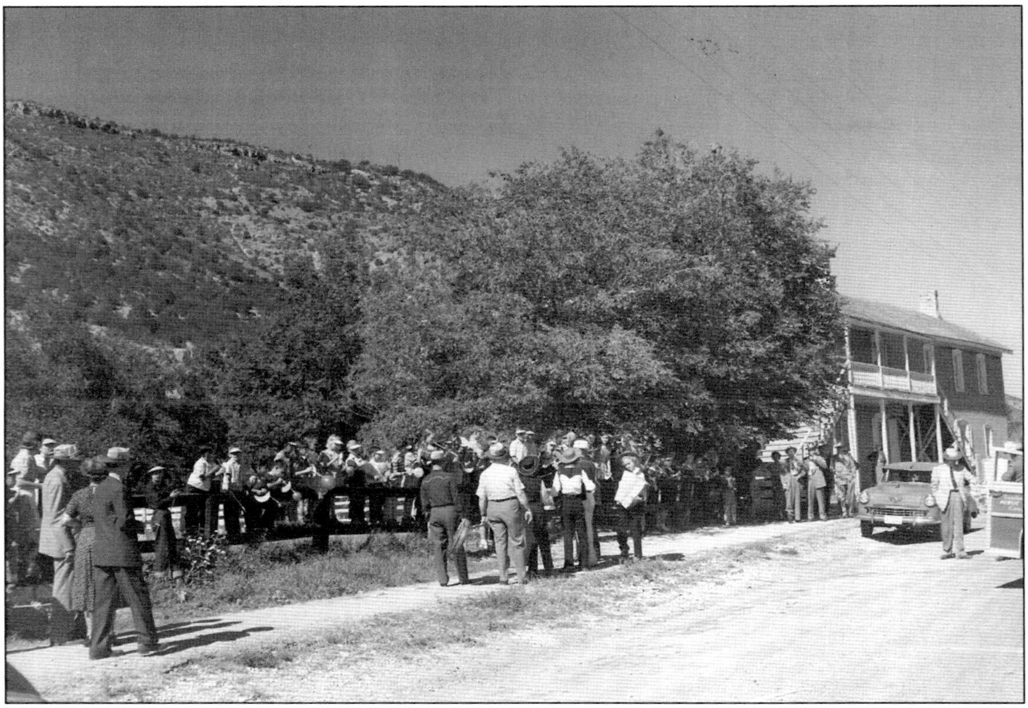

Two

The Hondo Valley

"Billy the Kid's hideout!" is proclaimed by several places along the Hondo Valley. And while this is true in many instances, the beautiful valley ironically located along the Billy the Kid Scenic and Historic Byway (U.S. 70/380) hardly needs the Kid to entice visitors. The charming atmosphere and landscape are all it needs to lure travelers into the valley.

The best time to take a scenic drive through the Hondo Valley is unquestionably in either the spring or the fall. In the spring, many beautiful fruit trees are in blossom, and likewise in the fall, when the leaves gain a golden orange hue, one can stop at the numerous fruit stands to buy the last produce of the season before winter comes. The half dozen or so villages one comes across on the drive west consist of (in order) Riverside, Picacho, Tinnie, Hondo, San Patricio, and finally Glencoe.

Most of the first settlers in the Hondo Valley were Hispanic, and many of their descendants still live there with the same surnames, such as the Anayas, Montoyas, Sanchezes, Salcidos, Torreses, and the Anallas. The first settlers in the Picacho area came from the Rio Grande Valley in the late 1860s with flocks of sheep and goats, and they used the Rio Hondo as a source for water. Eventually the Anglo cattlemen would move into the area as well, and many of their ranches still stand, such as the Diamond A. The elegantly named town of Tinnie used to be known as Las Cuevas (the caves), since early settlers used the caves for their homesteads. Tinnie was also known as Analla, named for an early settler in the area. The village of Hondo was originally known as La Junta because it was at the junction of the Ruidoso and Bonito Rivers. San Patricio is especially unique. At first a quick hideaway for outlaws such as Billy the Kid in the Lincoln County War, it eventually became home of artist Peter Hurd and even houses a polo field.

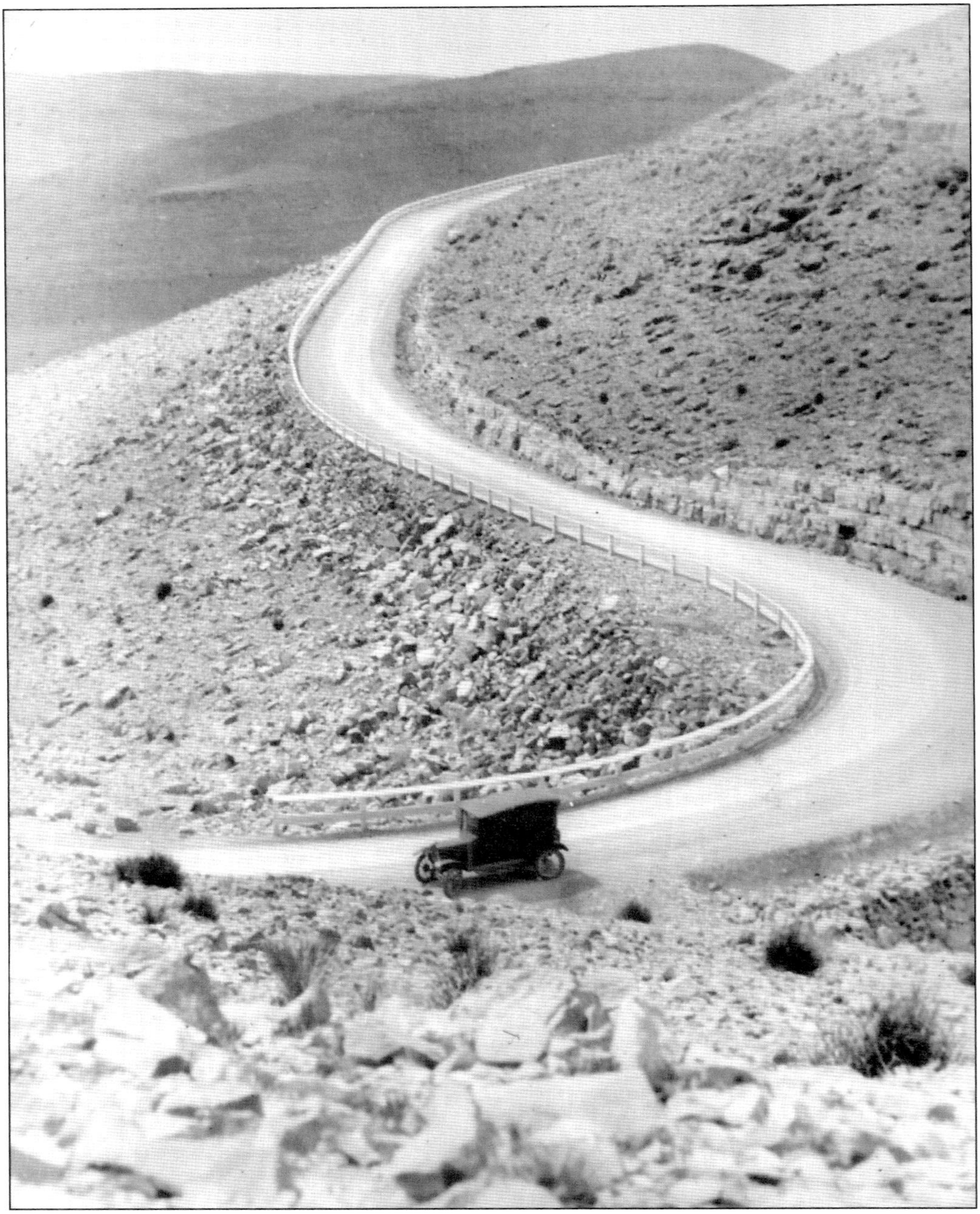

Pictured above, a motorist descends the steep and rocky Picacho Hill on the old stage road that is today no longer in use. Although it is often associated with the nearby settlement of Picacho, Picacho Hill is actually closer to Riverside, the first settlement one will encounter when heading west into Lincoln County. (Courtesy HSSNM #1768.)

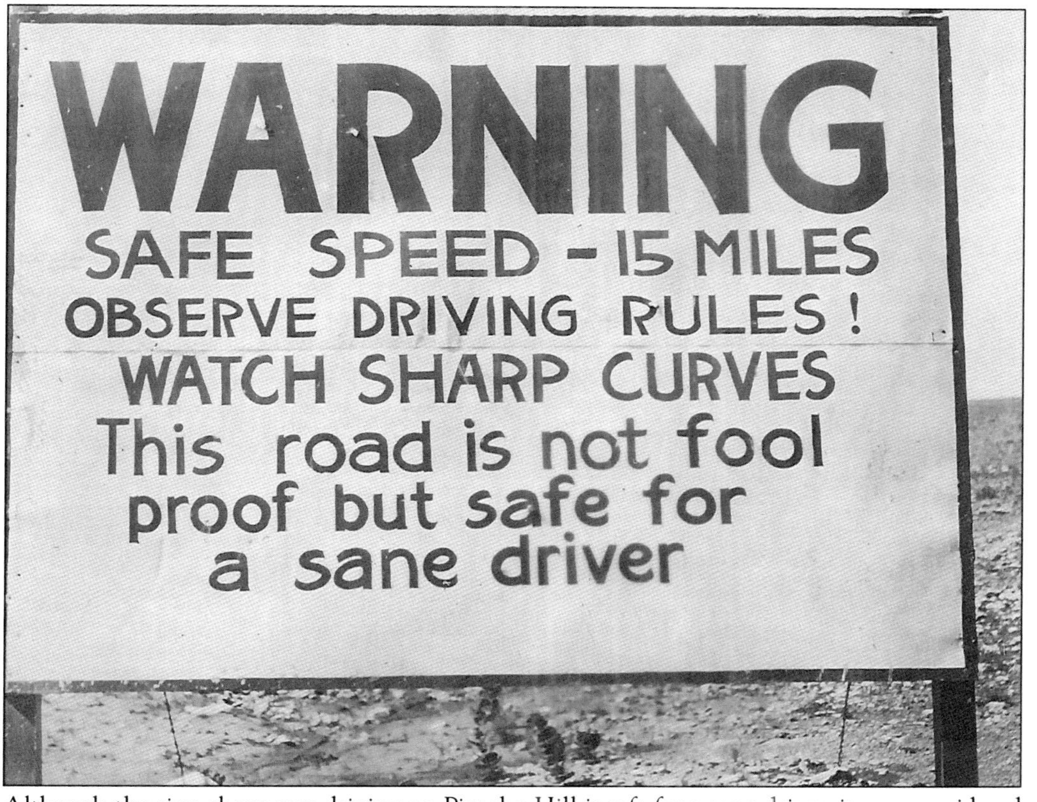

Although the sign above says driving on Picacho Hill is safe for a sane driver, it was considered extremely hazardous for inexperienced drivers due to its steep slope. Picacho Hill is one of the first landmarks one will see when entering the Hondo Valley heading west. Today the old road being traversed by the automobile below is no longer in use, but if one looks closely as they drive by Picacho Hill, they can still see its now lonely contours curving around the hillside. (Above, courtesy HSSNM #30941; below, courtesy HSSNM #2693A.)

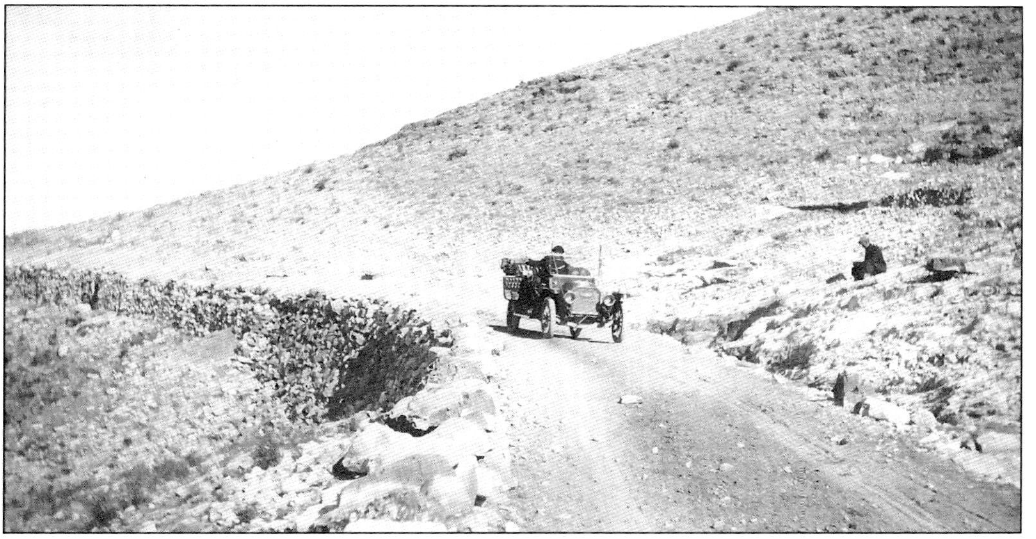

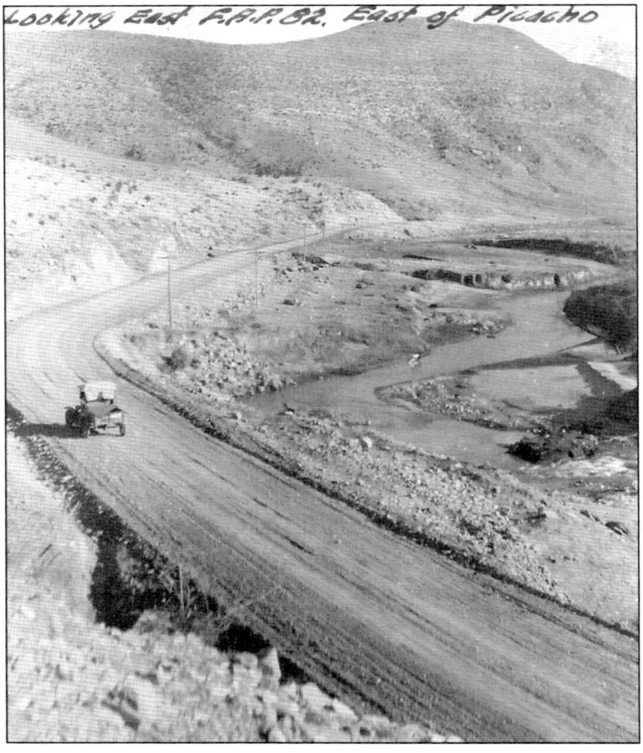

In the image to the left, an old truck drives along the road near the banks of the Hondo River, which can be seen in the right of the photograph. Pictured below, the Old West crosses paths with the advancement of the modern era as a horse drawn buggy and an automobile pass each other on the old stage road along the Hondo Valley near Picacho. (Left, courtesy HSSNM #3094A; below, courtesy HSSNM #3094B.)

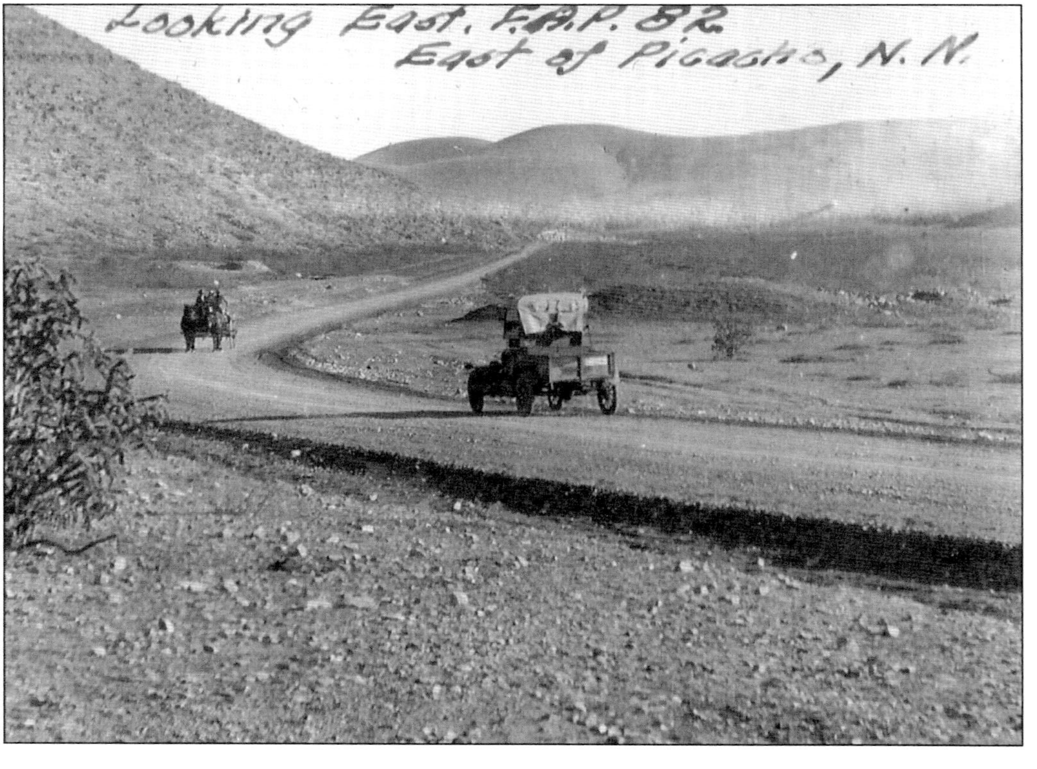

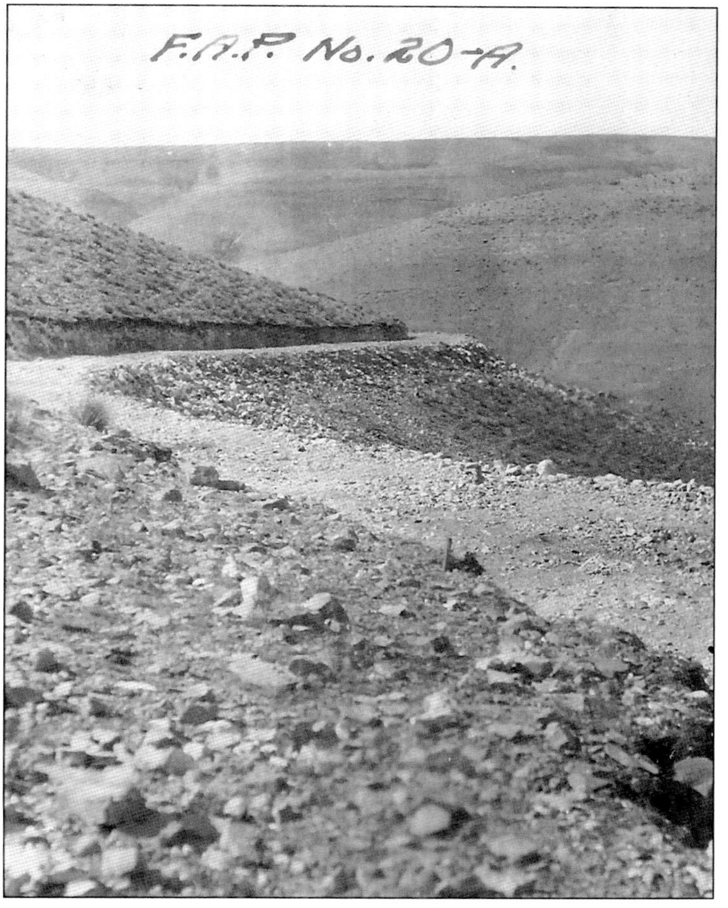

As can be seen in these images, the Upper Hondo Valley keeps with the rocky visage common in Southeastern New Mexico, but when one begins to enter the lower Hondo Valley, the scenery becomes much more lush and green. All of the photographs on these two pages come from the early 1920s when the road was being extensively worked on as part of the Federal Aid Project (FAP). The bottom image shows the FAP working on a guardrail for the old road. (Right, courtesy HSSNM #3094C; below, courtesy HSSNM #3094D.)

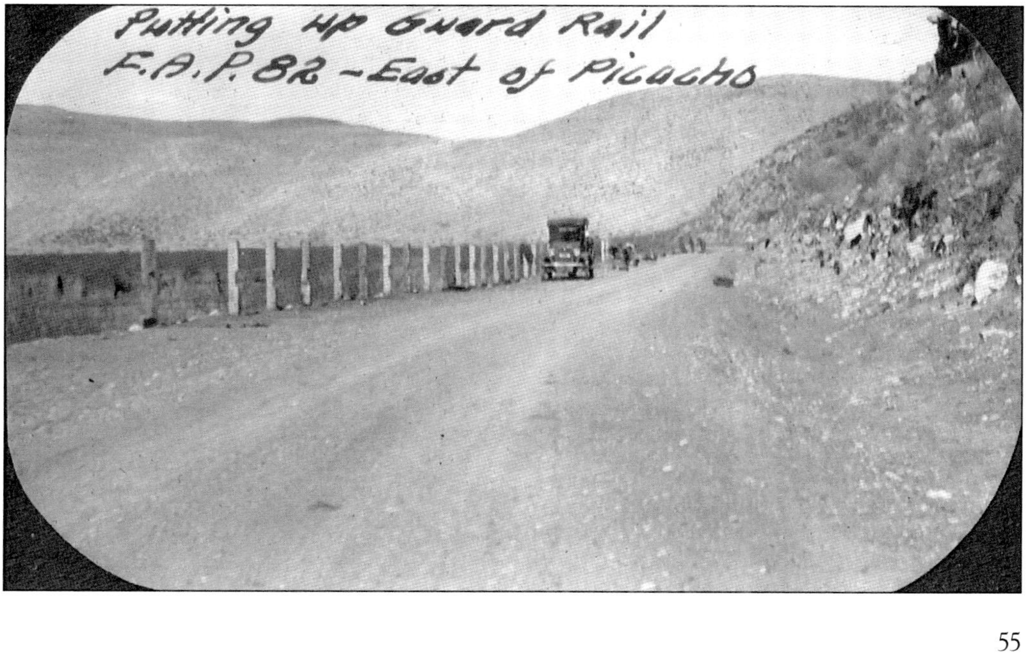

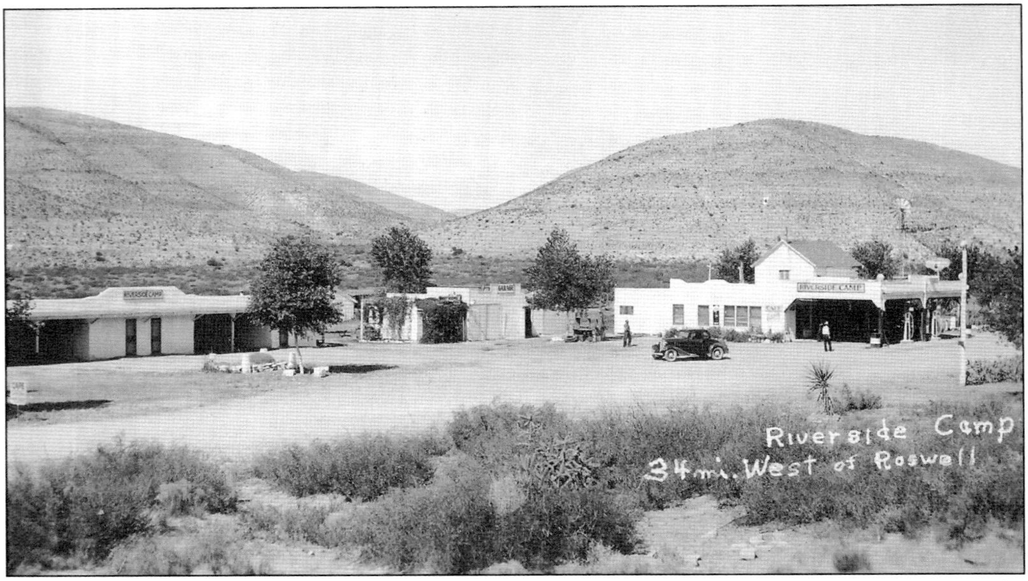

The first settlement one passes while headed west in the Hondo Valley is that of Riverside. Riverside Camp, shown above, was originally named Big Hill Filling Station by its owner W. O. Norman. The name was changed to Riverside Camp in 1930 after Norman sold it. (Courtesy HSSNM #5031.)

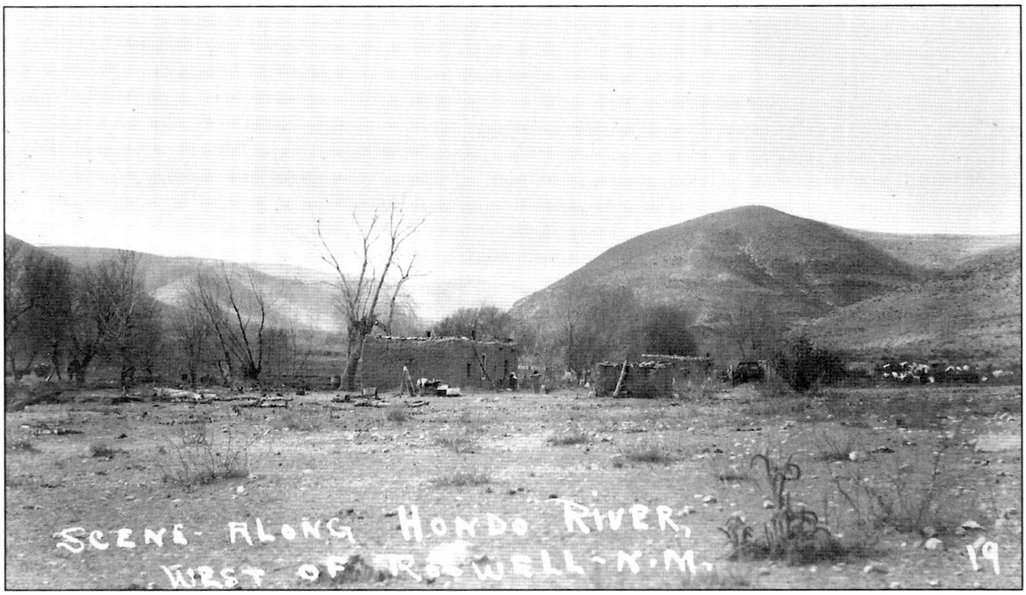

As one continues into the Hondo Valley after passing Riverside, the rise in population will become noticeable. Adobe homes like the one above used to smatter the landscape, and today many scattered homes and ranches can be seen off of the road in the valley below the highway. (Courtesy HSSNM #5557.)

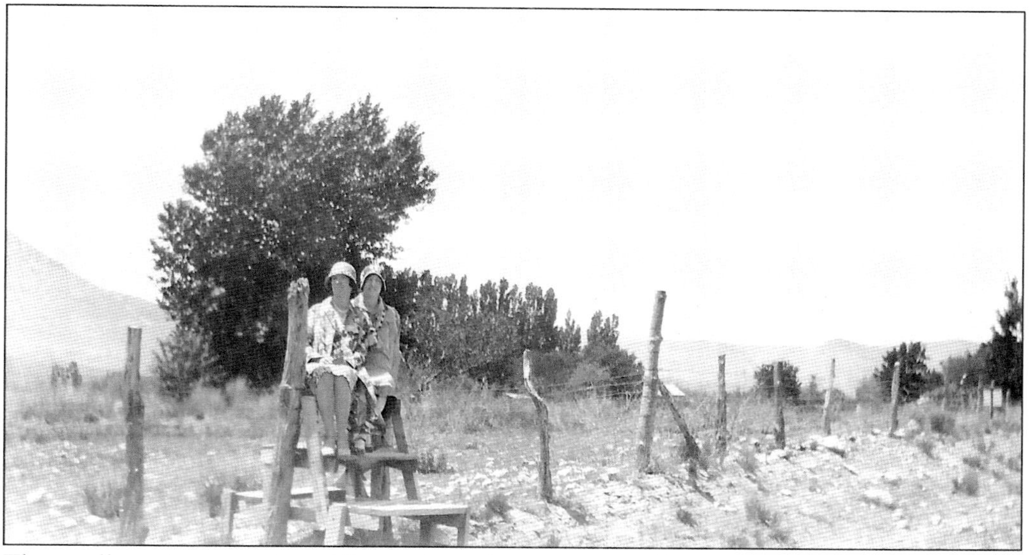

The small rural community of Sunset is in the same area of Riverside and Picacho. Annie L. Snorf and another woman sit on wooden steps near a barbed wire fence at the Sunset Ranch. (Courtesy HSSNM #2309D.)

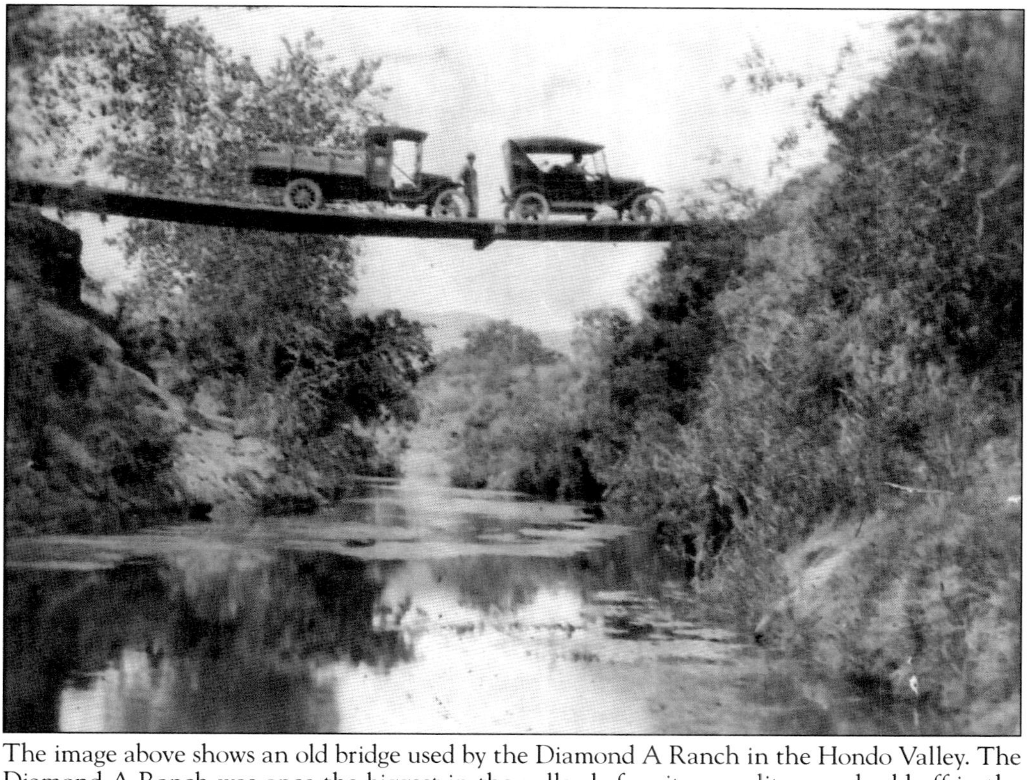

The image above shows an old bridge used by the Diamond A Ranch in the Hondo Valley. The Diamond A Ranch was once the biggest in the valley before it was split up and sold off in the 1940s. (Courtesy HSSNM Larkham Album 1 #739.)

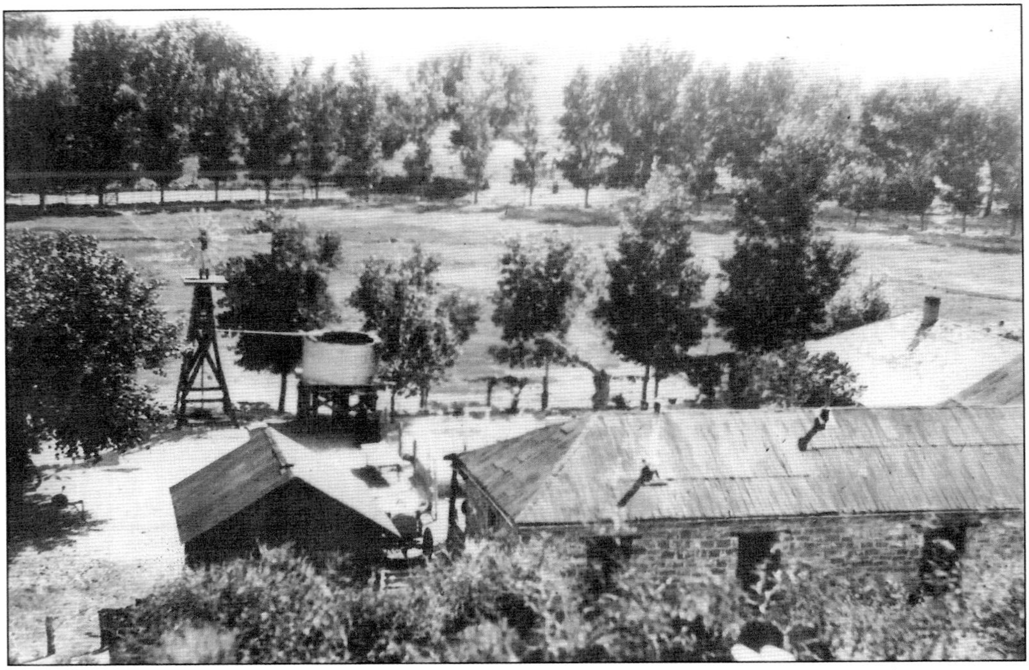

The Diamond A Ranch, seen above and below, began as the Circle Diamond Cattle Company, which came to the Picacho area in the 1870s. Eventually the Circle Diamond was annexed by the Diamond A Cattle Company, which itself became part of the Bloom Land and Cattle Company, growing to more than 800,000 acres. The Diamond A Ranch has gone through many different owners and foremen, the better-known ones being Capt. Burton C. Mossman, J. P. White, and Robert O. Anderson. (Above, courtesy HSSNM #2309G; below, courtesy HSSNM #2309A.)

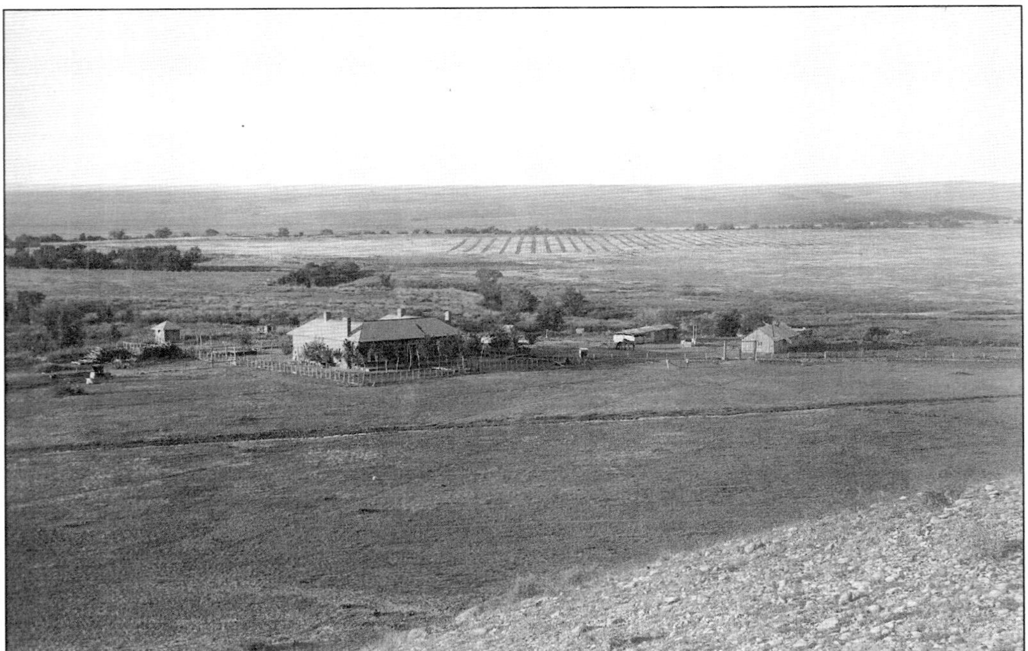

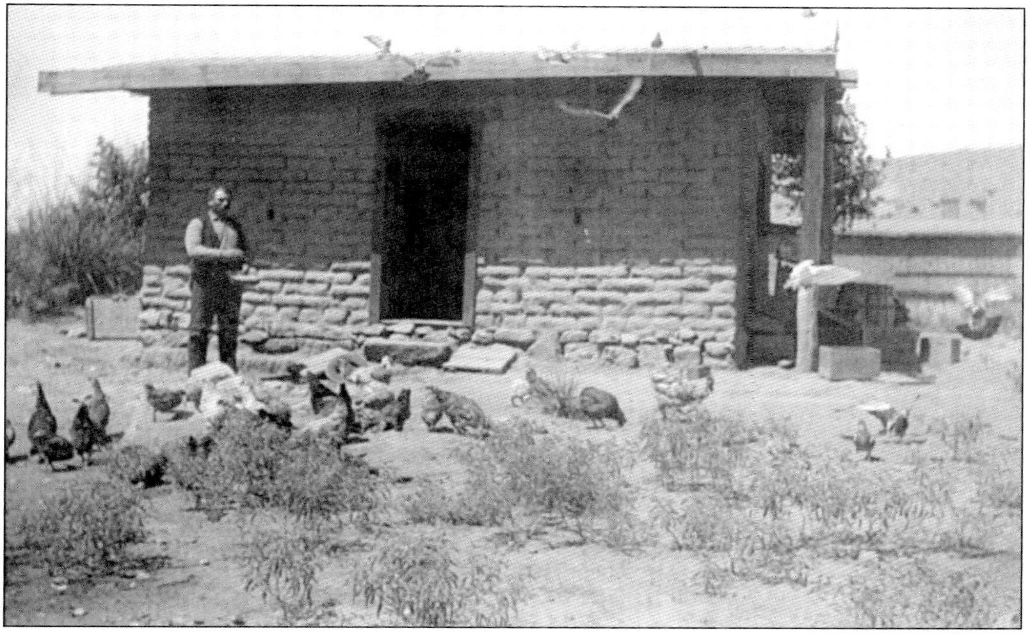

Pictured above feeding chickens, James Sutherland was a former ranch foreman at the Diamond A Ranch. Sutherland also had his own ranch, the Sutherland Ranch, which can be seen in the c. 1932 photograph below where Ethel Folds and another woman take their horses to the watering hole. (Above, courtesy HSSNM #1797B; below, courtesy HSSNM #5550.)

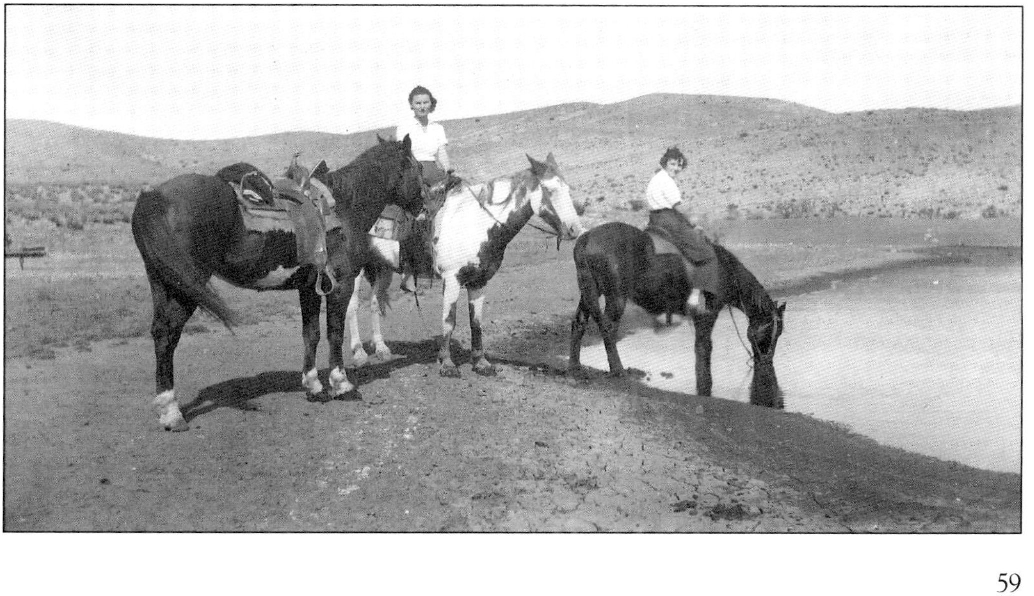

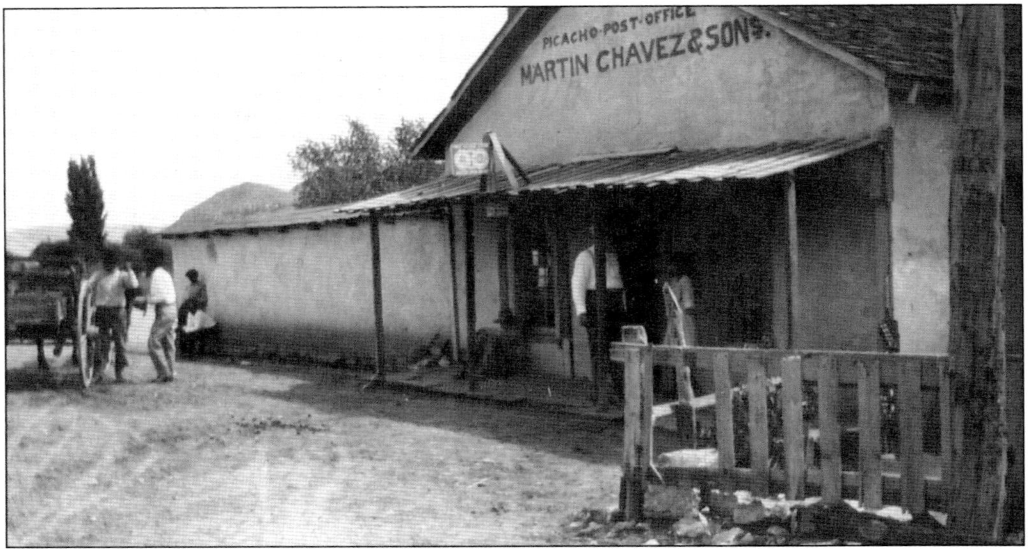

The postmaster of the Picacho Post Office (above) in its early years was Martin Chaves, none other than the man who had been the leader of the Regulators during the Five Day Battle in Lincoln when the Alexander McSween home was burnt down. Chaves had 20 to 30 men under his command at the time of the war. (Courtesy HSSNM #226.)

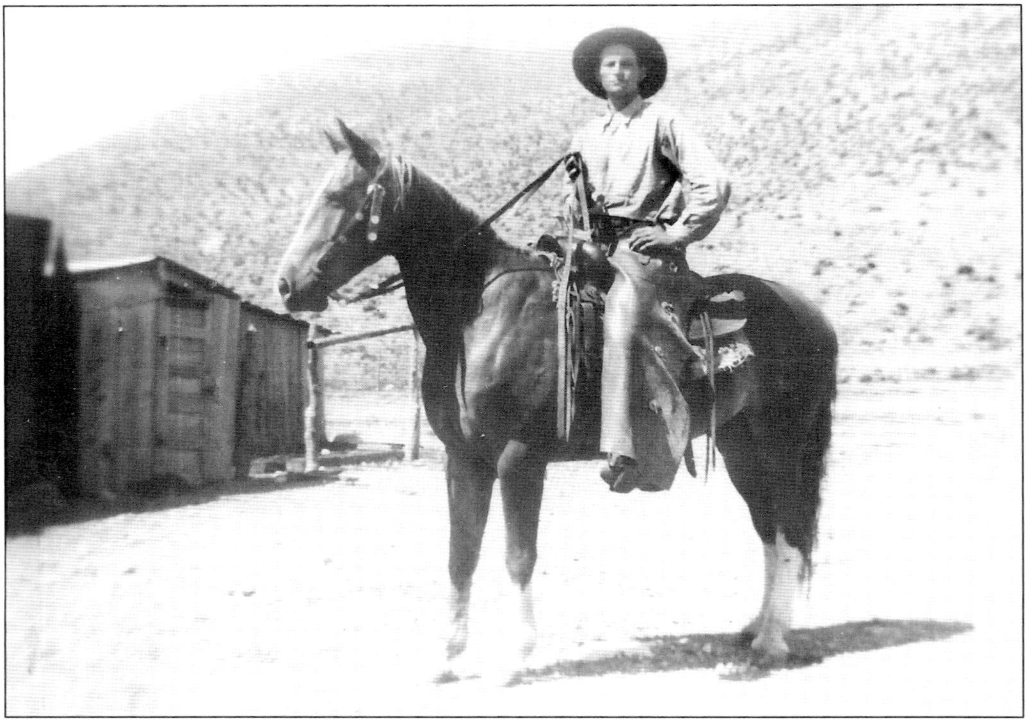

Above is Lewis Purcella, a well known old-time cowboy in the Picacho and Tinnie area of the Hondo Valley. In the caption on the back of this photograph, Purcella fondly recalls when "Preacher Pryor" used to hold services in the Hondo Valley. "Everyone turned out when Brother Pryor came to our community," Purcella said. (Courtesy HSSNM #4018.)

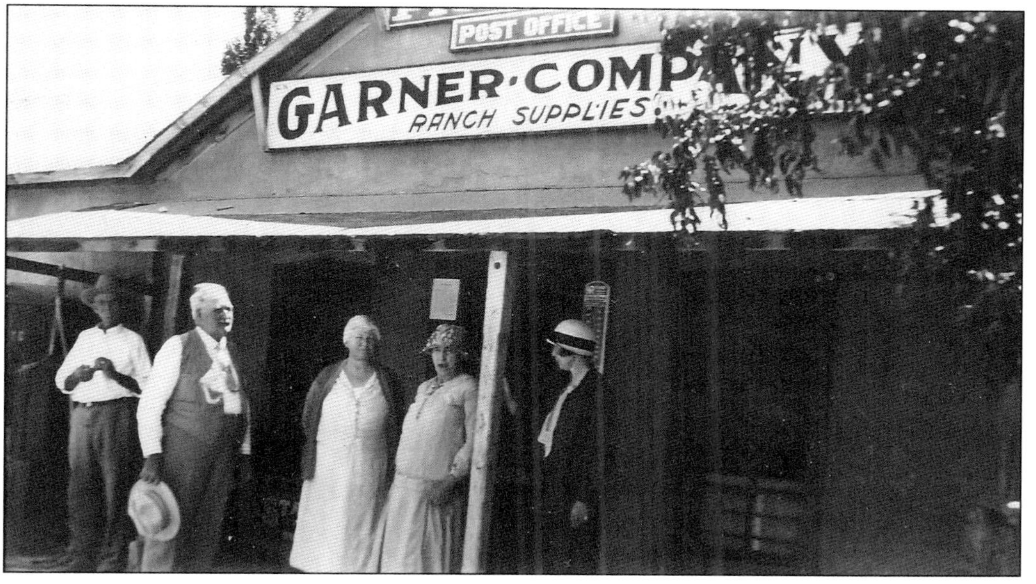

Eventually the Picacho post office, which also served as a general store and hotel, was taken over by the Garner brothers, Byrd and Lawrence. Byrd Garner was commissioned postmaster in 1915, when the mail was still brought by Porfiro Chaves on horseback from Lincoln. Later that year, mail would begin arriving by automobile. After the Garners, Albert Pruitt, former mayor of Roswell, took over the post office in 1932. During the World War II years, Picacho seemed like a ghost town, but the post office persevered and stayed in operation under Viola K. Sandoval. Unfortunately the historic building would burn down in 1946. A new post office was built by Polly Pruitt soon thereafter. Notice the horse drawn carriages in the bottom photograph compacting the dirt road next to the first store in 1923. (Above, courtesy HSSNM #2800A; below, courtesy HSSNM #3094Z.)

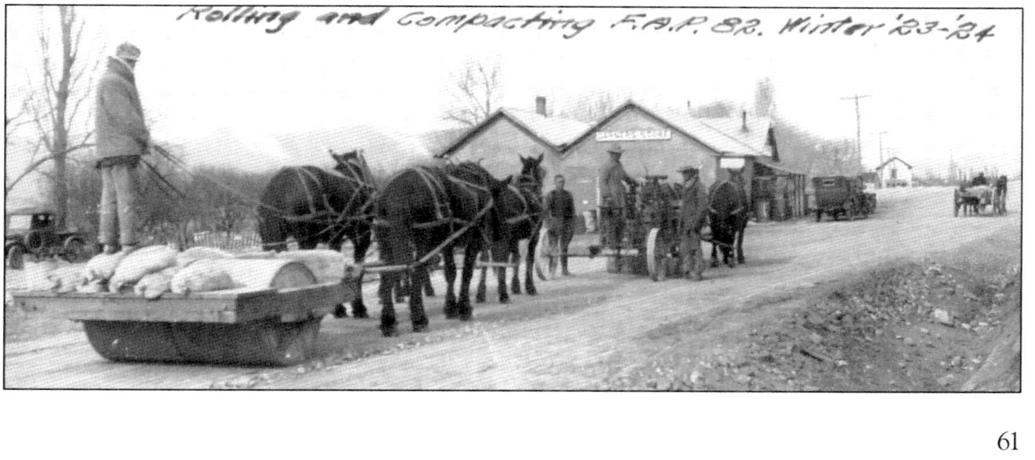

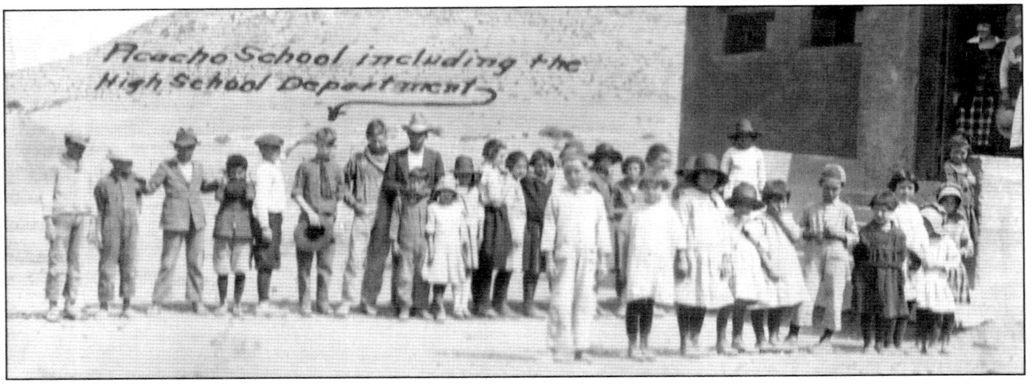

The entire class of the Picacho School, comprised of all grades through high school, is shown above in the c. 1920s image. Picacho has always had a small population of mostly Hispanics and a few Anglos. In the 1950s, the population of the small ranching community was as small as 200 people, which had gone down from nearly 300 in the 1930s and today is even smaller. (Courtesy HSSNM #3094M.)

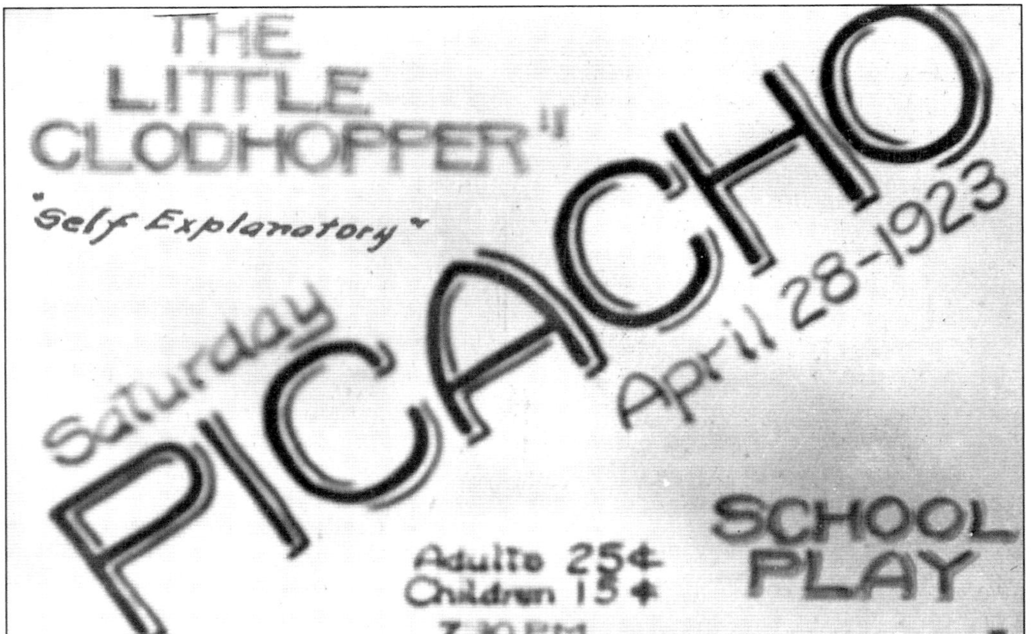

Above is a vintage homemade ad for a Picacho School play from 1923 called *The Little Clodhopper*. Clodhopper was a slang term at the time for an irritating, clumsy person, but the term also applies to a type of a broad-soled shoe worn by country people. More likely than not, *The Little Clodhopper* was Picacho's own homespun Dennis the Menace. (Courtesy HSSNM #3094D.)

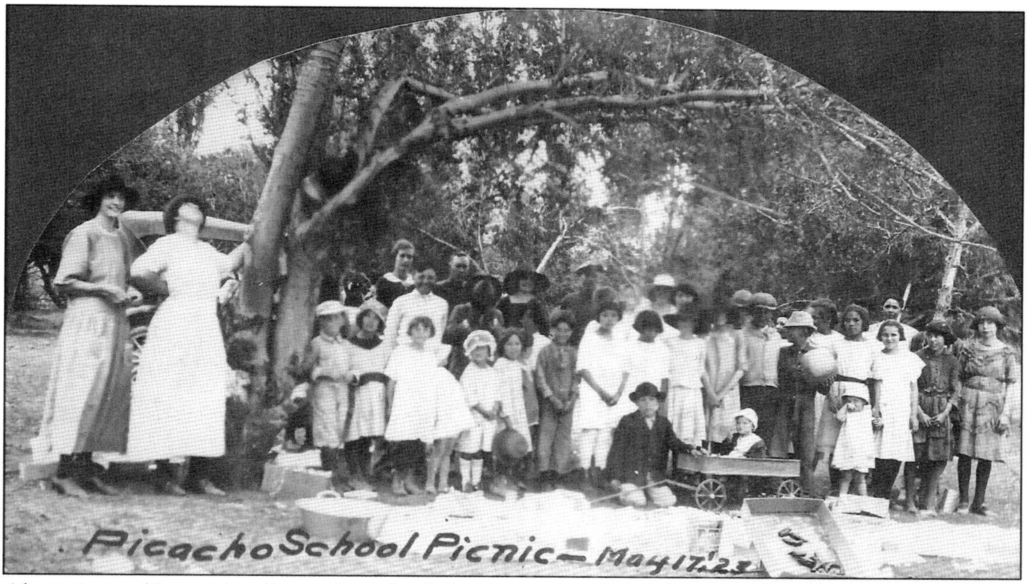

Above is an old snapshot from a Picacho School picnic on May 17, 1923. They likely took the picnic somewhere in the valley, which has many heavily foliaged areas. (Courtesy HSSNM #3094K.)

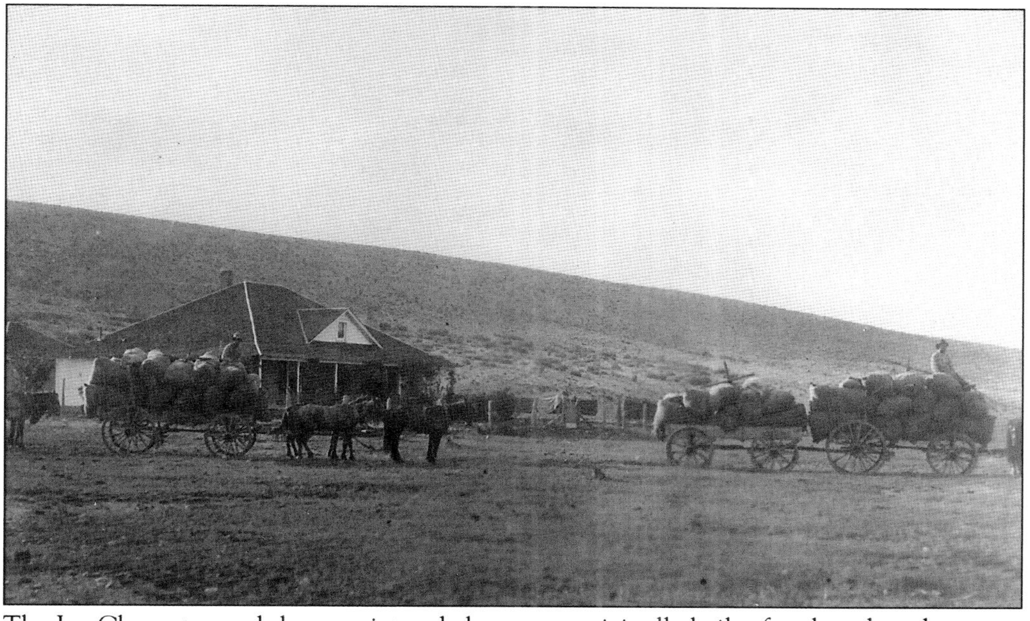

The Joe Clements ranch house, pictured above, was originally built of rock and mud, as were many others in the Hondo Valley. The ranch house is obviously a newer structure. The Clements ranch was located about 20 miles south of Picacho. (Courtesy HSSNM #2692.)

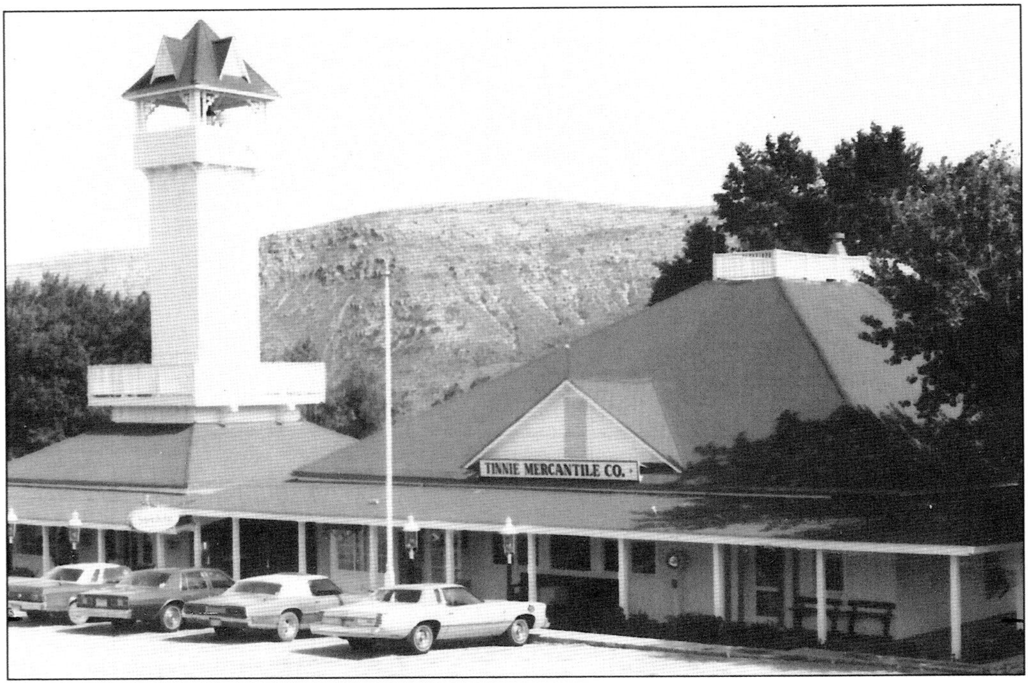

The most recognizable facet of Tinnie is the Tinnie Mercantile and Silver Dollar Restaurant, which can be seen above. Believe it or not, the well-known restaurant, which entices travelers from many miles away, actually began as the tiny mercantile and post office built in the late 1800s seen below. The structure above is not a completely new building, however. If one looks at these two photographs closely, the original building can be seen peeking out from the new. Tinnie got its name in 1909 from the daughter of then postmistress Oney Raymond, Tinnie Raymond. (Above, courtesy HSSNM #4070A; below, courtesy HSSNM #1326A.)

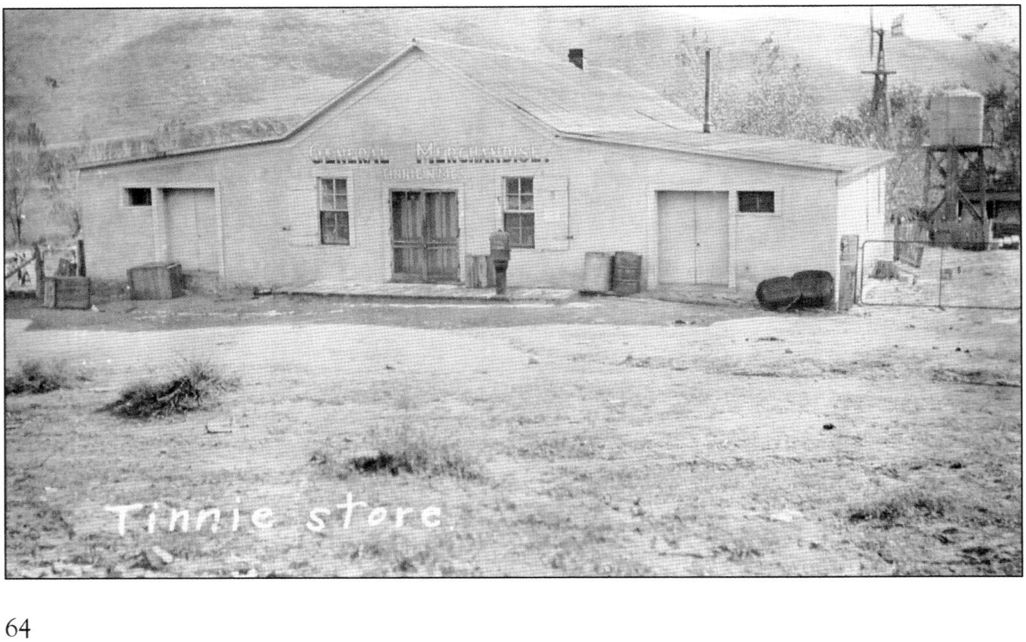

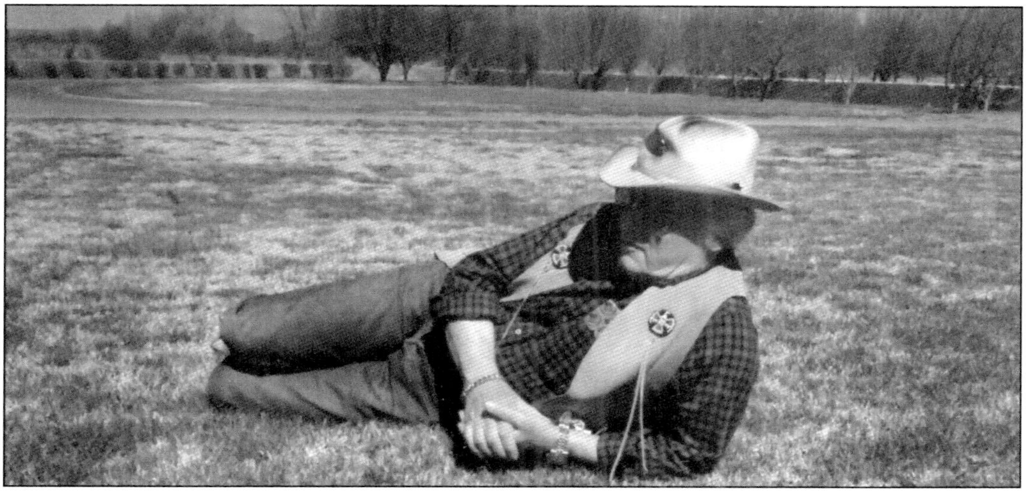

Tinnie Mercantile and Silver Dollar Restaurant received a major renovation in 1959 from Robert O. Anderson, pictured above reclining at his Circle Diamond Ranch. Anderson was one of the richest men in the United States and was, at the time, living nearby at his ranch, shown in the drawing by Sydney Redfield below. Since there were no nice restaurants nearby that he could take his company to, he decided to build one by adding a porch, a large tower, and a pavilion onto the old mercantile in Tinnie for a cost of several hundred thousand dollars. The renovation did not stop there; Anderson commissioned San Patricio artist John Meigs to oversee the artwork and decor of the building, some of which came from as far away as San Francisco. The restaurant is a staple in the Hondo Valley to this day. (Above, courtesy HSSNM, #4457B; below, courtesy HSSNM #3212F.)

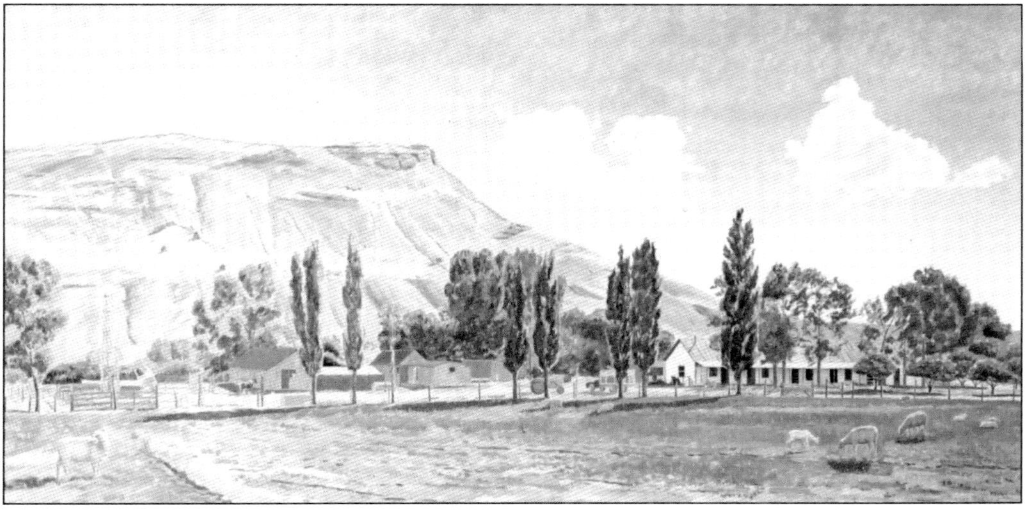

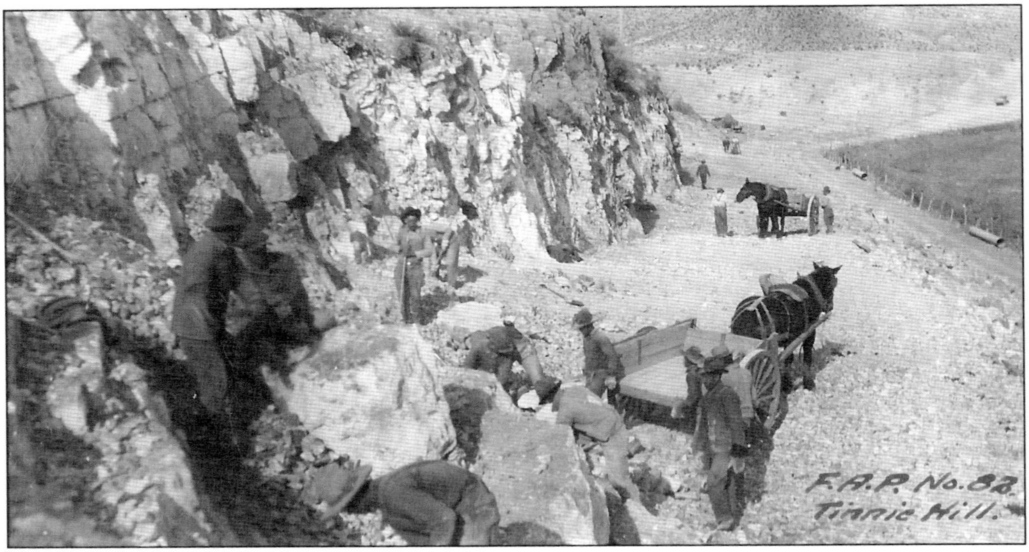

The two images on this page show Federal Aid Project workers removing rocks in the process of building the road. Pictured above, they are working on Tinnie Hill, hauling away large rocks with a horse drawn carriage. The men atop Sunset Hill below look to have just come back from lunch, as the man on the right is holding his outstretched stomach. (Above, courtesy HSSNM #3094J; below, courtesy HSSNM #3094E.)

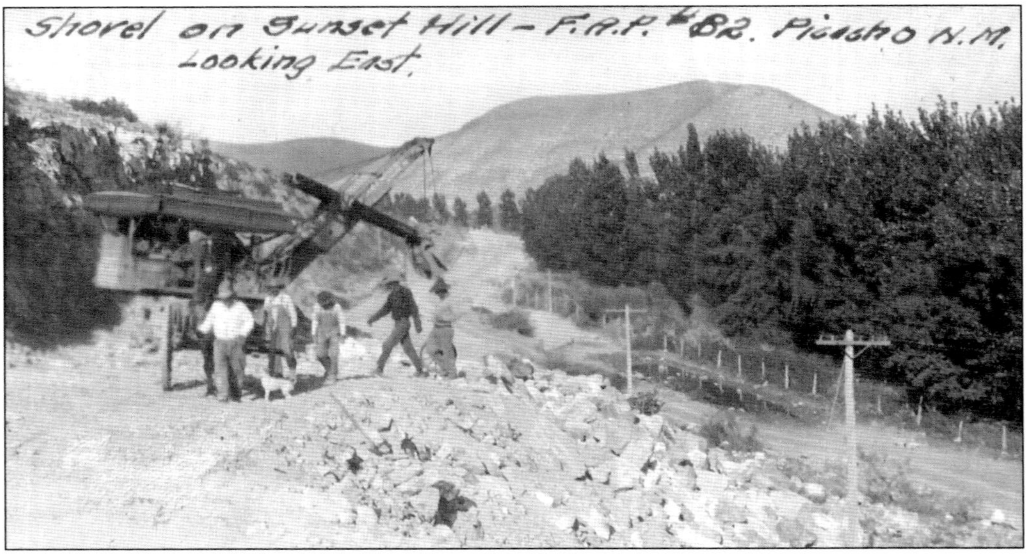

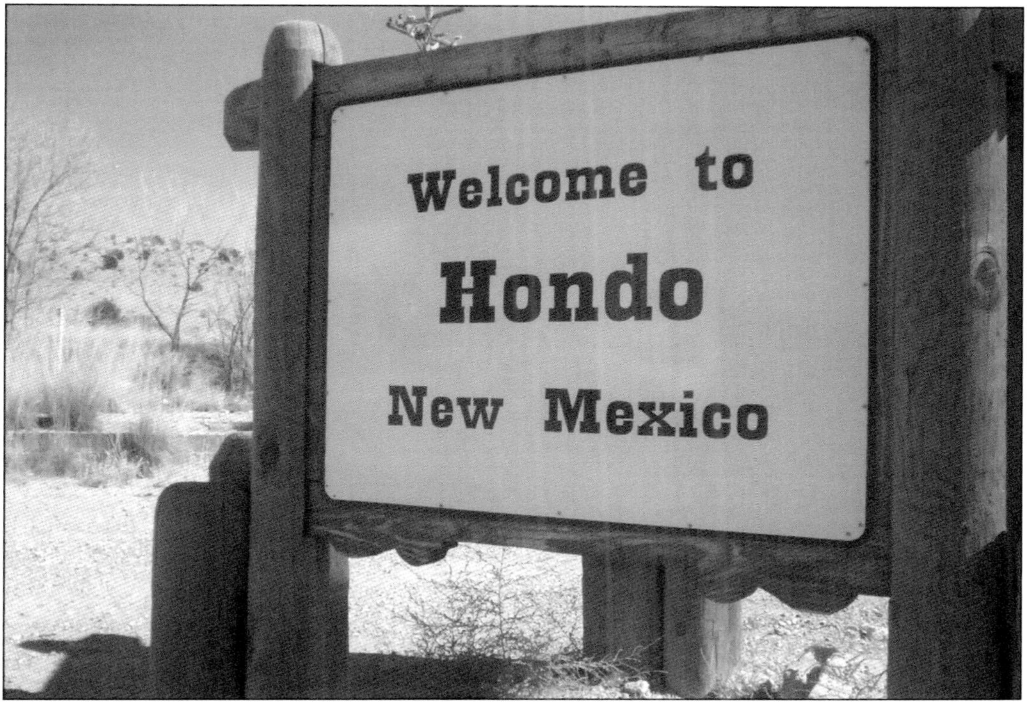

After Tinnie, Hondo is the next town a motorist will encounter along the Billy the Kid Scenic and Historic Byway, and the beautiful landscape is dotted with the occasional pond like the one below. Hondo's primary claim to fame is its first-class fruit produced from apple orchards in the area. Also in the area is the famous Hondo Iris Farm. Hondo derives its name from the Hondo River (*hondo* means "deep" in Spanish), although it was originally called La Junta. Lincoln County War villain James J. Dolan is actually buried in the old Hondo cemetery. (Above, Author's collection; below, courtesy HSSNM #6192.)

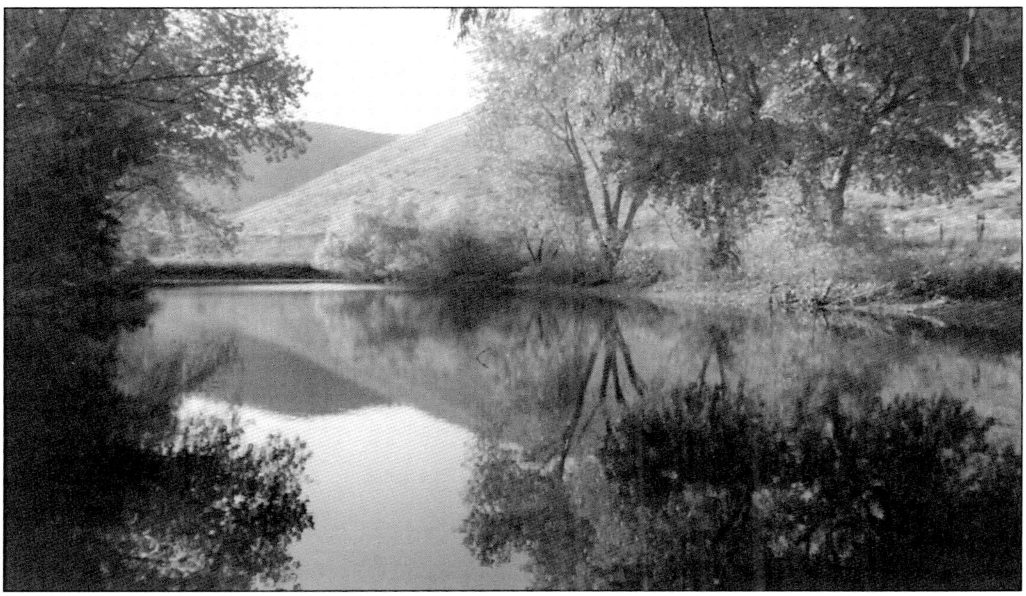

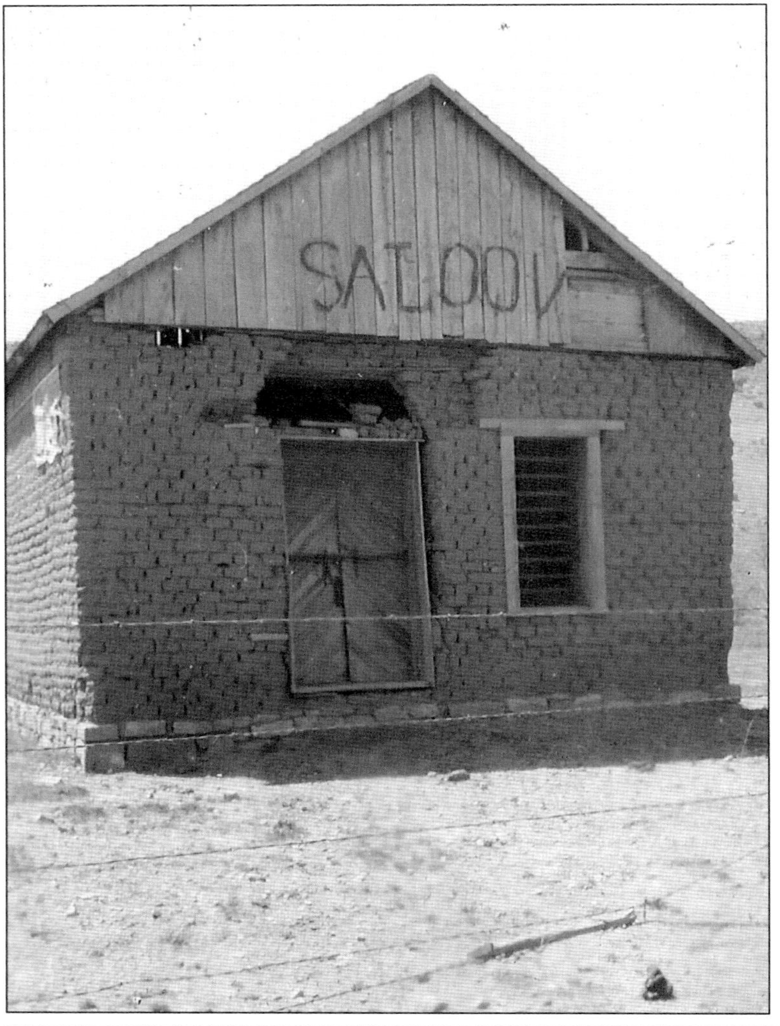

This old saloon was located in the village of Hondo. An old newspaper item says that, back in the 1870s, gamblers at the Hondo Saloon would wager everything from their bridle, saddle, and their horse if they had nothing else to gamble. Below is another beautiful Hondo Valley view. (Left, courtesy HSSNM #2275A; below, courtesy HSSNM Larkham Album 9 #1993-2.)

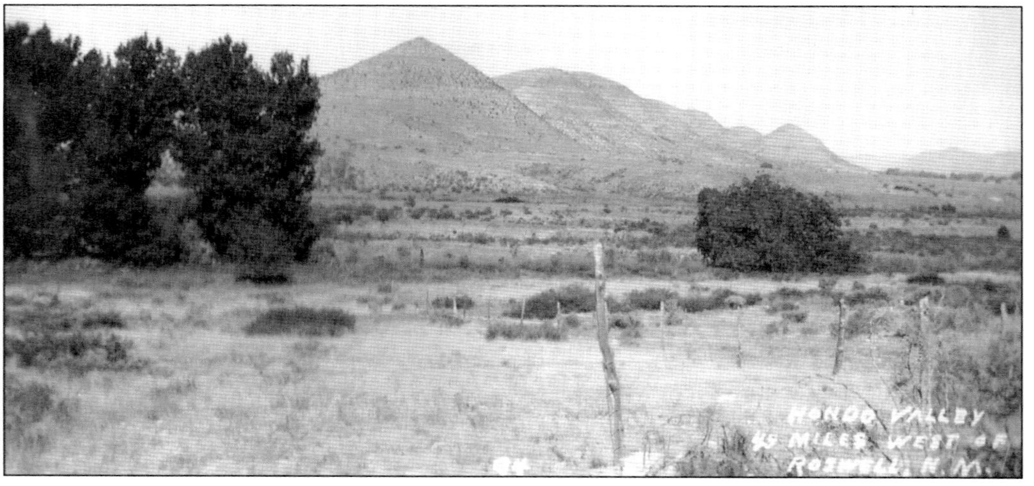

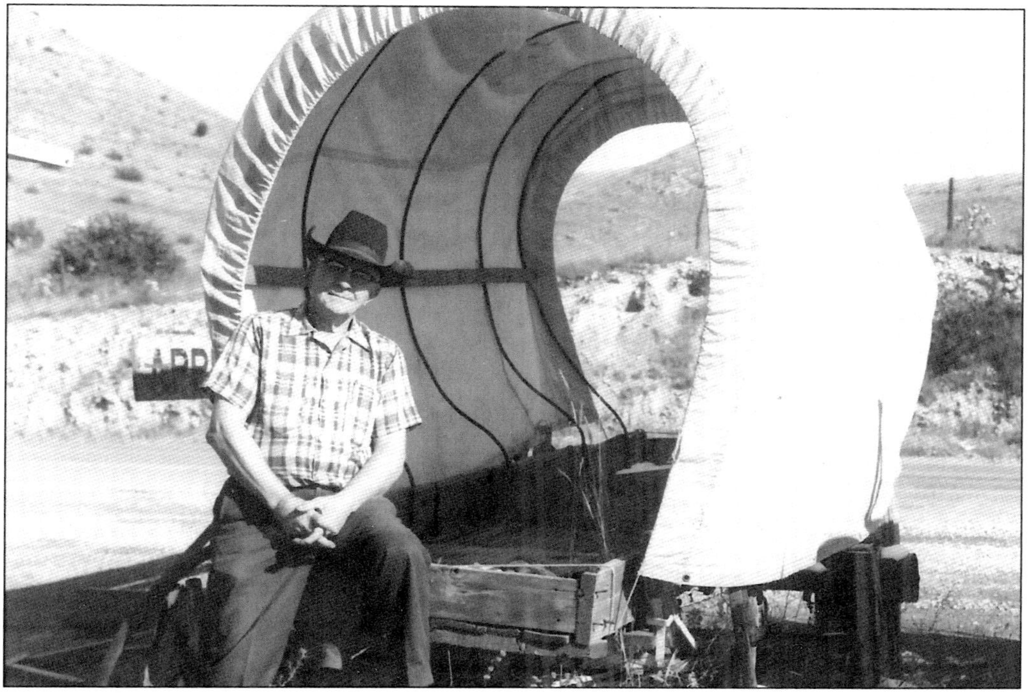

Fruit stands are a longtime staple of Hondo, as many of them dot the landscape along the road, enticing travelers to stop and savor fresh fruit. This man poses on an old wagon in front of his fruit stand, Bradley's Fruit Stand, in Hondo. The Casey family owned the wagon Bradley is sitting on when they first entered the Hondo Valley back in the 1800s. Unfortunately when the new road was built, many of Hondo's fruit stands were closed down, although there are still plenty to stop at today. Pictured below, boosters of the Eastern New Mexico State Fair stop to entertain in Hondo in the 1950s. (Above, courtesy HSSNM #4030; below, courtesy HSSNM #2885A.)

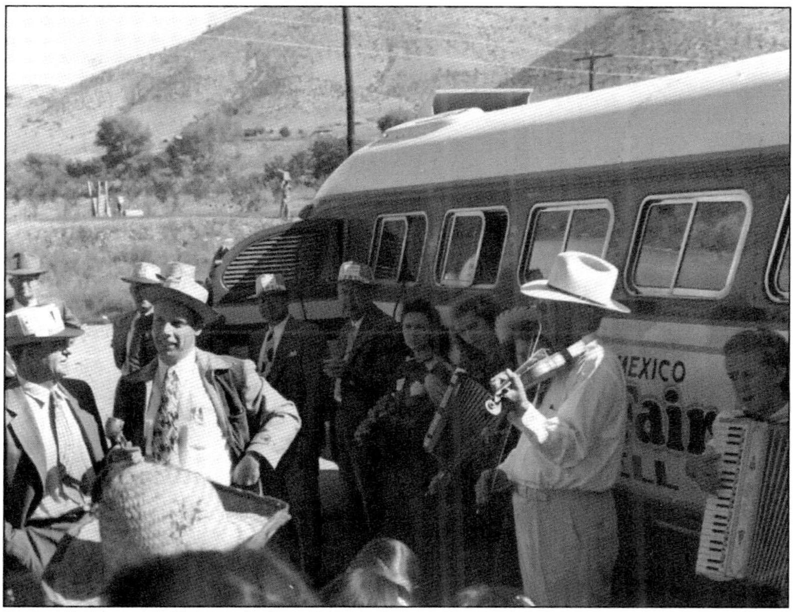

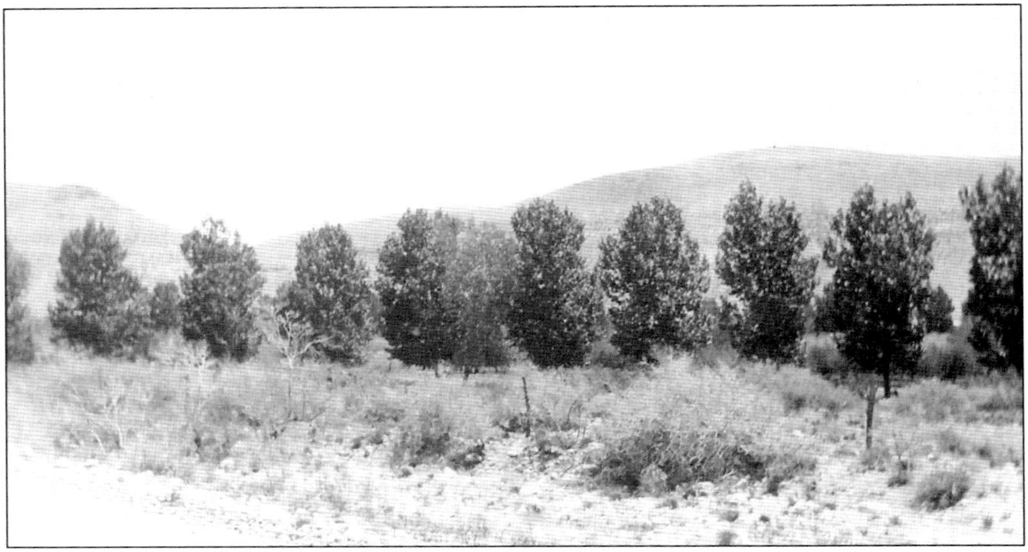

After passing through Hondo and a little ways before reaching San Patricio, one will pass Tunstall Canyon (below) where the young Englishman John H. Tunstall met his doom at the hands of a sheriff's posse on his way to Lincoln. (Above, courtesy HSSNM #2273A; below, courtesy HSSNM #5556.)

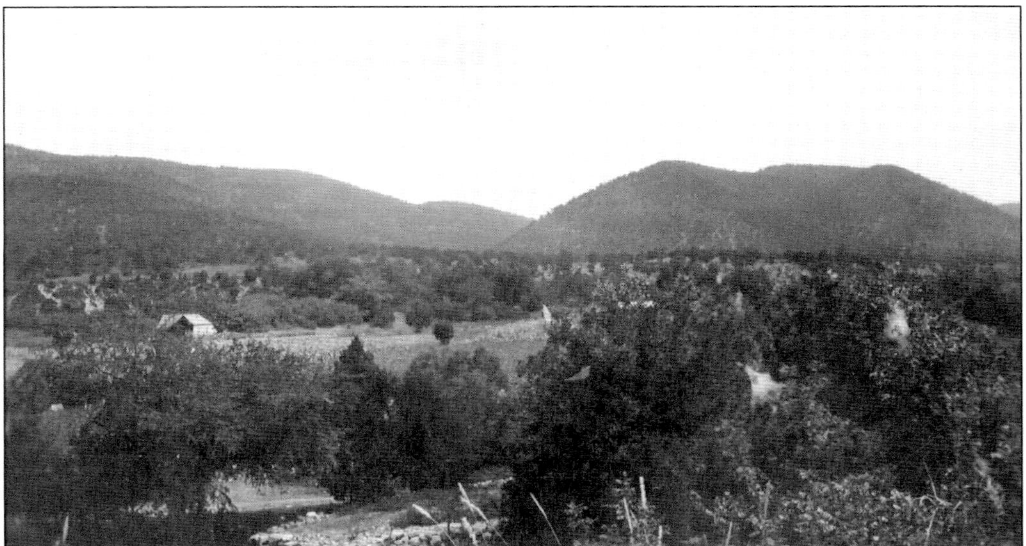

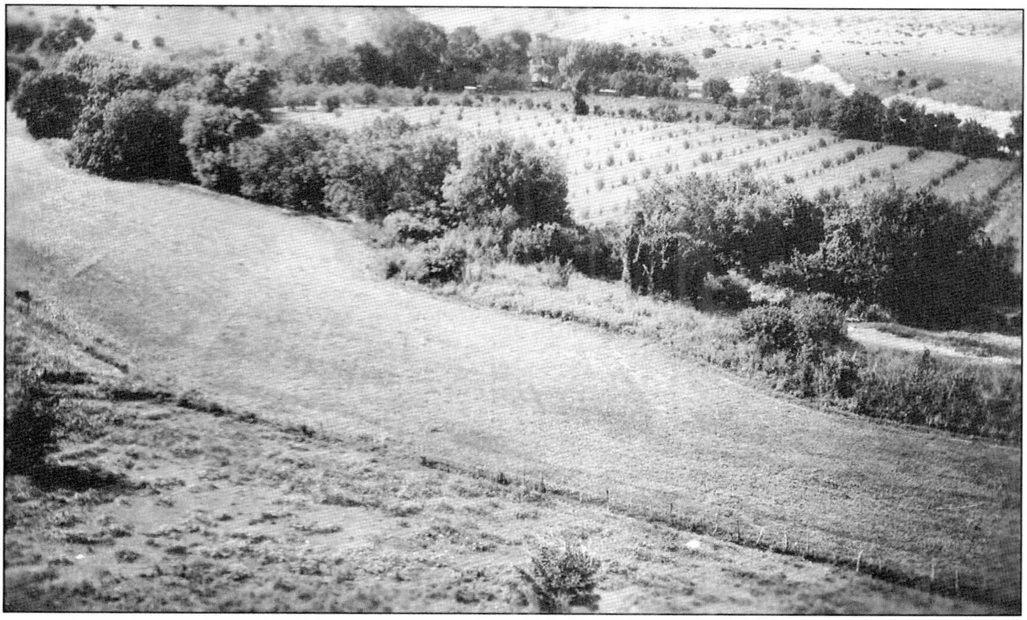

Driving along the Billy the Kid Historic and Scenic Byway, the view above of lush trees and fields is a common one. Below a horse drawn carriage crosses the Hondo River. Today the river rarely gets that full. (Above, courtesy HSSNM #099B; below, courtesy Eleanor Bonnell.)

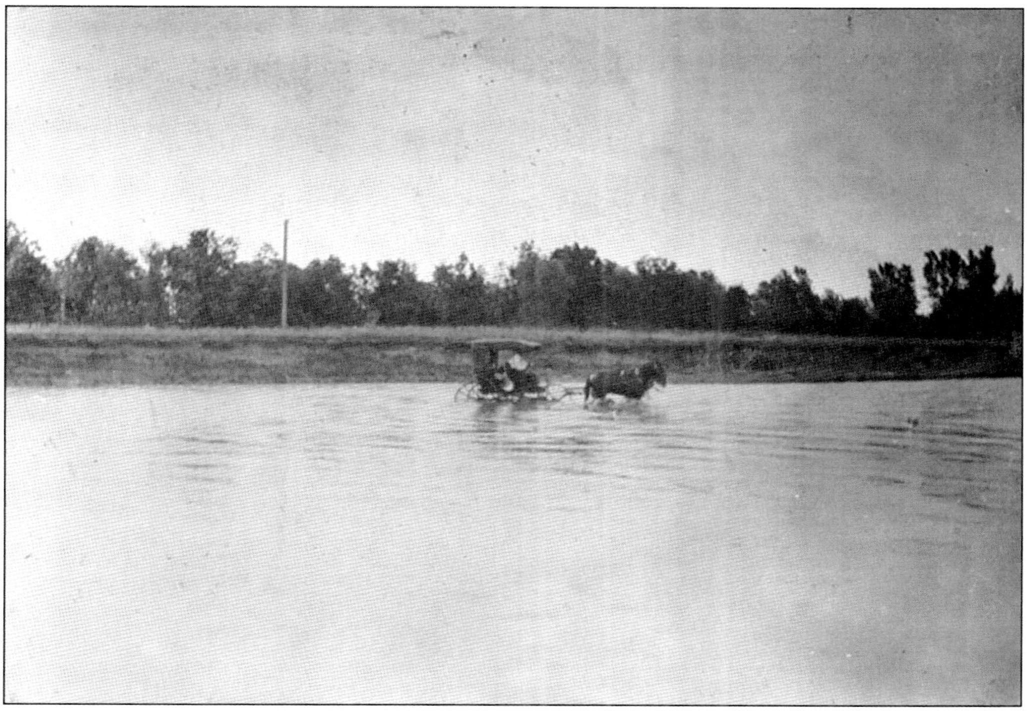

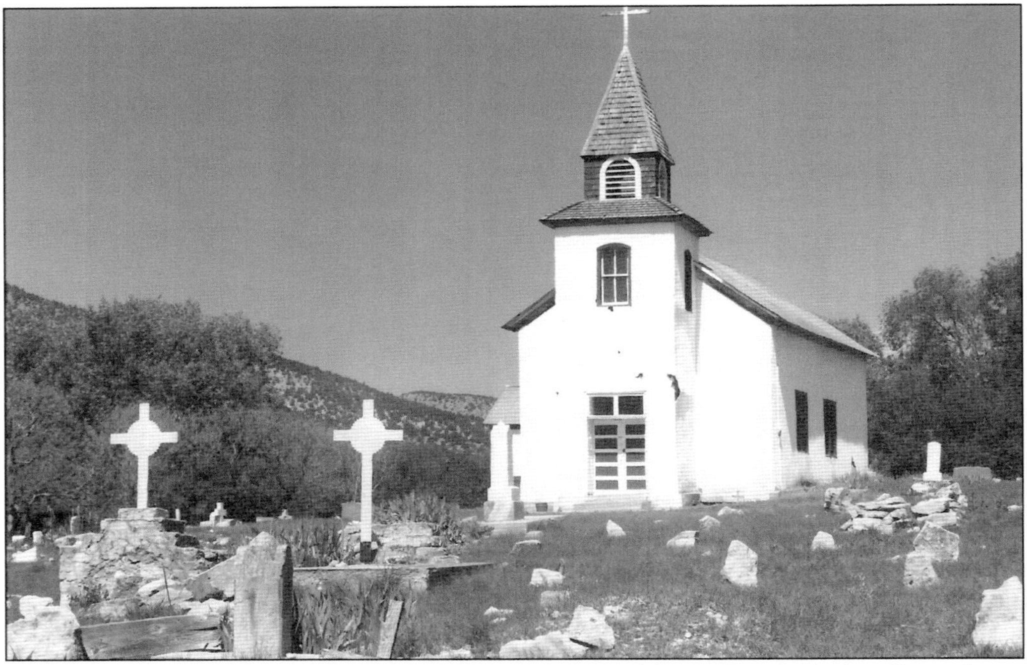

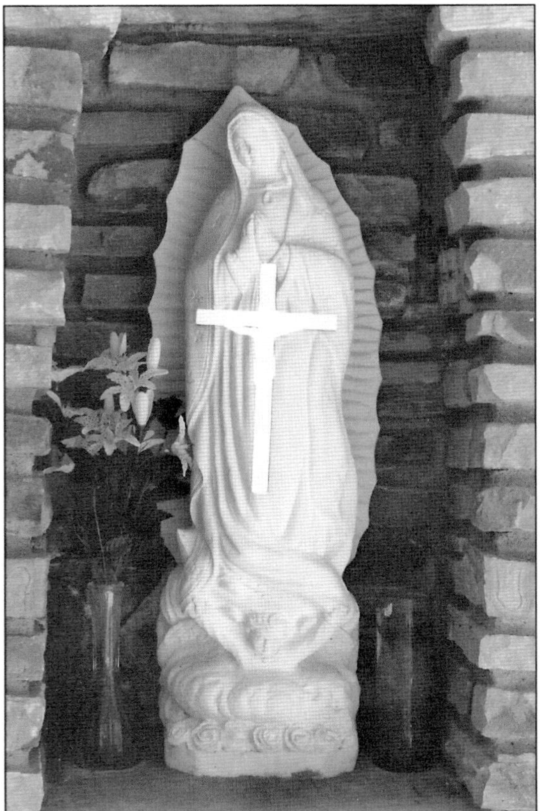

Legend has it that the little village of San Patricio was named by a young Irish priest traveling with a group of hunters through the valley sometime in the mid-1800s. The green valley in early spring reminded him so much of his native Ireland that he named the spot San Patricio after St. Patrick, and the name stuck. The first church in San Patricio would be dedicated to St. Patrick as well. Above is a well-known San Patricio church, and to the left is the Mother and Child statue at St. Jude Church in San Patricio. (Both courtesy HSSNM.)

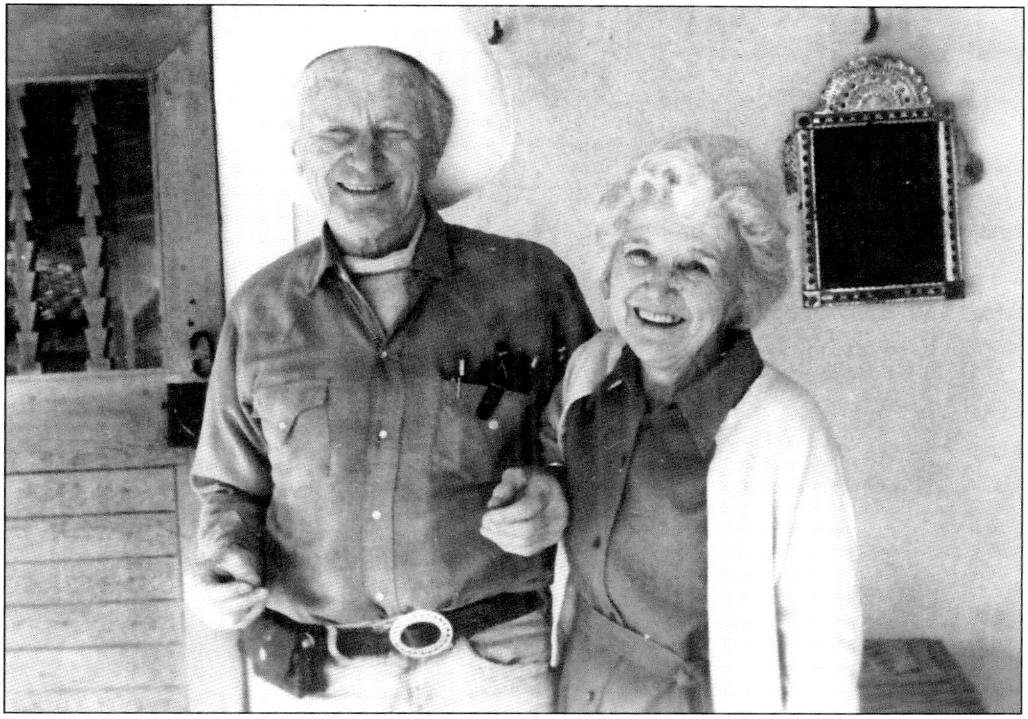

Pictured in the joyful candid photograph above are Peter Hurd and his beloved wife, Henriette Wyeth-Hurd. Peter Hurd studied art under Henriette's father, N. C. Wyeth, the famous illustrator who had worked on such classic books as Jules Verne's *Mysterious Island*. Henriette left her home in the East when she married Hurd in 1929. The two moved to their beautiful Sentinel Ranch home, below, in San Patricio in 1933. Henriette was also a respected painter, well known for her florals and still life oils. Today Michael Hurd, Peter and Henriette's youngest son, is also a painter and manages Hurd La Riconanda Gallery and Guest Homes at the elegant Sentinel Ranch in San Patricio. (Above, courtesy HSSNM #1134; below, courtesy HSSNM #1158B.)

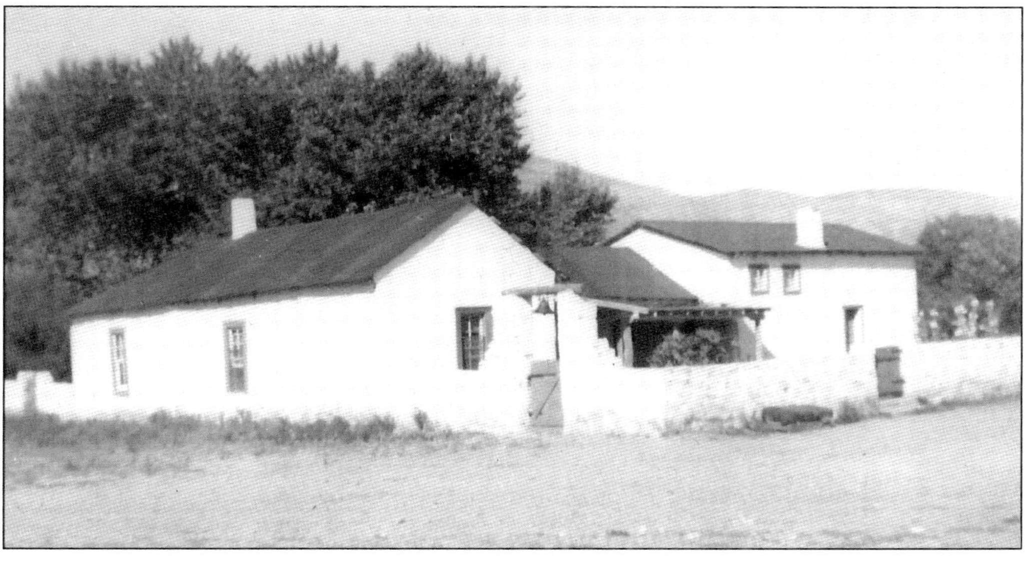

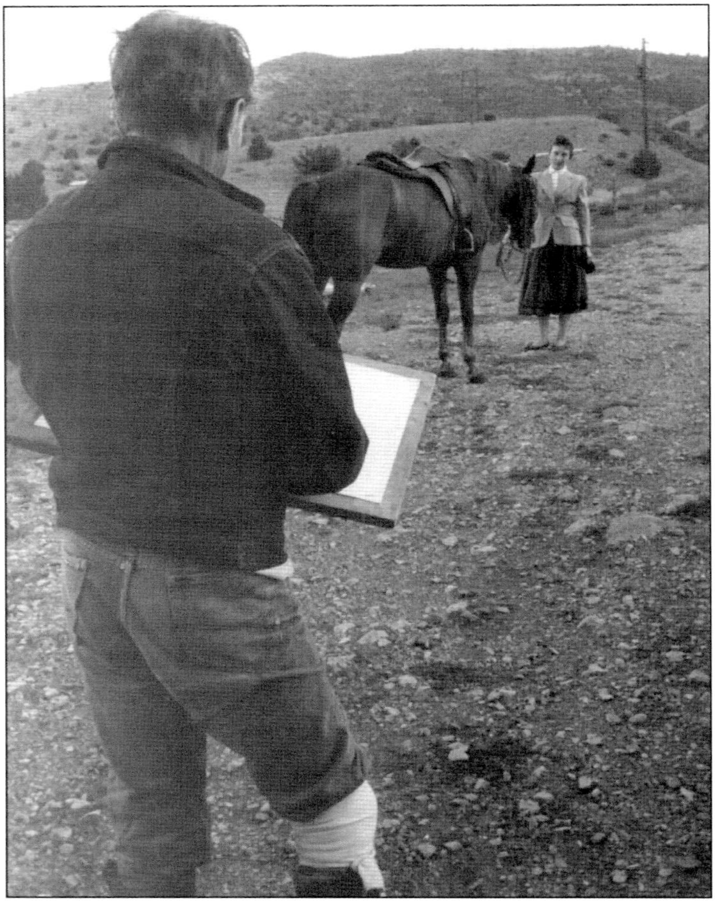

There is only one other man linked as indelibly to Lincoln County as Billy the Kid, and that man is Peter Hurd. Hurd is ironically the first person to play the Kid in *The Last Escape of Billy the Kid*, New Mexico's longest running folk pageant. But, of course, it is Hurd's beautiful paintings that are as indigenous to the Hondo Valley as the rolling hills that populate the work that made him famous. Hurd is out on the range doing preliminary work and sketches on various subjects in these two photographs by Ken Cobean of Roswell. (Left, courtesy HSSNM #2119G; below, courtesy #2119I.)

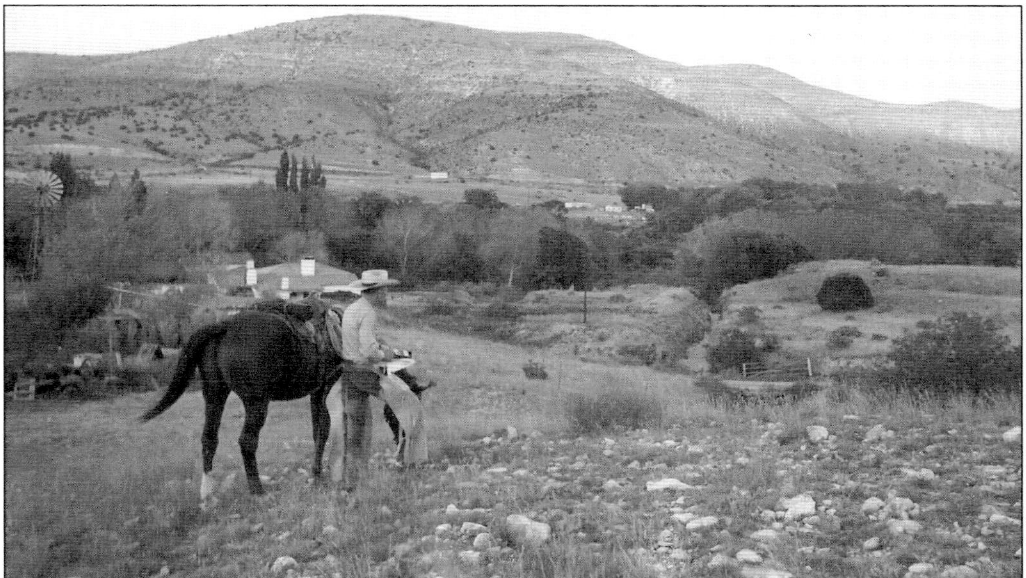

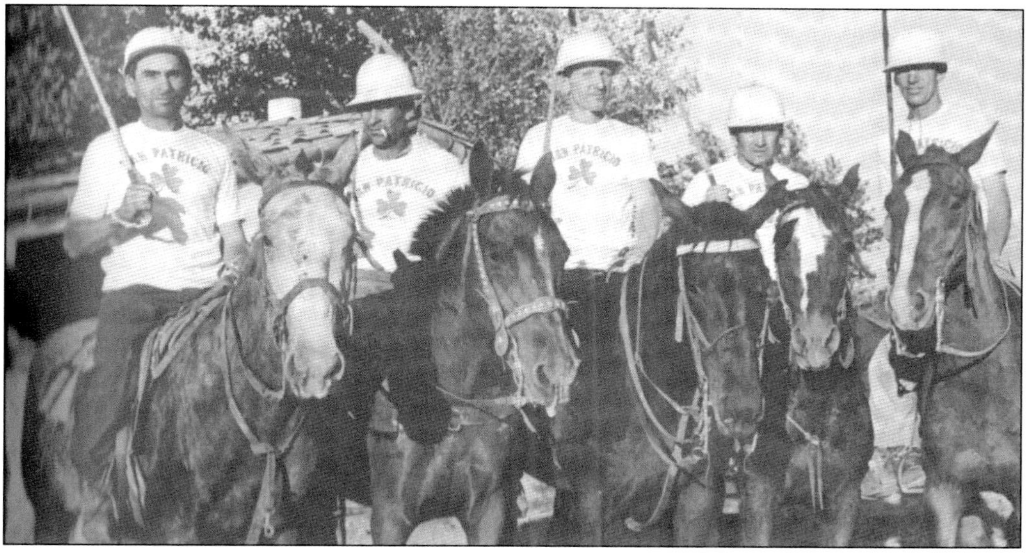

One of the facets that sets San Patricio apart in the Hondo Valley and in Southern New Mexico in general is its elegant polo field. Polo, a game played on horseback and popularized by the British, may seem a bit out of place in the Southwest, but the polo field in San Patricio, with its lush greenery and backdrop of rolling hills, certainly sets it apart from other polo fields across the United States. Peter Hurd and his polo team can be seen above, and below is the San Patricio polo field in action. (Above, courtesy Michael Hurd; below, courtesy HSSNM #6357A.)

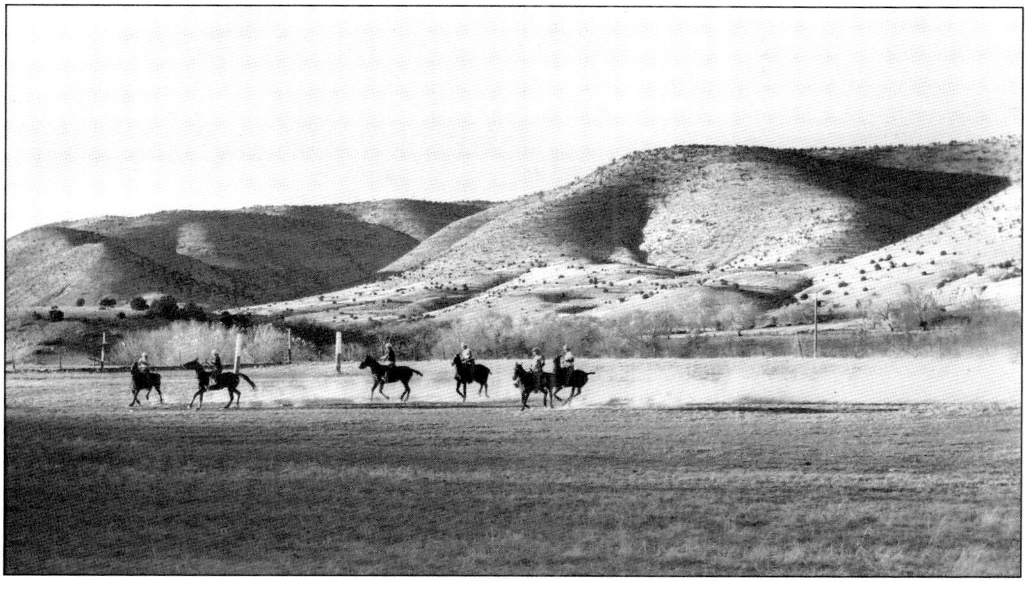

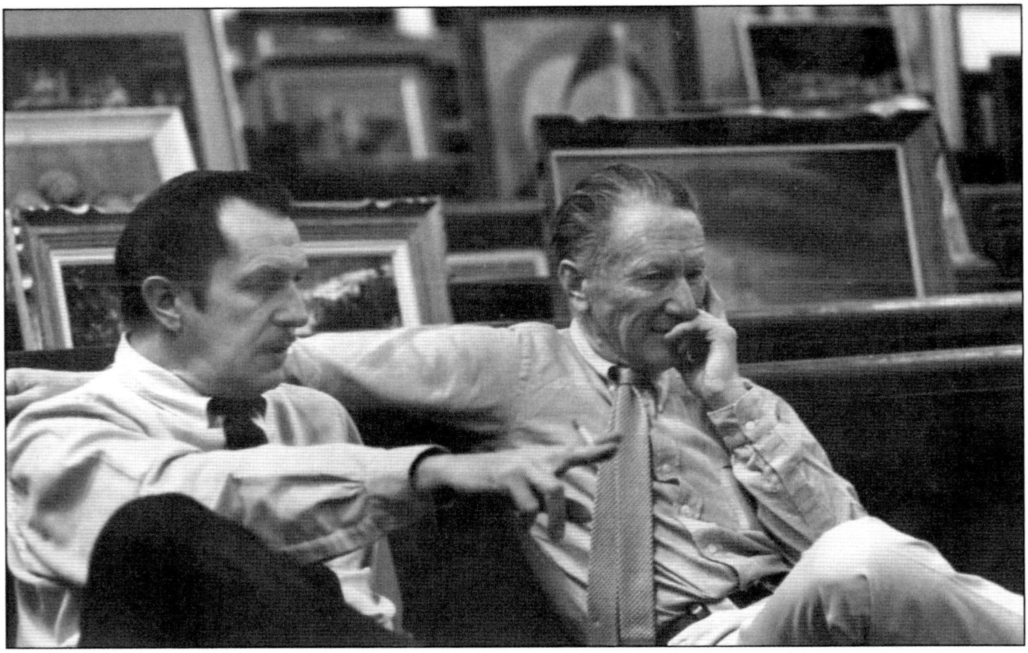

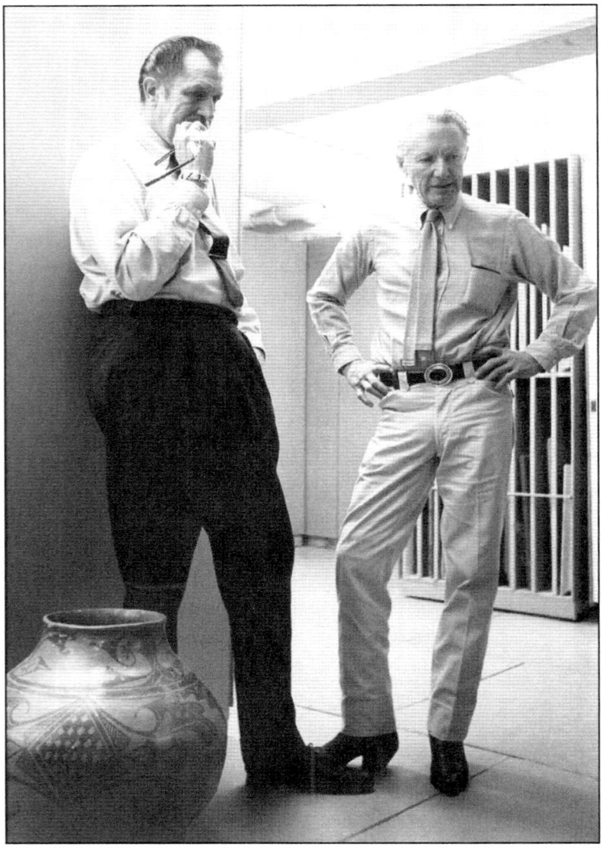

Many famous faces came to San Patricio to visit Peter Hurd, such as famed horror star and art collector Vincent Price, who can be seen conversing with Hurd in these two images. Other celebrities to visit San Patricio included Burl Ives, Helen Hayes, Linda Darnell, Charles MacArthur, a prince from Thailand, and Pulitzer Prize winning author Paul Horgan. (Above, courtesy HSSNM #2119J; left, courtesy HSSNM #2119K.)

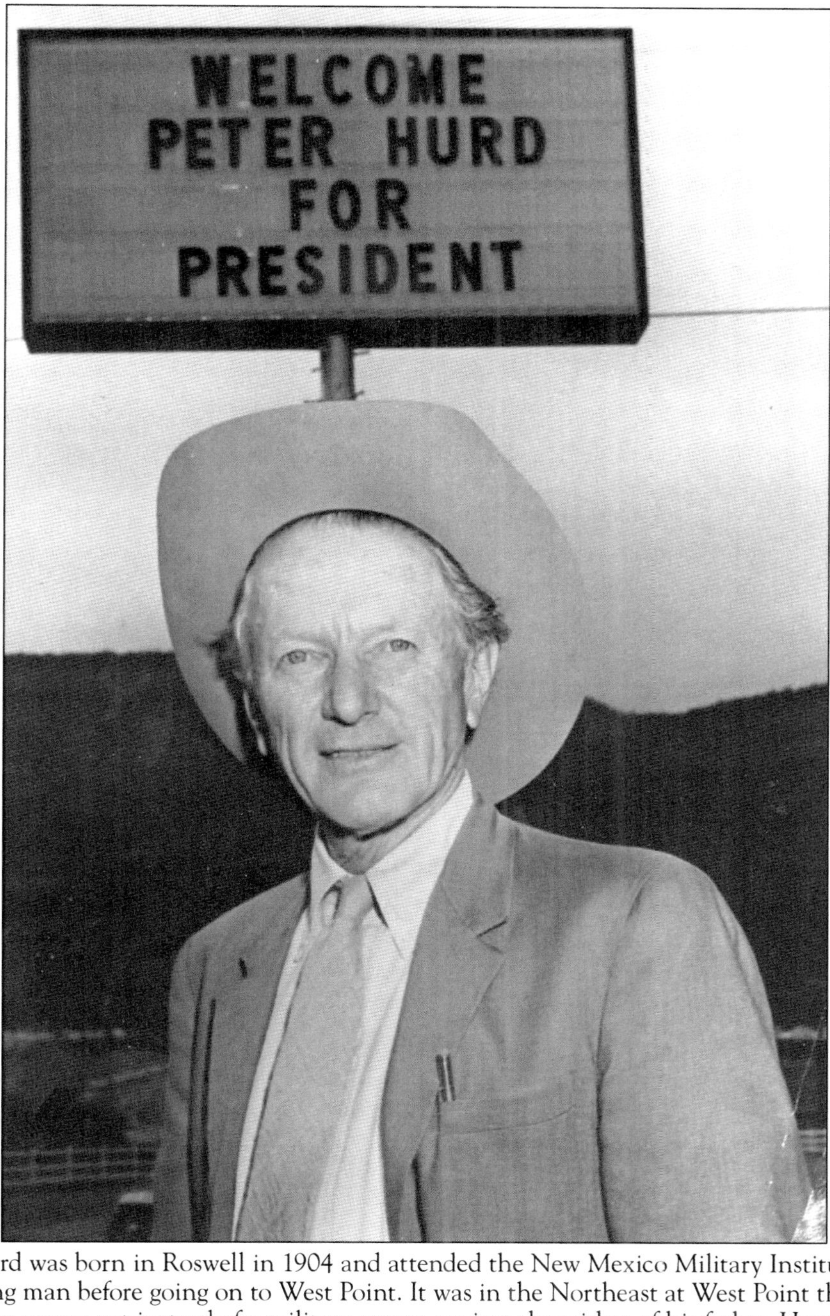

Peter Hurd was born in Roswell in 1904 and attended the New Mexico Military Institute there as a young man before going on to West Point. It was in the Northeast at West Point that Hurd decided to pursue art instead of a military career, against the wishes of his father, Harold. Hurd began taking classes at the Pennsylvania Academy of Fine Arts in Philadelphia. It would be there that Hurd began his five-year apprenticeship under N. C. Wyeth and would meet his wife, Henriette. At the Sentinel Ranch in San Patricio, Hurd produced his most recognizable work, even working with *Life* magazine and the WPA. Hurd passed away in Roswell in 1984. The marquee above Hurd reading, "Peter Hurd for President" may have been a reference to his painting of Pres. Lyndon B. Johnson. (Courtesy HSSNM #2587.)

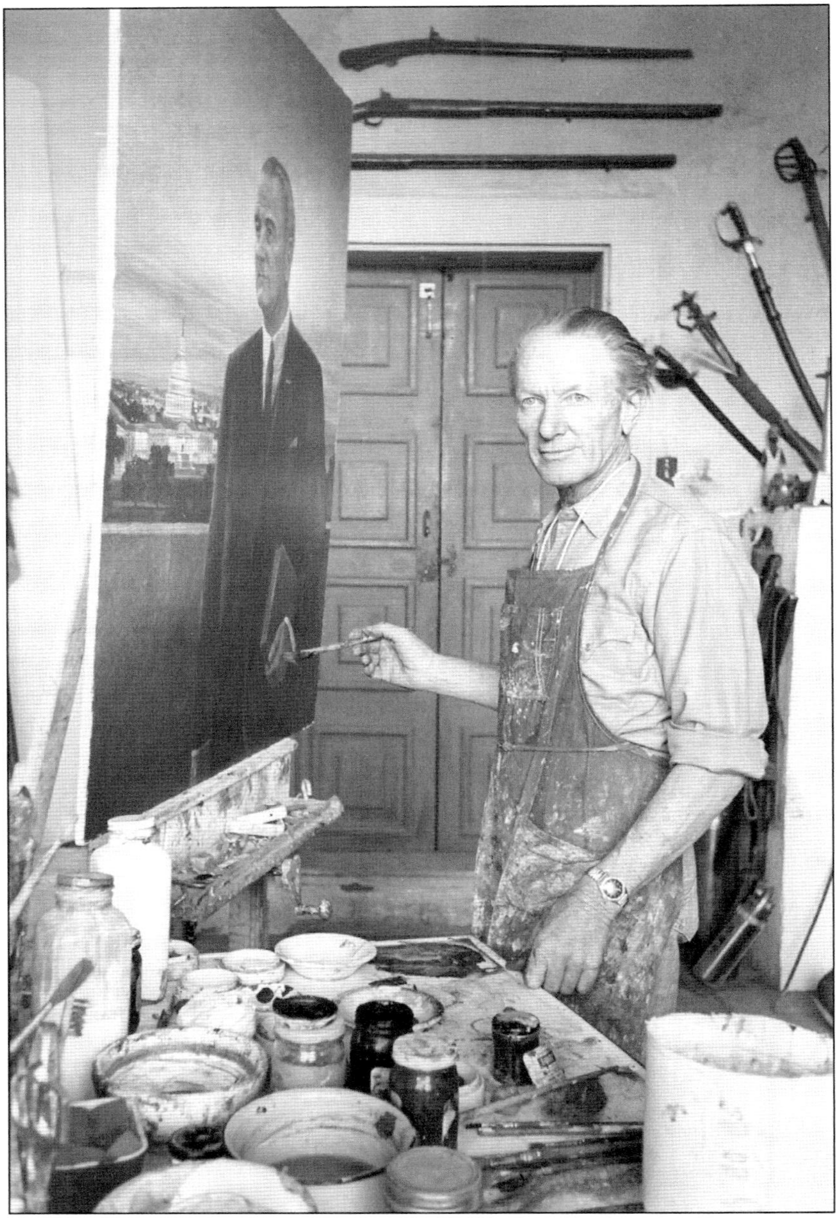

One of Peter Hurd's most memorable escapades was when he was commissioned by the White House to paint the presidential portrait of then president Lyndon B. Johnson. Hurd was offered a $6,000 commission to paint Johnson, which would be difficult for Hurd, since Johnson would never pose for him. Hurd had been flown in a helicopter down to Camp David where Johnson—according to an interview with Hurd conducted by Minor Huffman—was to give Hurd 45 minutes of his time. However, when Johnson walked in to meet Hurd, who had just begun to sketch the president from an old photograph, Johnson muttered, "Humph! Looks like an old drunk to me," and then laughed. When Hurd told the president that he would need for him to pose for a good three hours, Johnson grunted again and denied him. In a photograph above by Ken Cobean, Hurd works on the portrait of Johnson in his studio around 1965. (Courtesy HSSNM #2119B.)

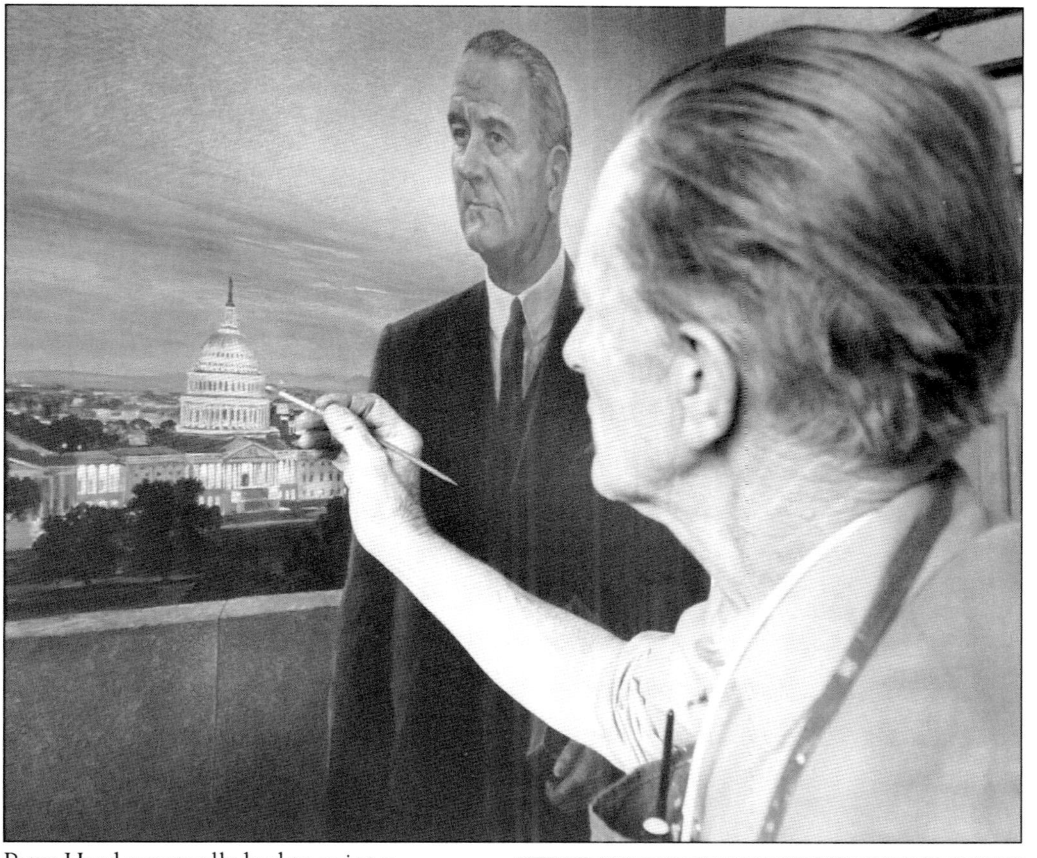

Peter Hurd eventually had to paint a portrait of President Johnson from an old photograph. The final result was rejected by Johnson, who reportedly said it was the "ugliest thing I ever saw." Eventually the Smithsonian acquired the portrait, and Hurd was flown in as the guest of honor when it was installed. While walking with a group of people, who may or may not have known Hurd was with them, Hurd stepped in front of the painting of Johnson and said in a mock Texas accent, "Hell fire, I don't blame ol' LBJ neither. Don't look any more like 'im than I do!" (Above, courtesy HSSNM #2119A; right, courtesy HSSNM #2119E.)

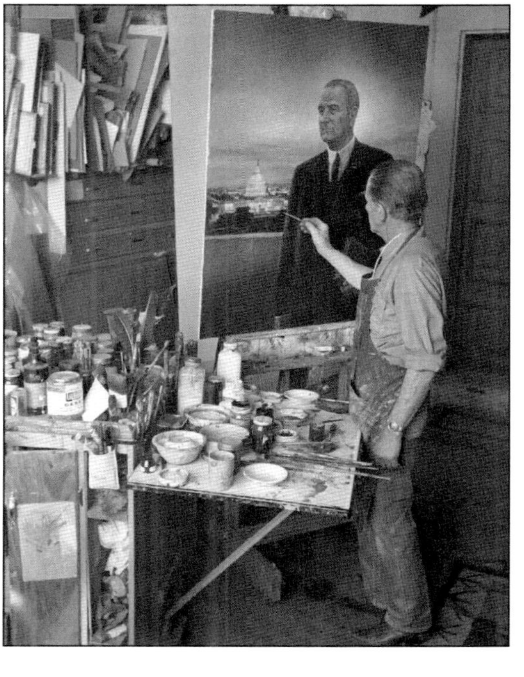

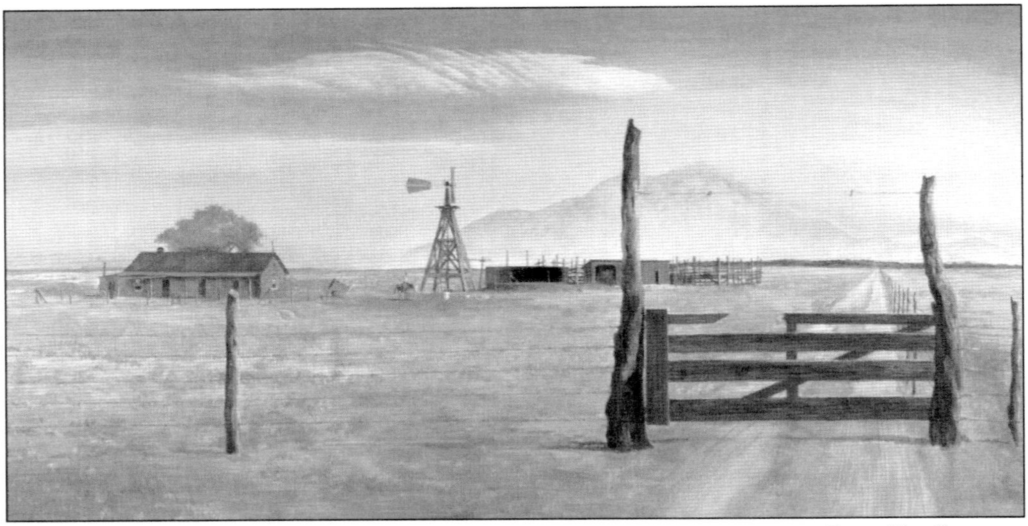

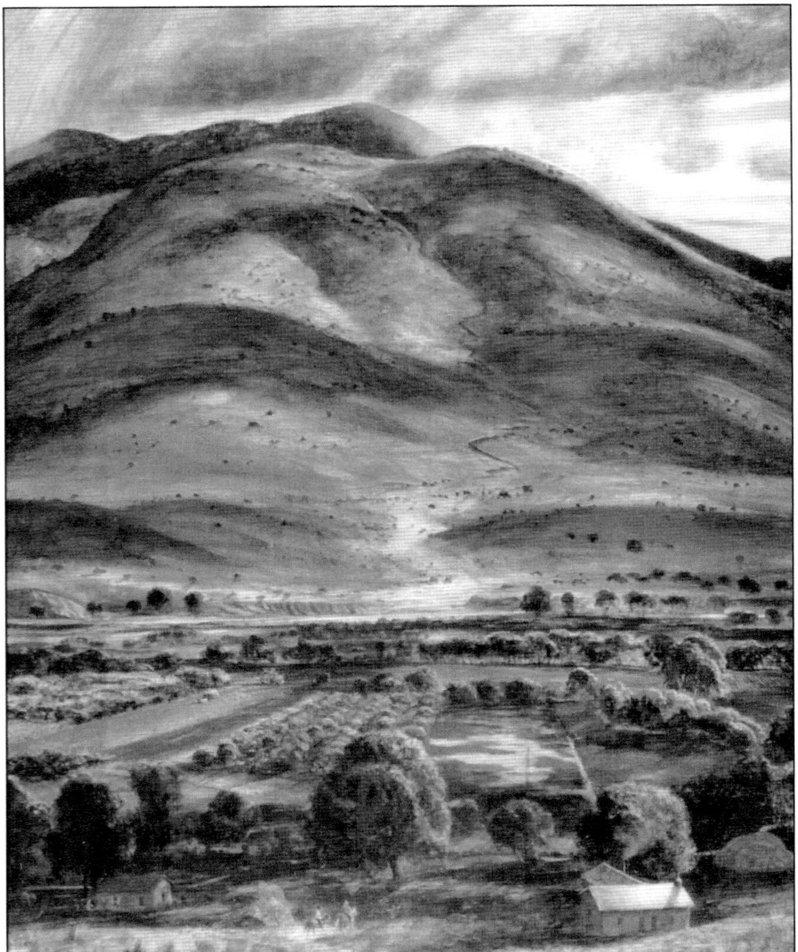

Peter Hurd's painting, *The Gate and Beyond*, c. 1952, depicts small ranch homes common in the Southwest, especially those west of Roswell before entering the Hondo Valley. The painting to the left is entitled *The Rainy Season*, c. 1947. (Courtesy Michael Hurd and the Roswell Museum and Art Center.)

The beautiful Hondo Valley–inspired landscape portrait to the right is entitled *The Valley Farm*, c. 1945. The beautiful female subject of the painting below, *Portrait of Carol*, c. 1958, is of Hurd's daughter, Carol. Today many of these paintings are proudly displayed at the Roswell Museum and Art Center in Roswell. (Courtesy Michael Hurd and the Roswell Museum and Art Center.)

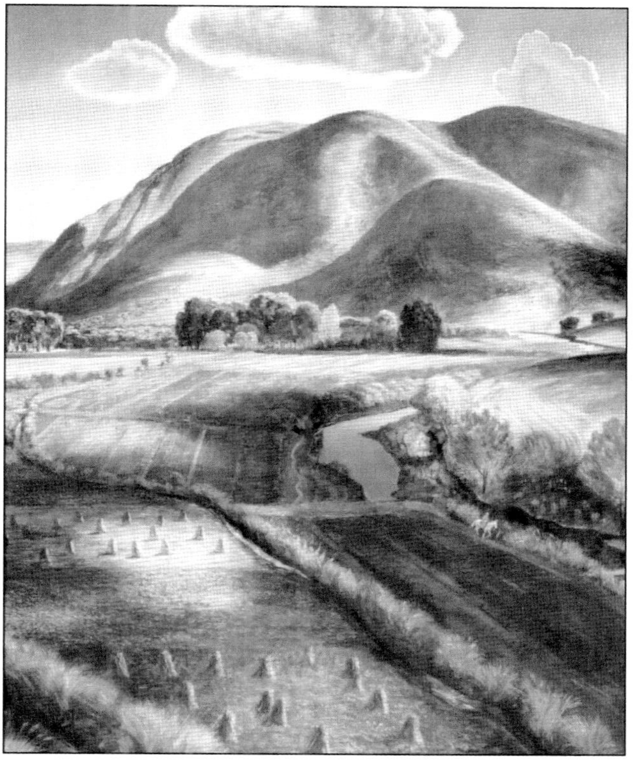

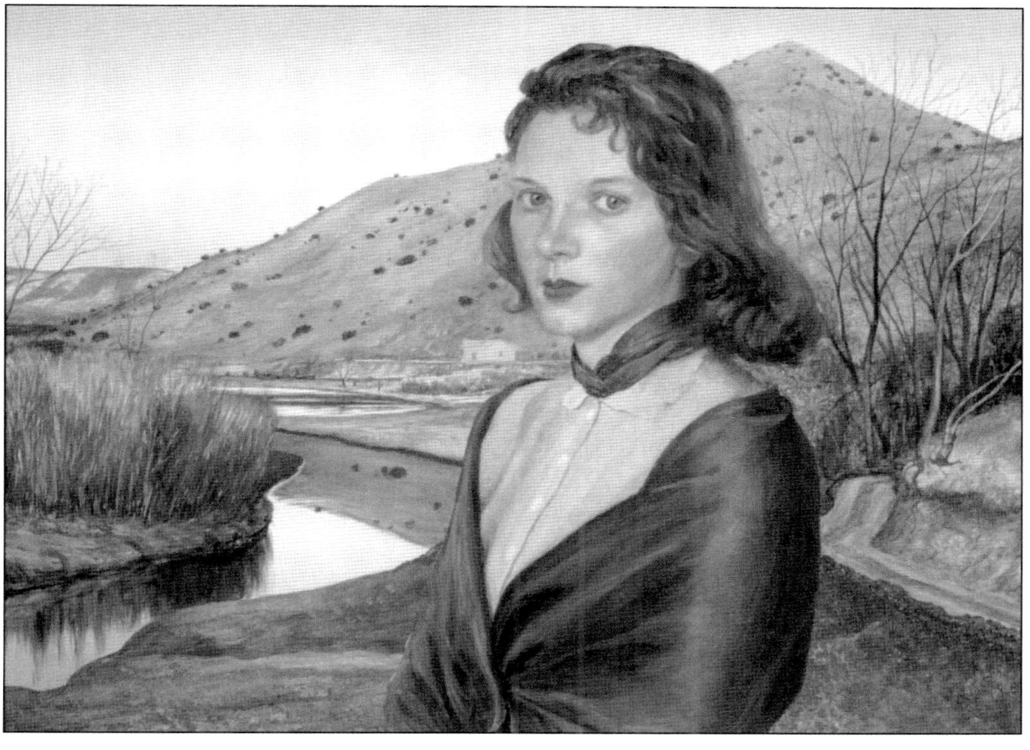

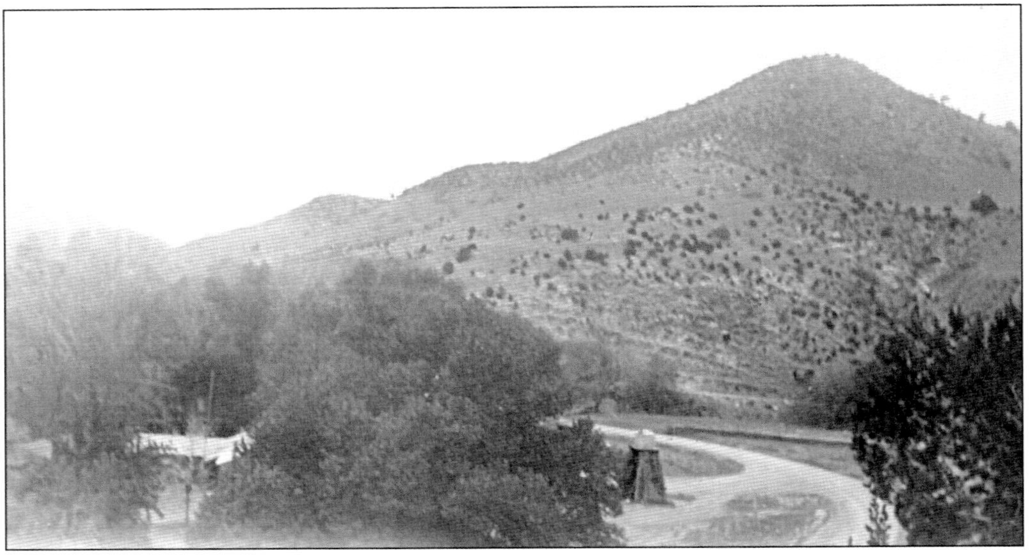

Before the Hondo Valley turns into the Ruidoso Valley, as motorists travel further westward, they will encounter the Bonnell Ranch and Farm, which used to be a popular resort. Back in its day, it was also the starting point for pack trips to White Mountain and also a stop on the passenger bus line between Roswell and Alamogordo. Above is the view from the mesa above the Bonnell Ranch, and below is the road to the Bonnell Ranch. Notice the old Conoco filling station to the right. (Above, courtesy HSSNM #2273B; below, courtesy HSSNM #4737B.)

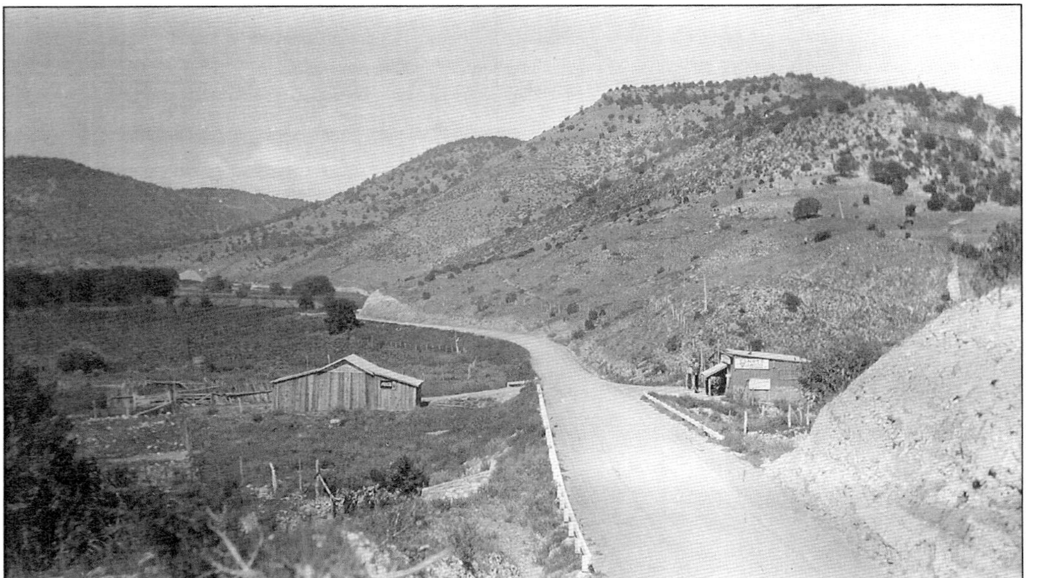

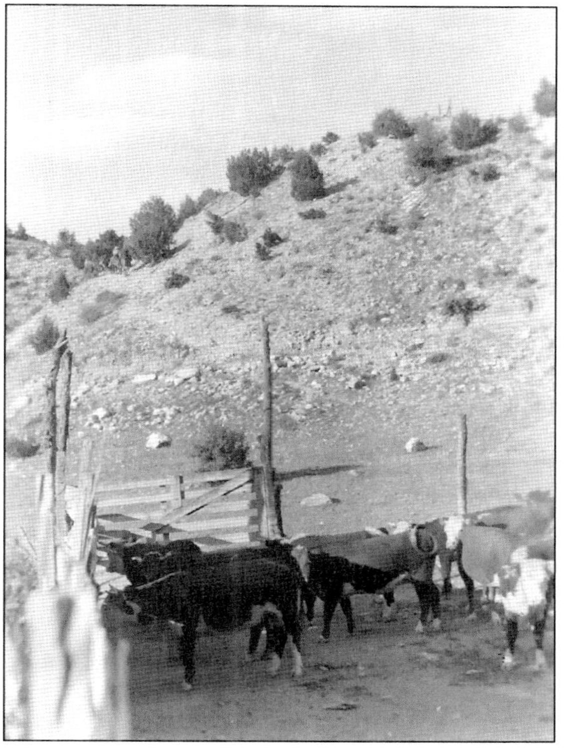

The first Bonnell in Lincoln County arrived in the boom town of White Oaks in 1880. Although Edwin R. Bonnell may have been too late to be part of the Lincoln County War, which had already ended, his lineage would end up entwining with it anyway when his sons married two of the Coe girls, Sydney and Agnes, whose father was Frank Coe of Blazer's Mill battle fame. Together the Coes and Bonnells planted a bevy of fruit trees in the valley and eventually started a popular resort, the Bonnell Ranch and Farm, sometime between 1915 and 1920. Right and below are different views of cattle at the Bonnell Ranch. (Right, courtesy HSSNM #4737C; below, courtesy HSSNM #4737F.)

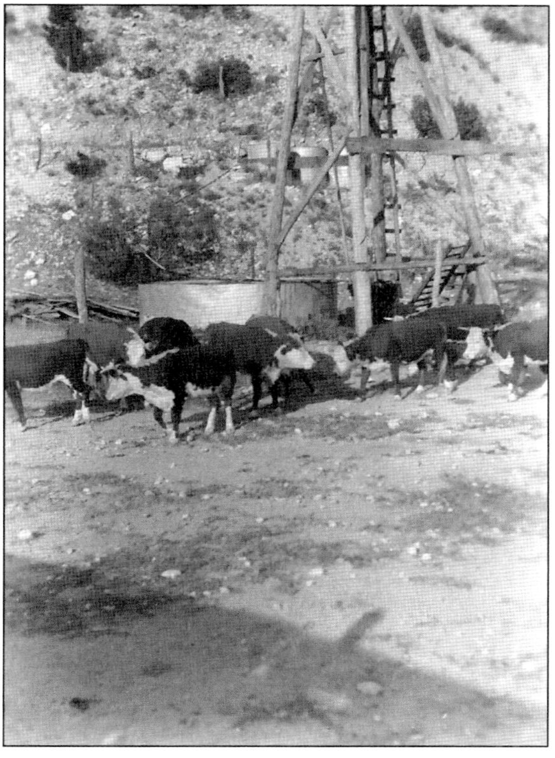

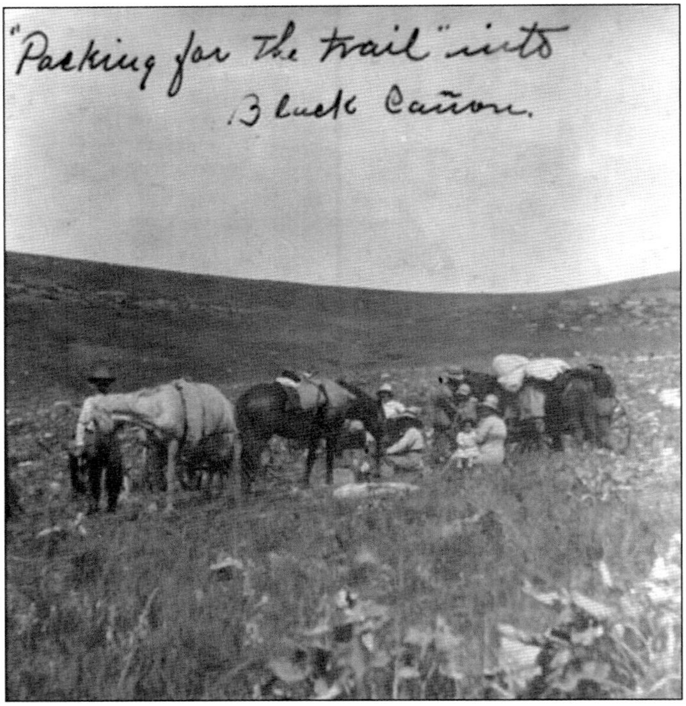

The Bonnell's grandchildren still fondly remember Bonnell Ranch memories, such as the many picnics and trail rides they took to various places in the Hondo Valley. Left is the Bonnell family on one of their many trail rides. In the image below, just "a few" of the grandchildren pose on and alongside the burro cart. Summer activities at the ranch included picnic trips to locales as far away as White Sands National Monument, hayrides, a dance every Saturday night, and most importantly, every August was harvest time for picking fruit, and almost everyone available helped out. (Both courtesy Eleanor Bonnell.)

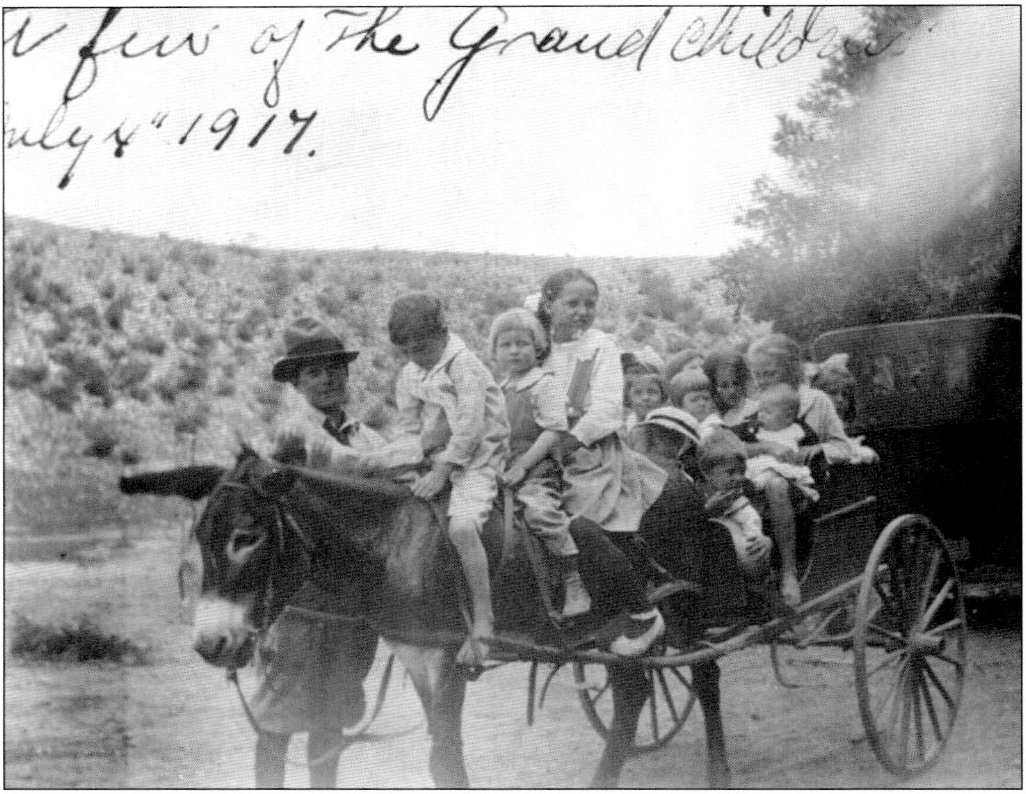

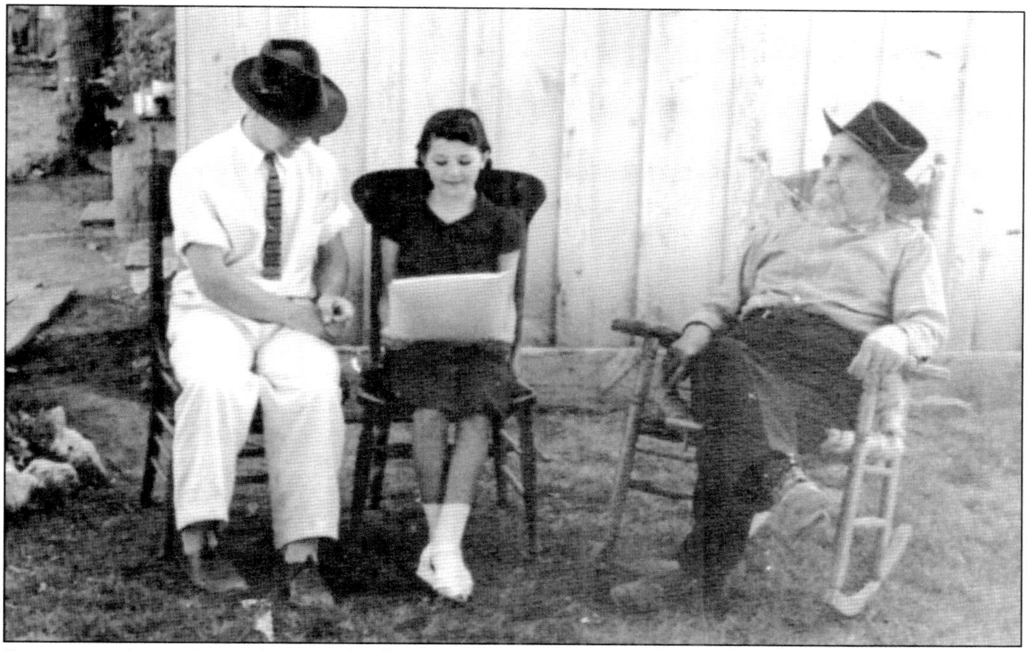

Sitting on the rocking chair in the far right of the photograph above is George Coe, pal of Billy the Kid and one of the longest living survivors of the Lincoln County War. Next to him are his granddaughter, Marie Coe Farrar, and Dan Storm. George Coe wrote a book on his exploits called *Frontier Fighter,* which he sold at his rural post office, general store, and fruit stand pictured below around the 1940s. Called the Rancho Linda Trading Post, the lettering on the front of the store reads: "The Home of Frontier Fighter, Fought and Rode with Billy the Kid, Geo. W. Coe. Books for Sale." (Above, courtesy HSSNM #4714; below, courtesy HSSNM #4075.)

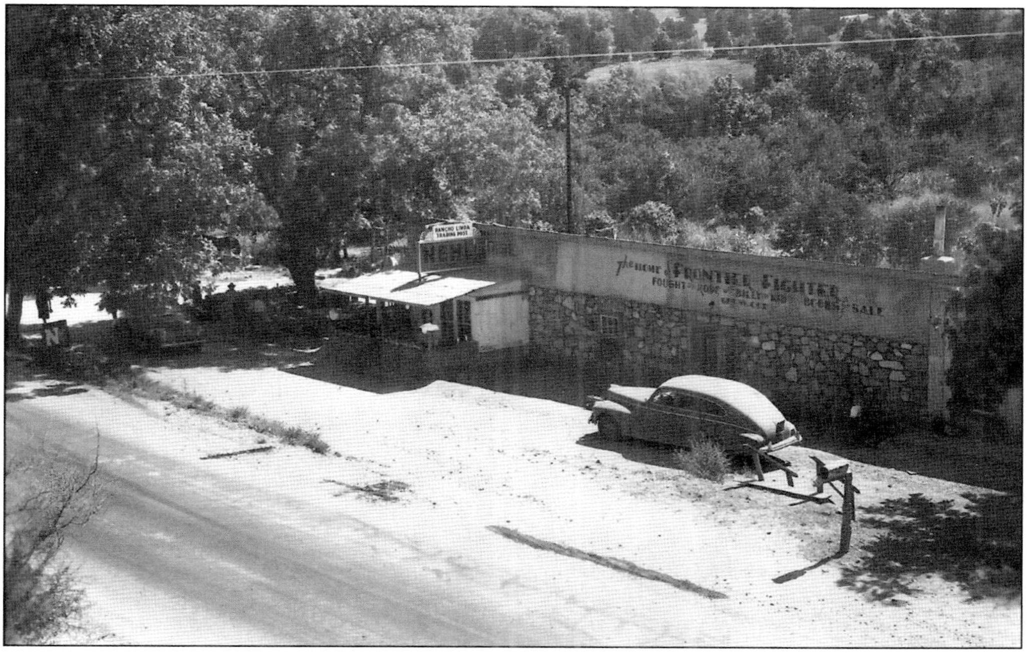

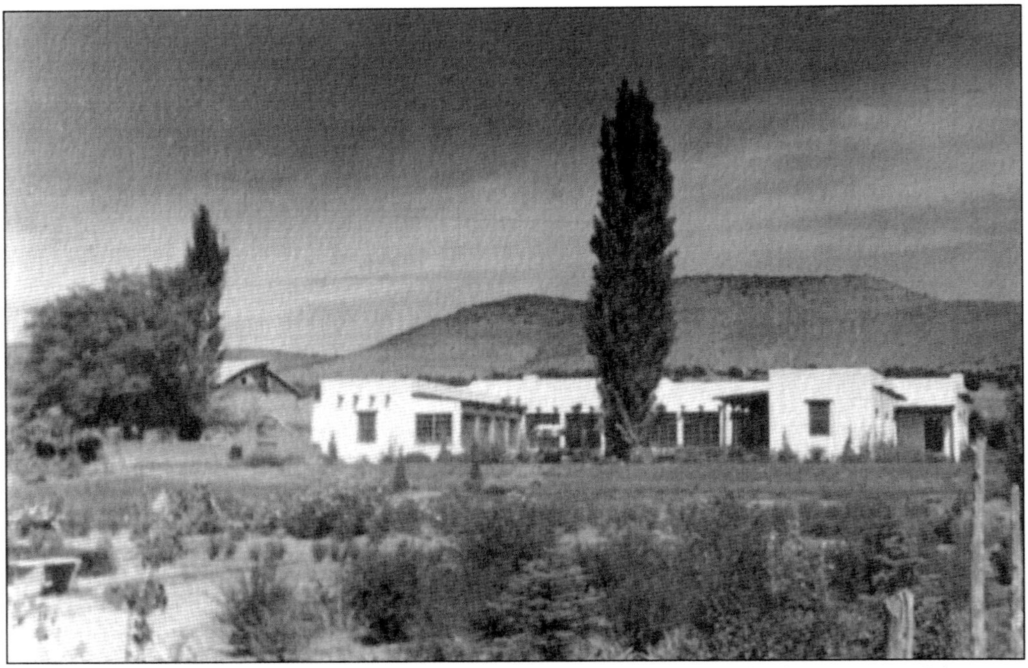

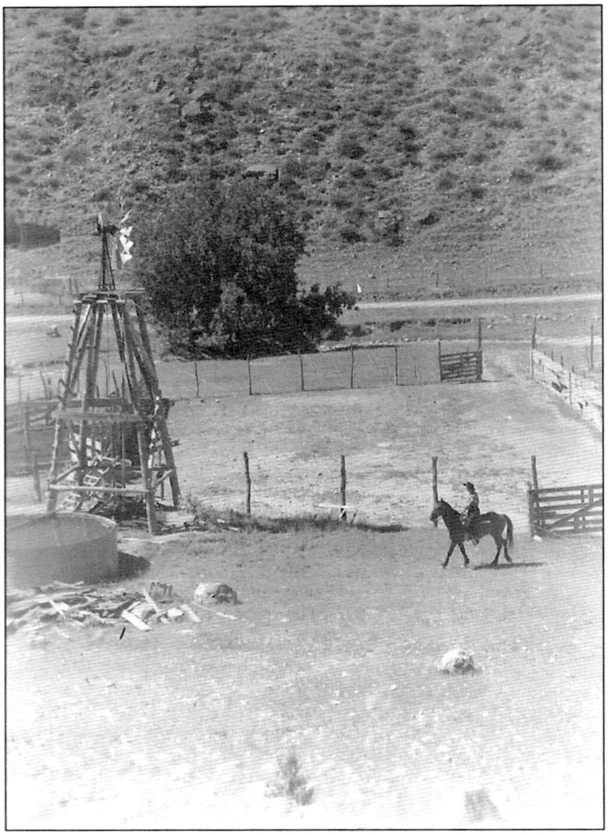

Above and left are views of the beautiful Wilbur F. Coe Ranch, or simply the Coe Ranch. The beautiful main living quarters are pictured above, and a ranch hand is inspecting the corrals at left. The town of Glencoe got its name from the Coe brothers themselves, and Jasper Coe was the first postmaster. Glen is a Scottish term for valley, and when combined with the Coe family name makes Glencoe. (Above, courtesy HSSNM #1249C; left, courtesy HSSNM #4738F.)

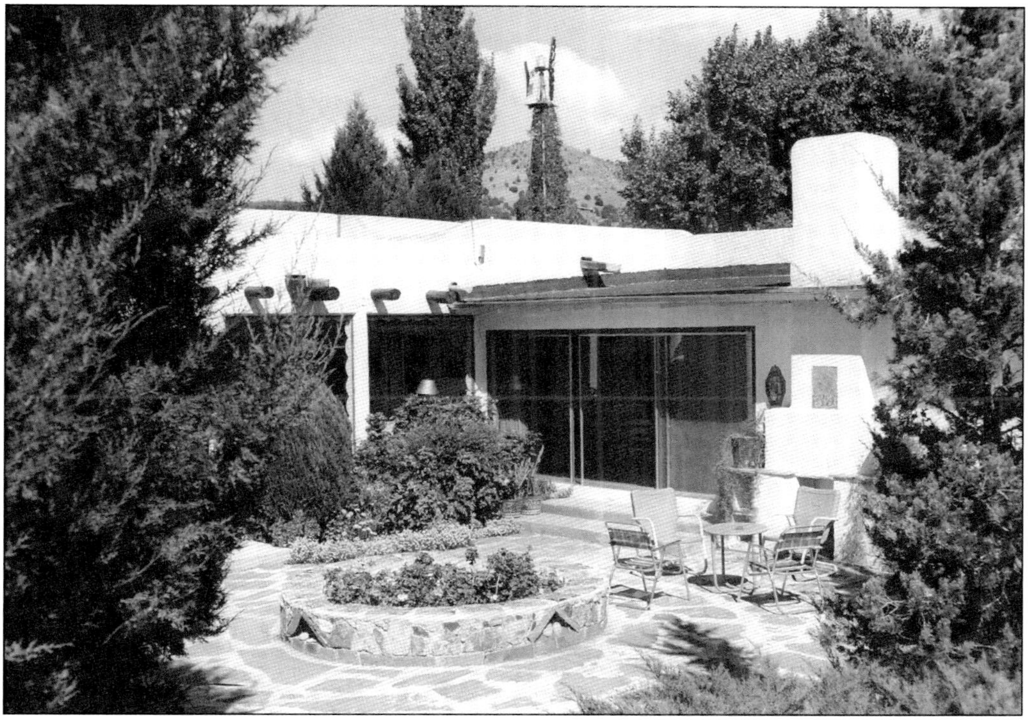

Here are two more photographs taken by Louis Philippe of the Wilbur Coe home, one of the outdoor patio and one of the living room. (Above, courtesy HSSNM #1249C; below, courtesy HSSNM #1249D.)

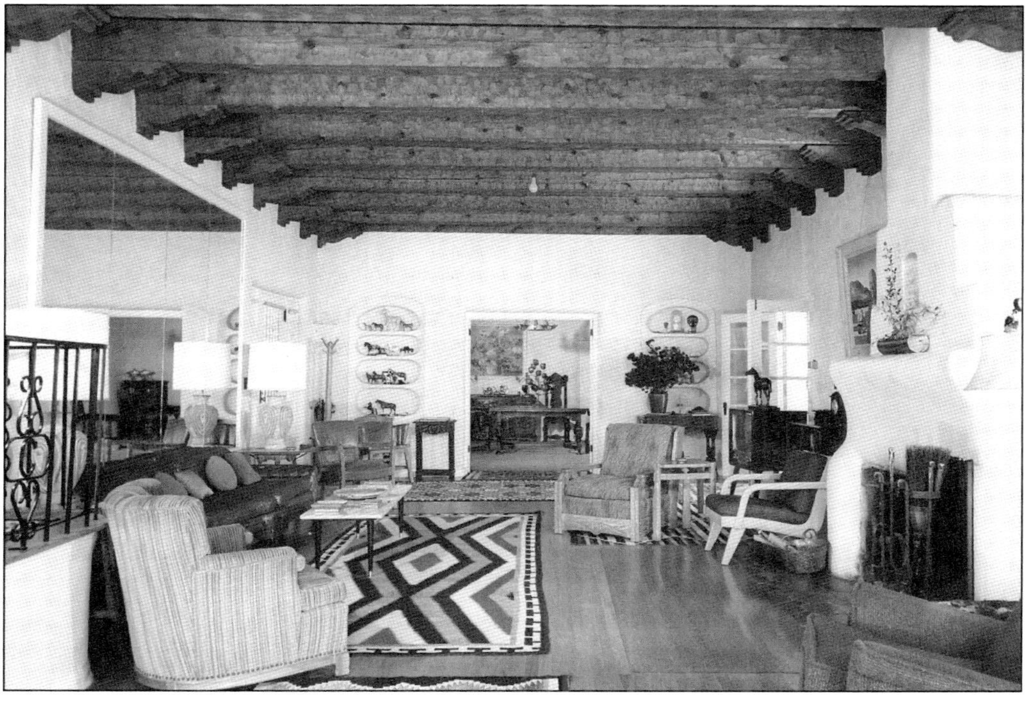

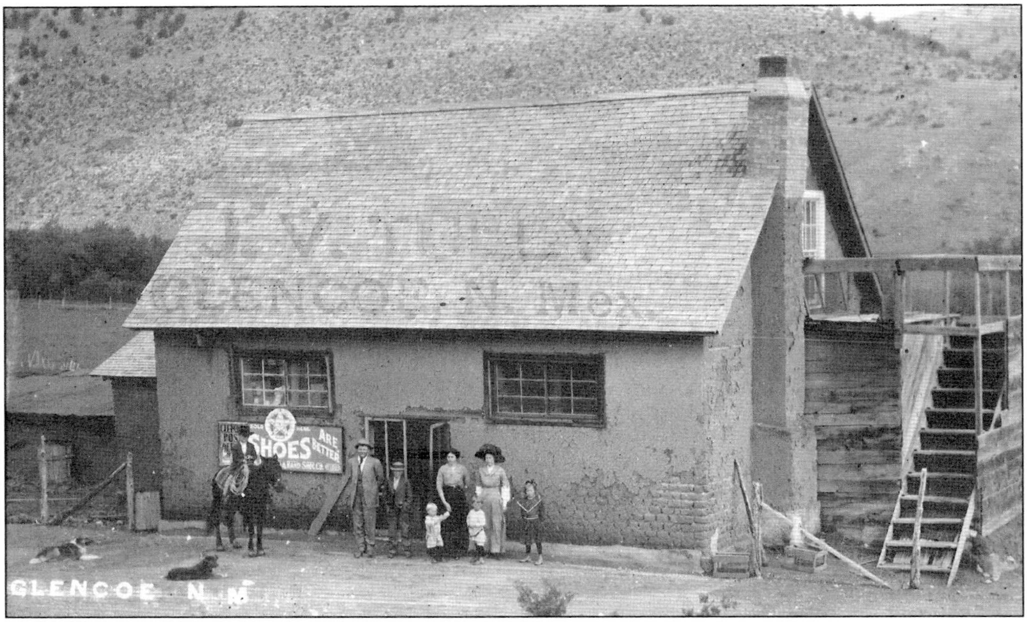

Another prominent family in Glencoe was the Tullys. Ora G. Tully, for instance, was postmistress in 1920. The J. V. Tully Store is shown above, and in a postcard from Tully's store below is a bridge in Glencoe. When the new highway was being constructed, the store and post office had to be moved to a new site on the highway. (Above, courtesy HSSNM #1780; below, courtesy HSSNM #3018.)

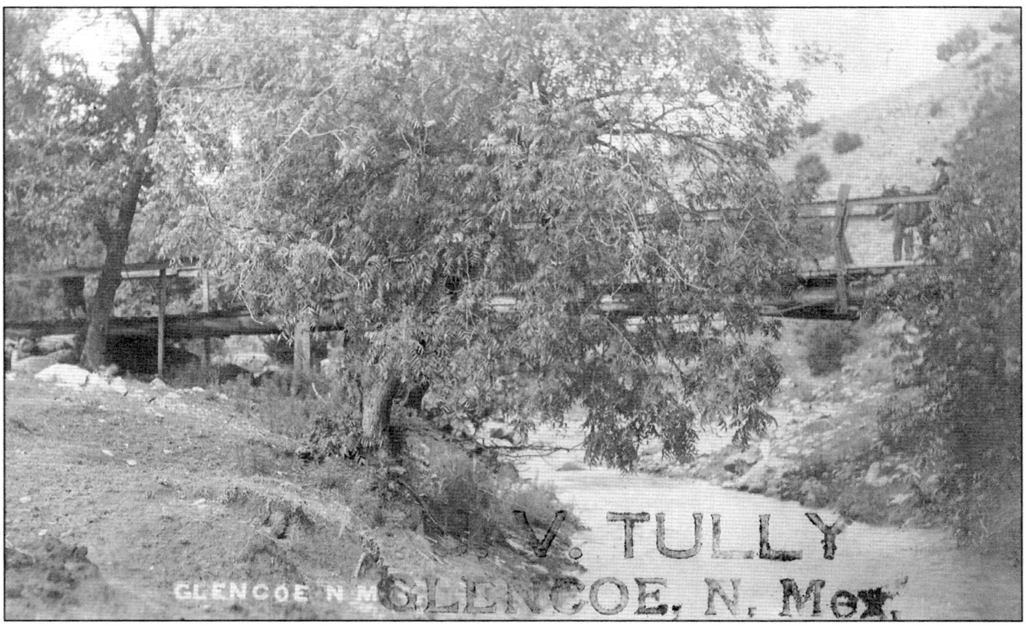

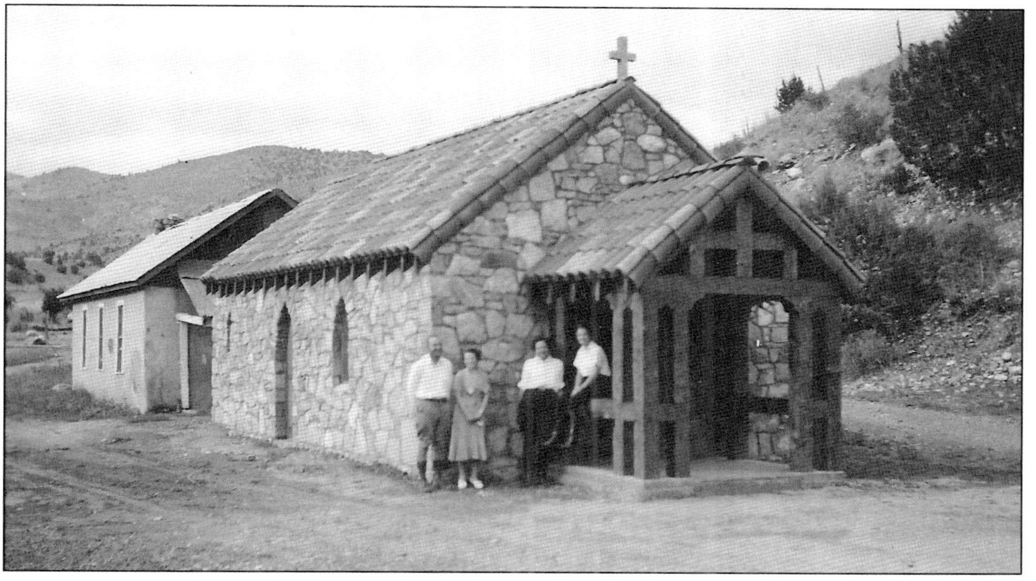

Although it is not very large, the St. Anne's Episcopal Church in Glencoe is a landmark thanks to its elegant design. Today the church is located in a groove just off of the main byway; motorists may not notice it anymore unless they know where to look. The Bonnell Store, run by Bert Bonnell, used to be located next to the chapel. (Above, courtesy HSSNM #4725B; below, courtesy HSSNM #4725C.)

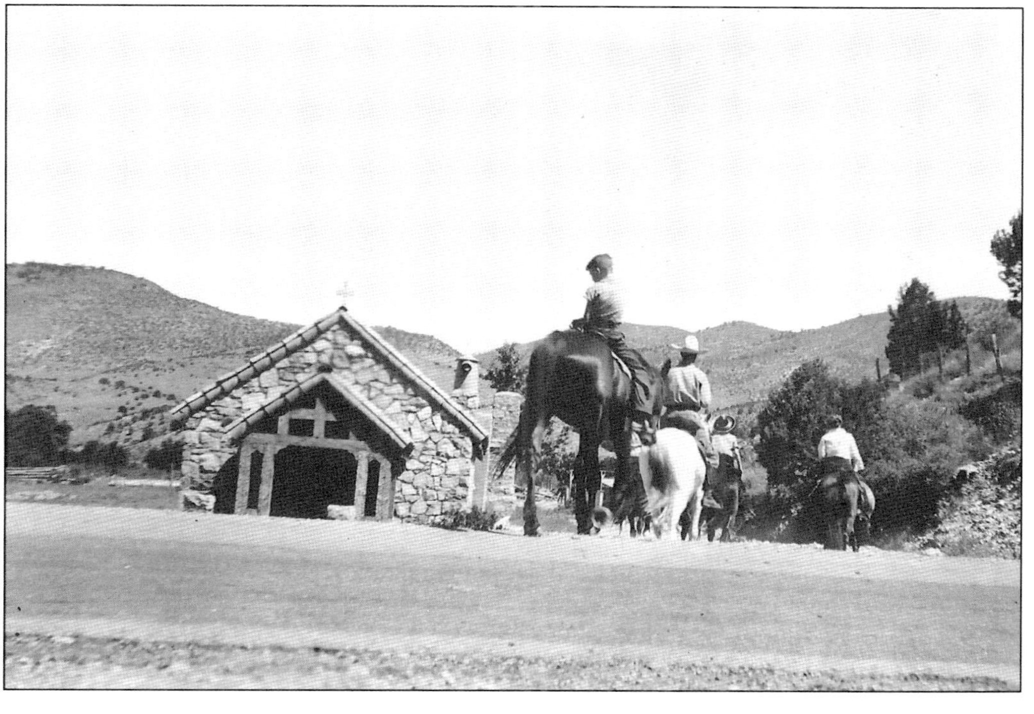

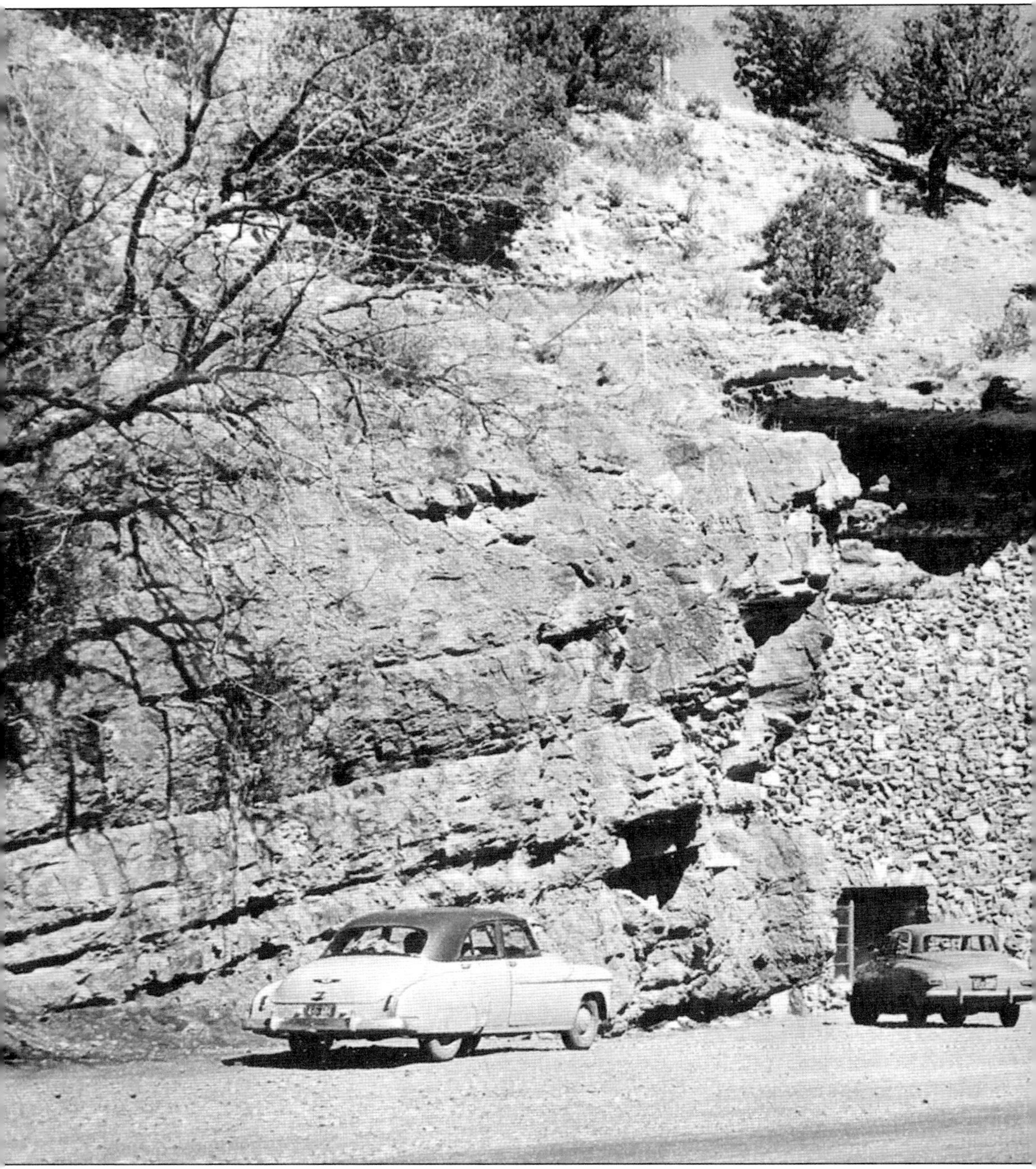

One of the most recognizable landmarks for travelers on the way to Ruidoso is Fox Cave. "We always used to stop at Fox Cave," remembers Peggy Stokes of Roswell. The caption on back of this postcard of Fox Cave reads: "Fox Cave on U.S. Highway 70, Hollywood, New Mexico. Fox Cave was once used as a hideout by Billy the Kid and roving bands of Apache warriors. It is located on Highway 70 between Roswell and Alamogordo, near Ruidoso, New Mexico, in the World's Largest Mountain Playground." The place called Hollywood, New Mexico, was located in Ruidoso

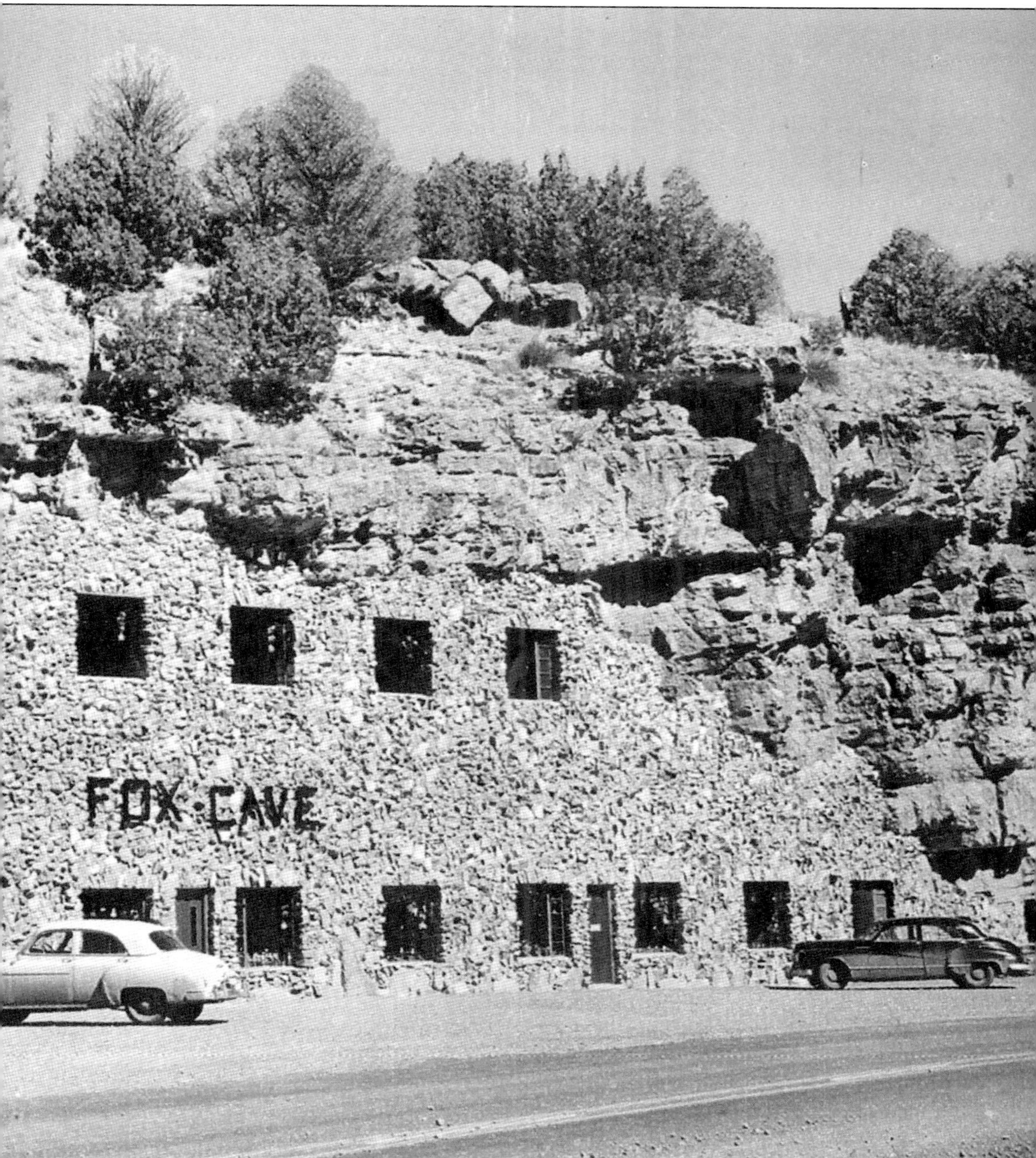

Canyon between Ruidoso and Ruidoso Downs, although it no longer exists today, swallowed up by the towns it resided in between. For a time, Fox Cave was closed down and lingered only as a monument to days gone by until it was reopened as Fox Cave and Gem Mine by an adventurous entrepreneur. The cave now hosts a wide collection of rocks, gems, books, DVDs and other novelties unique to Southeastern New Mexico. (Courtesy HSSNM #912.)

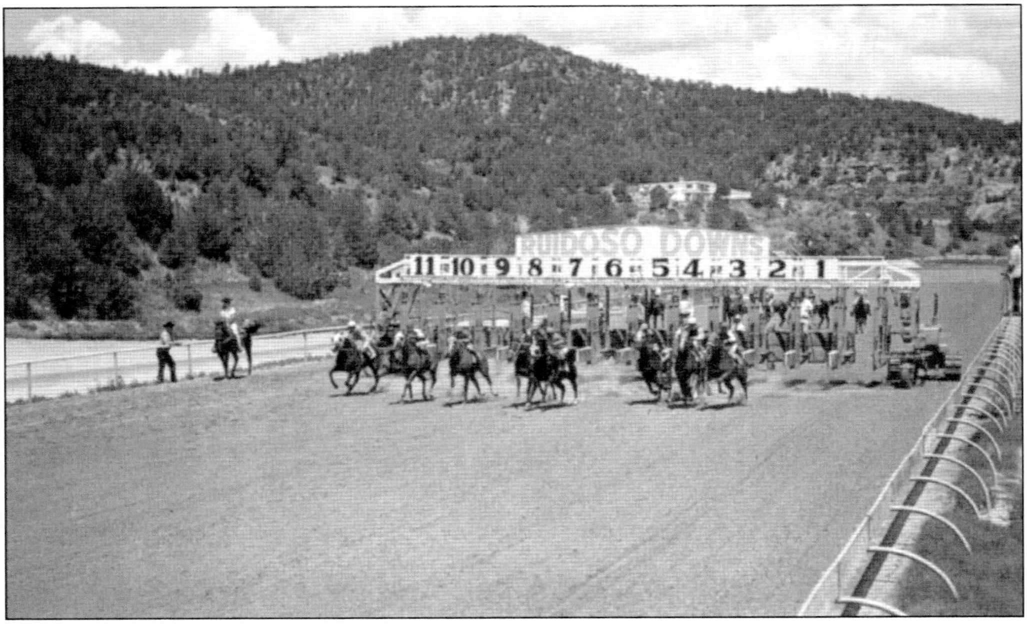

Ruidoso Downs, a town now famous across the West for the Ruidoso Downs Racetrack and Billy the Kid Casino, the Hubbard Museum of the American West, and the Lincoln County Cowboy Symposium, should not be confused with nearby Ruidoso, as the two are actually separate towns. These two postcards showcase the racetracks and the cool pines. (Both, author's collection.)

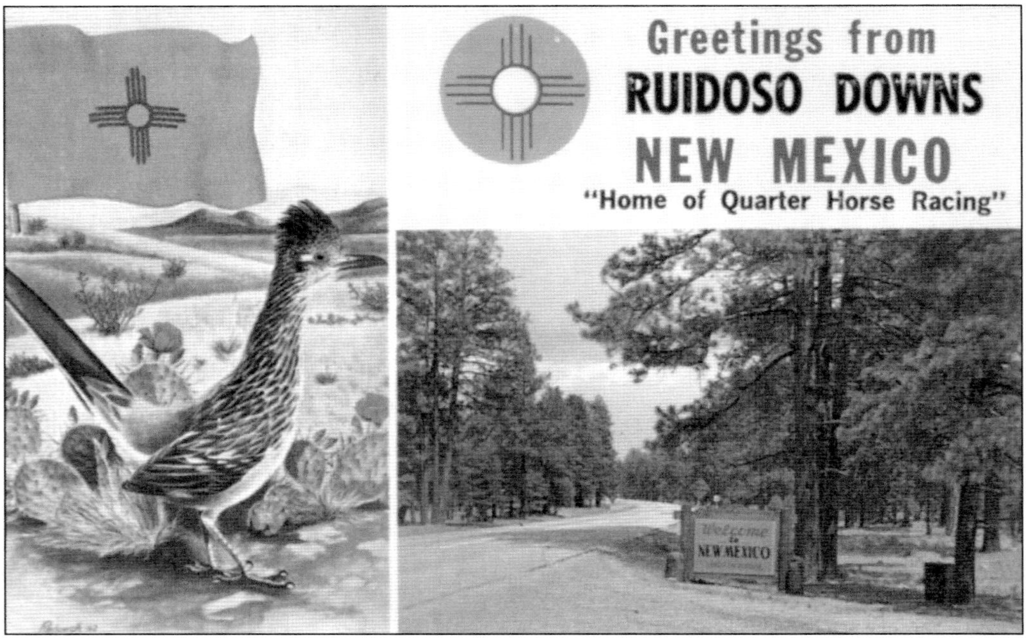

Three

Mountain Villages and Mining Towns

It is a surreal experience for someone living in the desert climate of Southern New Mexico to make the trip to Ruidoso. The hot arid air of the desert is gone and replaced with a cool breeze carrying the scent of pines in its wind. And as if that were not enough, if one is close enough, they can listen to the soothing ripples of the Ruidoso River. (*Ruidoso*, ironically, means "noisy" in Spanish).

The town of Ruidoso itself was named for the river and began with the Dowlin Mill in Flume Canyon in the late 1860s. It took some time, but eventually the town exploded and is now known as the "Playground of the Southwest." Although today it is the largest town in Lincoln County, the county seat remains in Carrizozo, which itself took the seat away from Lincoln village in 1913. Carrizozo started out as a railroad town, and although it has had its ups and downs, such as the railroad strike of 1923, which caused disastrous results to the town's economy at the time, it has survived handsomely into the present day.

While remnants of the Old West such as Ruidoso, Carrizozo, and Lincoln itself have survived into the 21st century in Lincoln County, many more did not. White Oaks for example, a booming town in the middle of a highly profitable gold rush, was once the richest and highest populated town in the whole county. Today, thanks to the hard work of caring citizens, it has narrowly avoided becoming a ghost town and boasts several museums.

Also in this vicinity are several other mountain towns such as Alto and Capitan. Alto is currently home to the Spencer Performing Arts Theater, and Capitan is known for being the home of the real flesh and blood Smokey Bear. Some communities in between Ruidoso and Capitan, like Angus and Bonito, are remembered by name only and are considered more or less part of the Ruidoso area. Some, like Ancho and Escondido (meaning hidden in Spanish), are long forgotten and only a few sparse ruins remain.

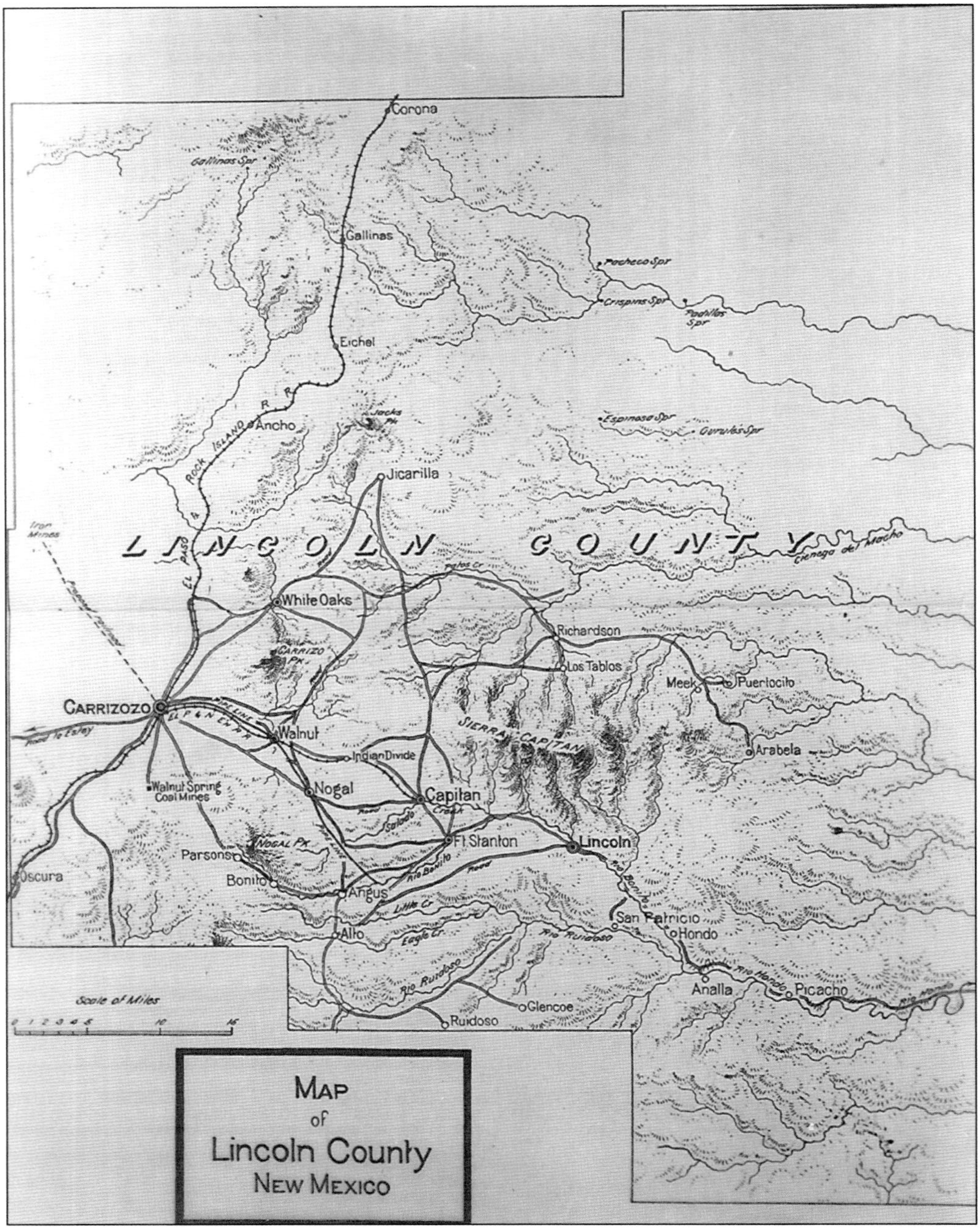

The map above shows Lincoln County in its present state. Although it used to be the largest county in all of New Mexico and the territorial United States, taking up all of Southeastern New Mexico in 1889, several smaller counties were carved out of Lincoln. These counties are Otero (south), Chaves (east), and Eddy (southeast). (Courtesy HSSNM #1545.)

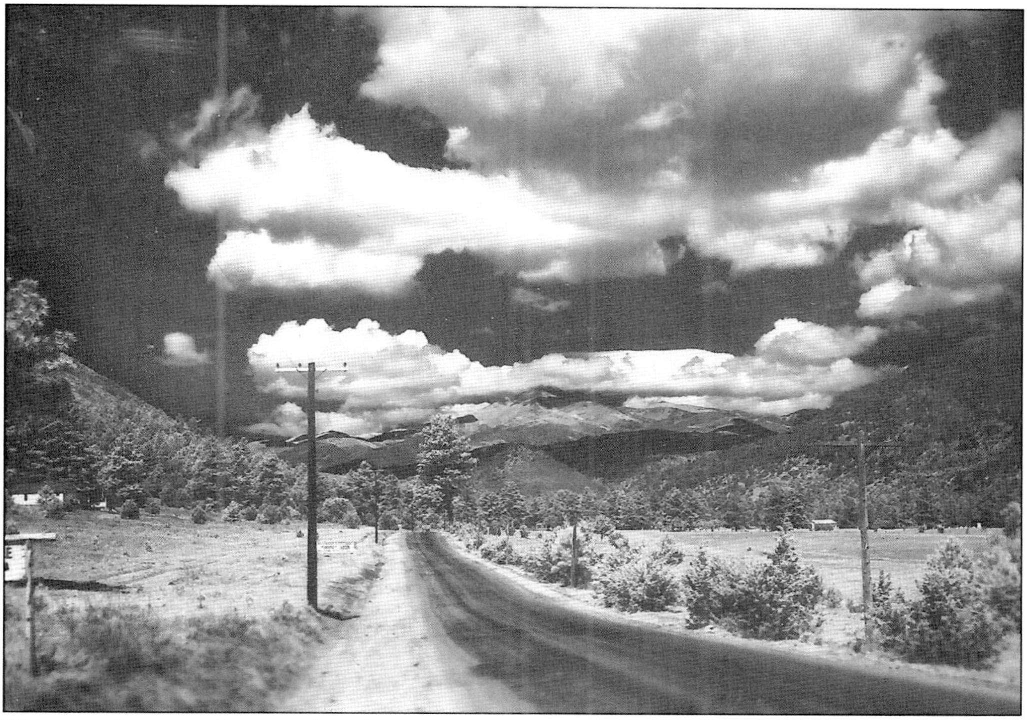

This page features photographs of the old road to Ruidoso by two of the area's best photographers. Paul Larkham took the c. 1940 image above with infrared film, which gives the sky its surreal look. Carmon Phillips was a famous Ruidoso photographer and curio shop owner (the old Dowlin's Mill in Ruidoso) who took this shot on the right of Highway 70 to Ruidoso. (Above, courtesy HSSNM Larkham Album 3 #481; right, HSSNM #5544.)

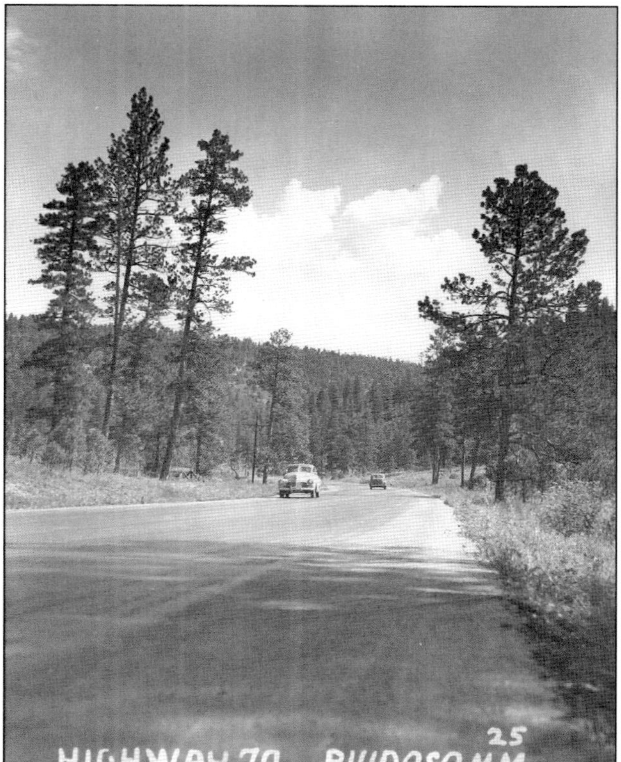

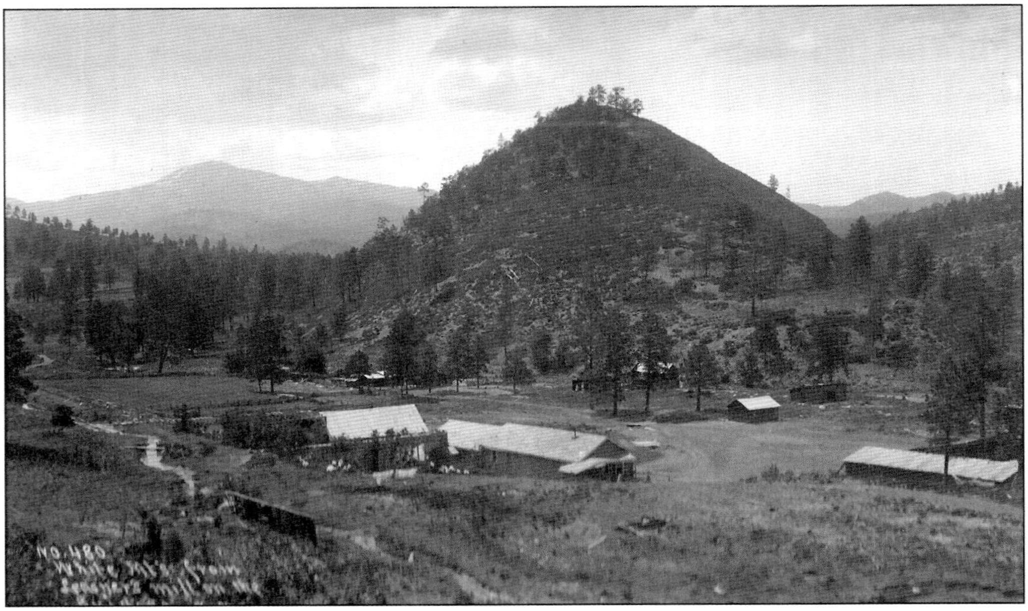

The beautiful but humble beginnings of Ruidoso can be seen above and below in the form of Dowlin's Mill. Dowlin's Mill began with brothers Paul and Will Dowlin, who came to the area in 1868. During the Lincoln County War, the mill was Billy the Kid's hideout, a fact proudly attested to by the town to this day. The old mill stands today, correctly touting itself as "Ruidoso's Birthplace" and has housed many different businesses over the years. The above image is from 1888, and the photograph below is from the 1920s or 1930s. (Above, courtesy HSSNM #589; below, courtesy HSSNM #1442A.)

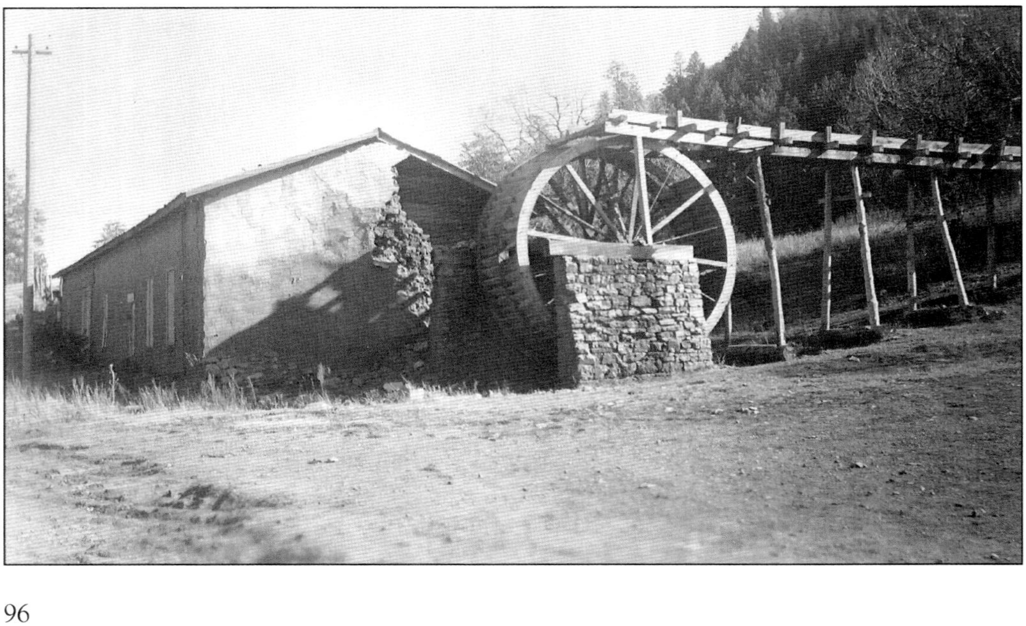

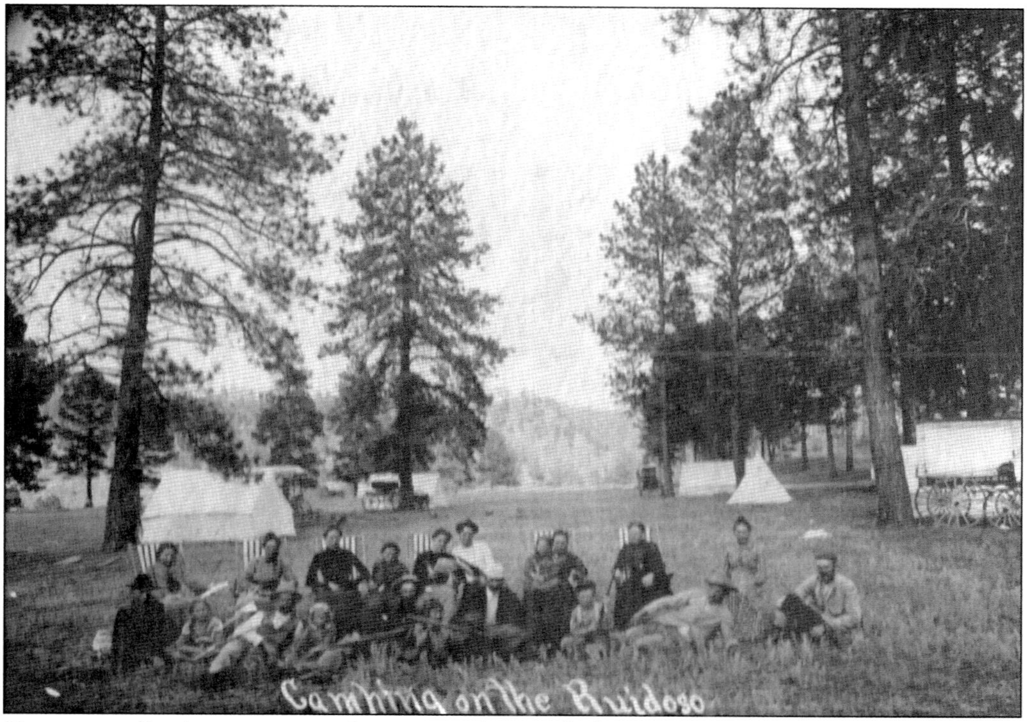

Camping in Ruidoso was a popular pastime for people from as far away as Roswell. Back in the horse and carriage days, Roswell was quite a ways away from Ruidoso. The campers above enjoy the serene atmosphere of the area. (Courtesy HSSNM #2162.)

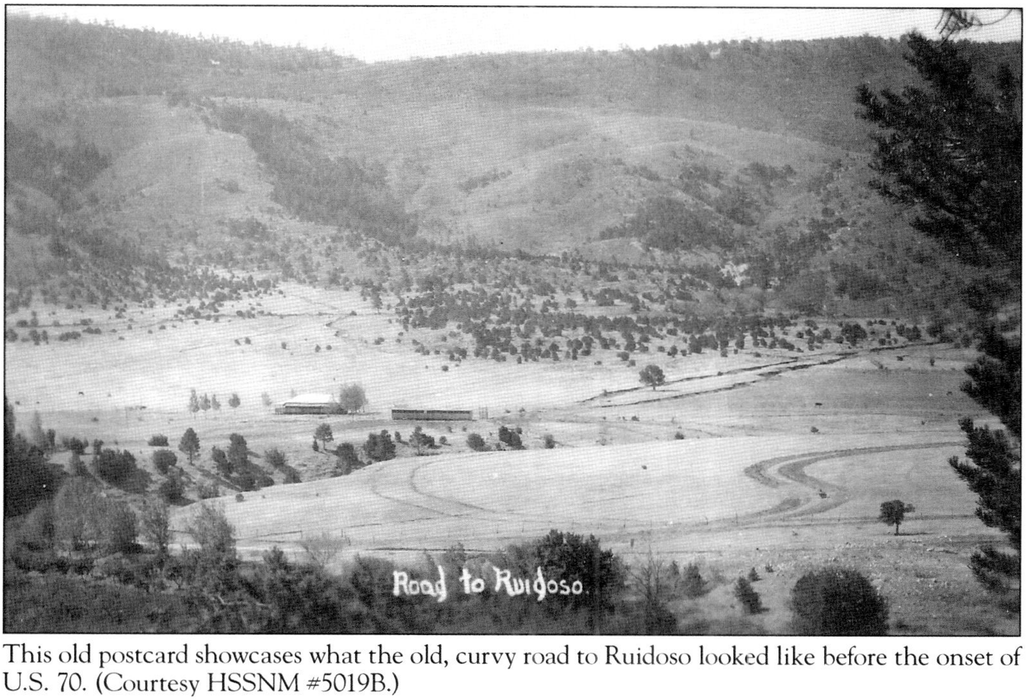

This old postcard showcases what the old, curvy road to Ruidoso looked like before the onset of U.S. 70. (Courtesy HSSNM #5019B.)

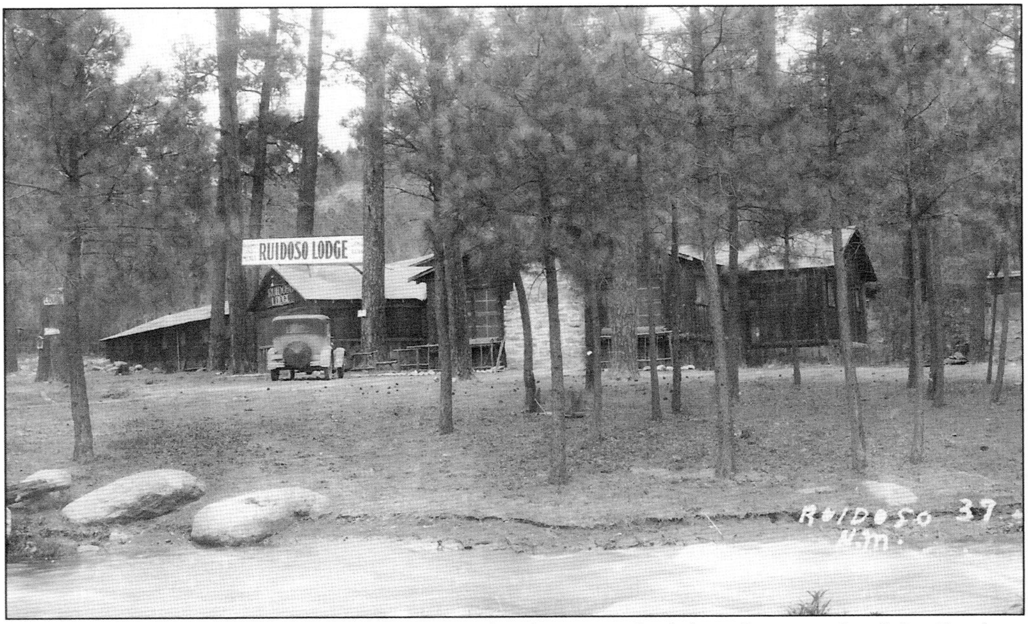

The rushing Ruidoso River can be seen in the foreground of this photograph of the Ruidoso Lodge. (Courtesy HSSNM #1599.)

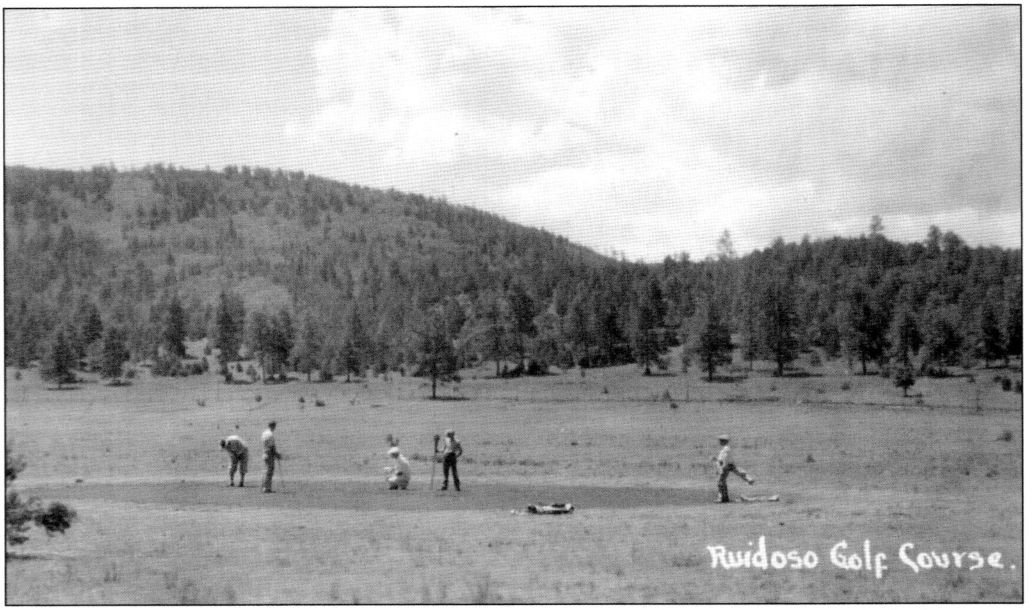

The background of cool pines gives this Ruidoso golf course a unique mountain look. (Courtesy HSSNM #995.)

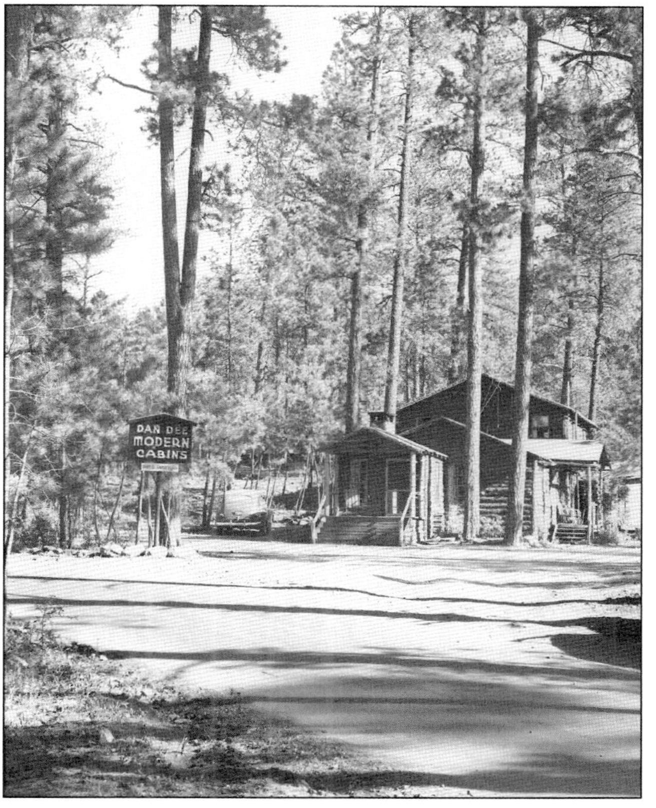

The image to the right shows Dan Dee Modern Cabins, which is still a favorite Ruidoso tradition for many today. The image below looks back at Ruidoso's Main Street when it was not congested and overflowing with traffic. This picture was taken sometime in the 1950s when the street was only occasionally overcrowded with tourists but not all the time like it is today. (Right, courtesy HSSNM #5103; below, courtesy HSSNM #5391.)

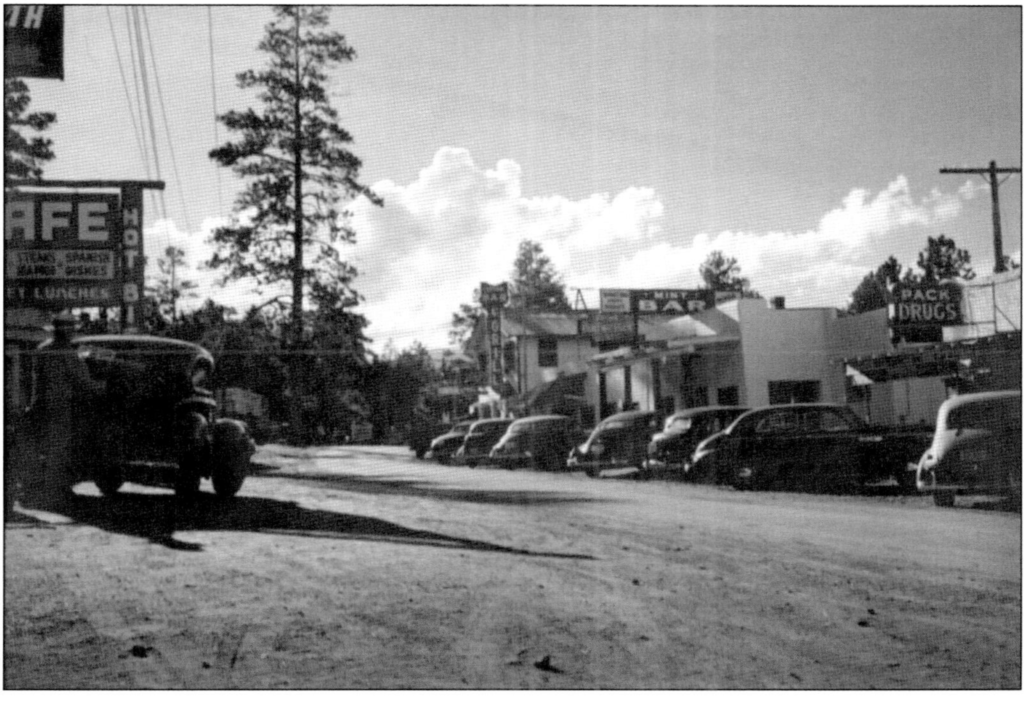

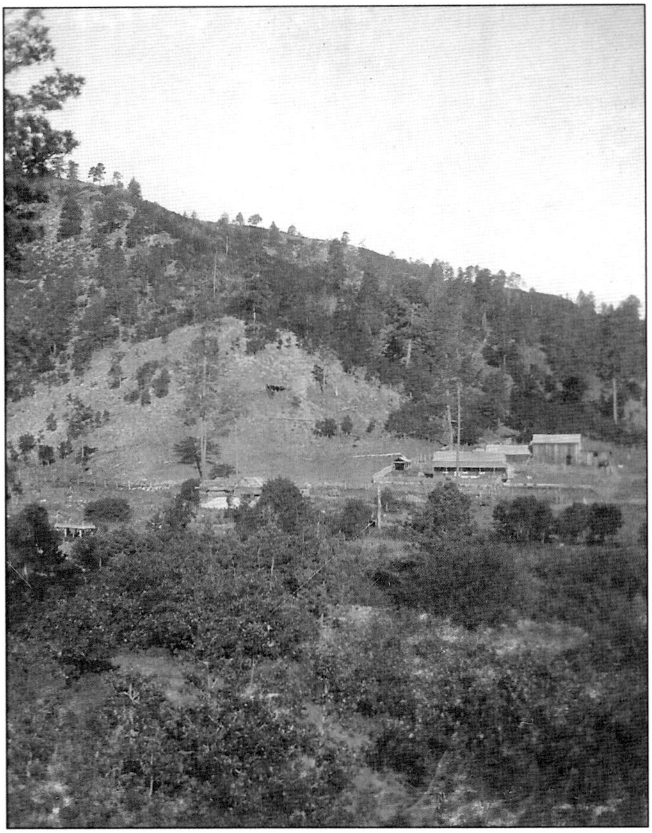

Believe it or not, the quaint mountain village of Bonito, which started out as a mining settlement, was the site of one of Lincoln County's most gruesome murders. On the night of May 5, 1885, there were two guests staying at the Mayberry Hotel, and one of them was a murderer. Mark Nelson, the mysterious young traveler, for no reason whatsoever killed the hotel owner and all of his family except for his daughter, Nellie, who left New Mexico soon after, never to return. Nelson also killed a saloon keeper and the manager of the general store. The next morning, Bonito residents remained locked in their homes, save for a brave few who went out and killed Nelson. Including the killer, eight total were dead. (Left, courtesy HSSNM #3493; below, courtesy New Mexico State University Library, Archives and Special Collections.)

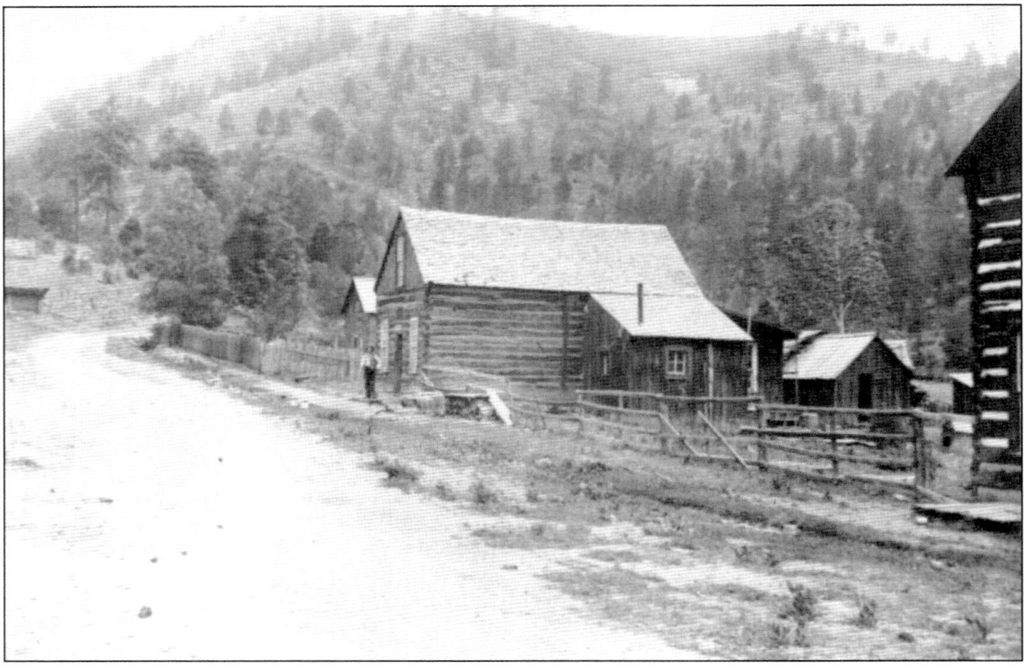

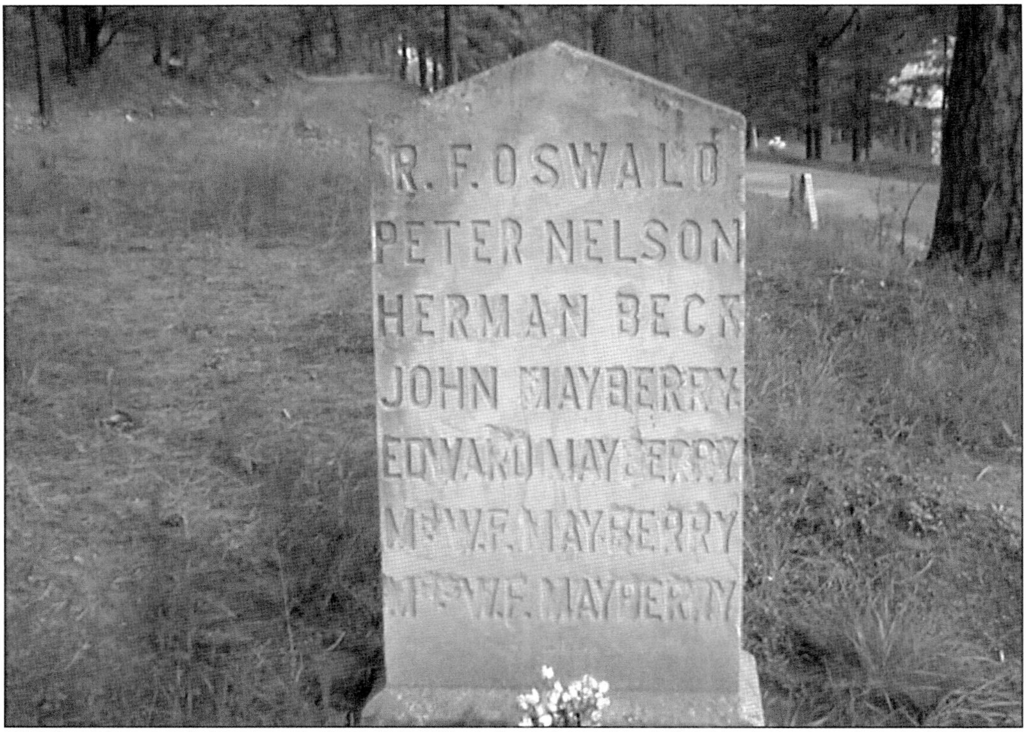

Bonito City is gone today. The buildings were dismantled and moved when the Southern Pacific Railroad constructed a dam in Bonito Canyon. Bonito Lake (sometimes called Bonita Lake), pictured below, remains today as a mainstay and popular fishing spot in the Ruidoso area. The graves of Mark Nelson and his seven victims were transferred from Bonito City to Angus, another nearby settlement. The victims were buried side-by-side; lore has it that Mark Nelson was buried upside down, headfirst into the ground to prevent his ghost from ever walking the earth. The victims' headstone is shown above in the Angus cemetery. (Above, courtesy James Owens; below, courtesy Carmon Phillips.)

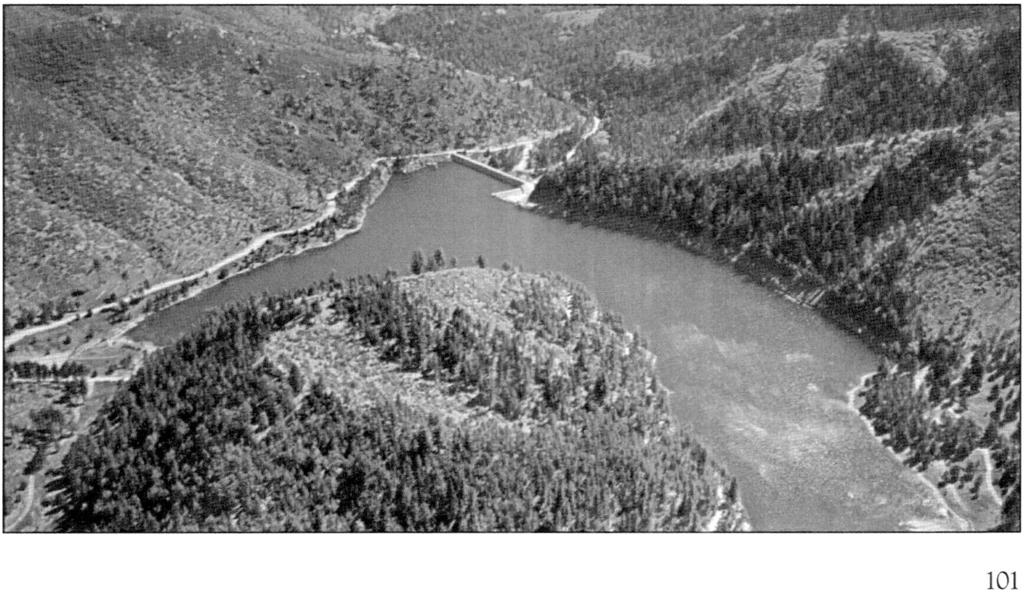

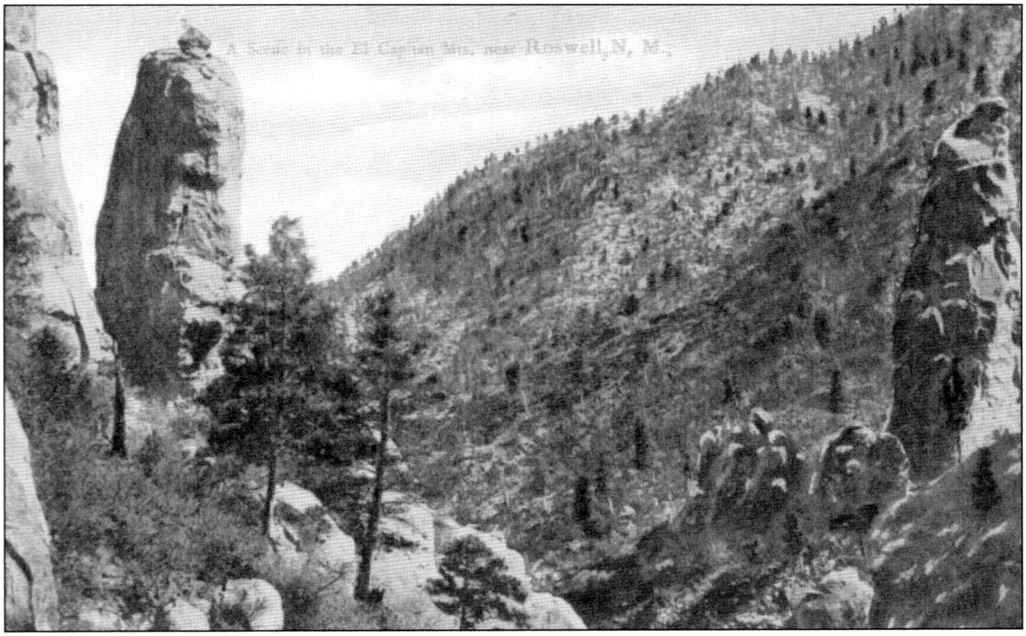

The Capitan Mountains are some of the most well-known formations in all of Southern New Mexico, and El Capitan, named for Capt. Saturnino Baca of Lincoln, can be seen all the way over in Roswell. This postcard showcases a scene high up in the Capitans. (Courtesy HSSNM #1410.)

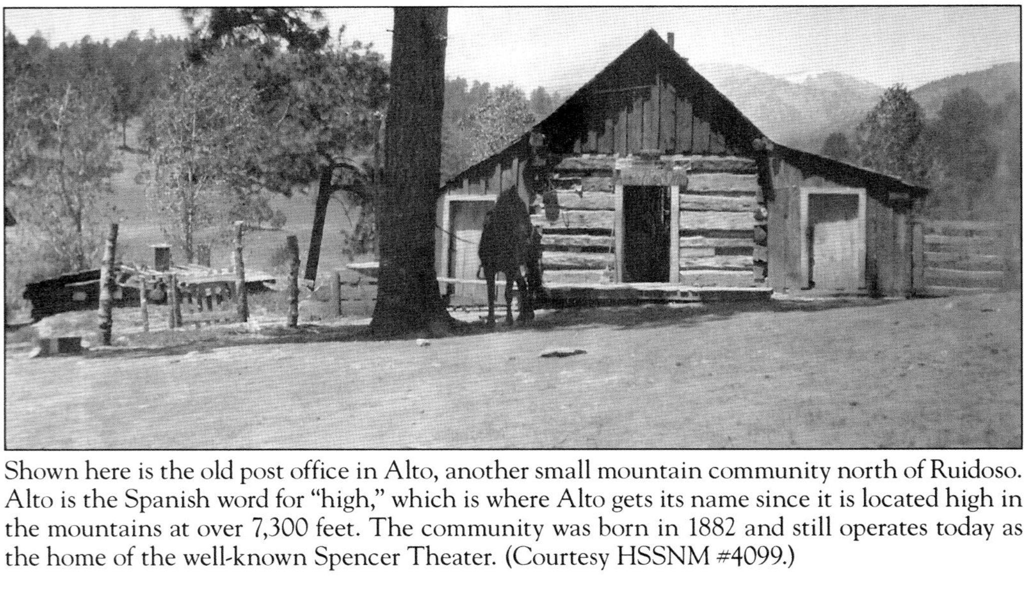

Shown here is the old post office in Alto, another small mountain community north of Ruidoso. Alto is the Spanish word for "high," which is where Alto gets its name since it is located high in the mountains at over 7,300 feet. The community was born in 1882 and still operates today as the home of the well-known Spencer Theater. (Courtesy HSSNM #4099.)

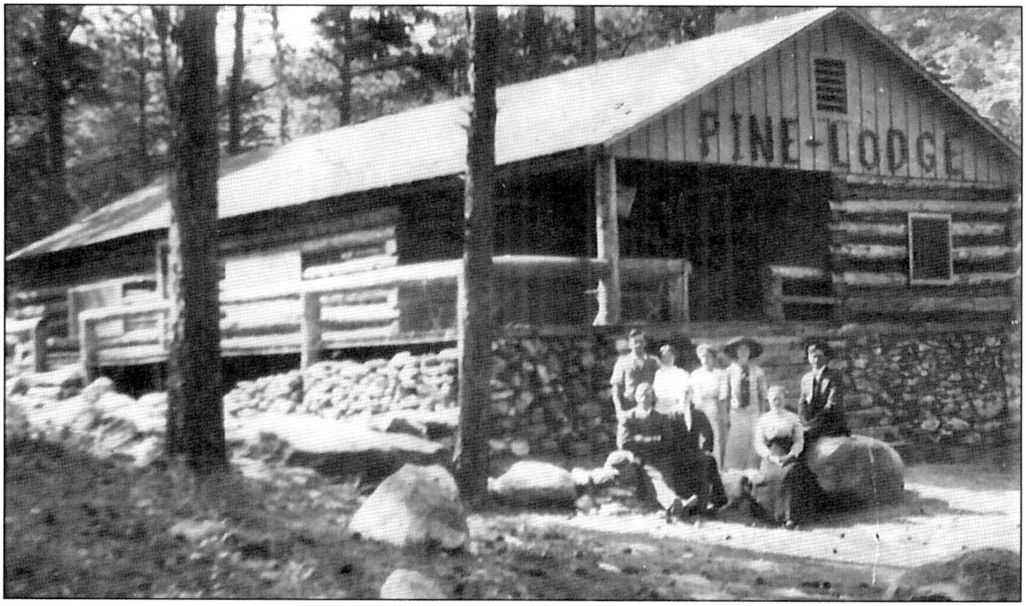

Pictured above, a popular spot to camp, especially for Roswellites, was Pine Lodge on the northeast side of the Capitan Mountains. Pine Lodge no longer exists today; the main lodge burned down sometime prior to 1980, and the road there is extremely rough, even if one has a four-wheel drive vehicle. Pine Lodge, mainly a summer cabin resort, was constructed in 1909. The smiling young man with the washbowl is James D. Cooley Jr., the son of Roswell writer James D. Cooley. The picture was taken at Pine Lodge around 1920. (Above, courtesy HSSNM #2671A; right, courtesy HSSNM #2500A.)

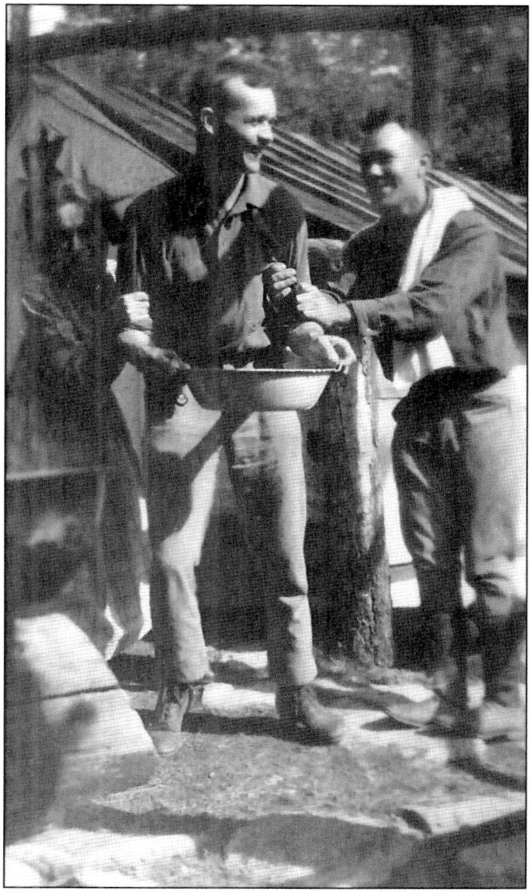

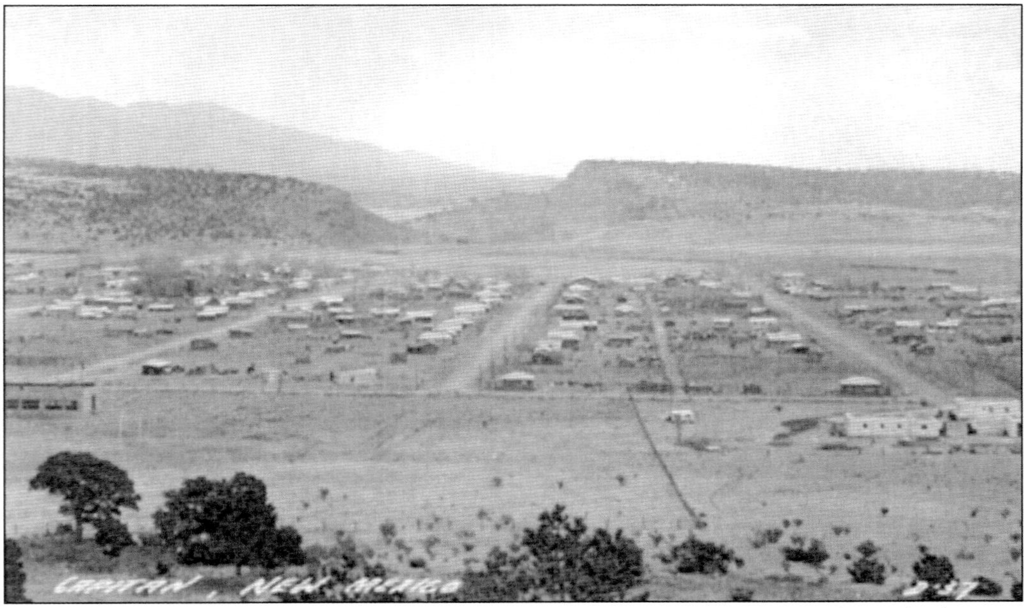

The mountain town of Capitan, flanked by the beautiful Capitan Mountains from which it gets its name, was originally called Gray for its first settler, Seaborn T. Gray. Gray started the first post office and general store in the area. Eventually land promoter Charles B. Eddy, who begat many towns in Southern New Mexico, purchased land in the area and platted a town site that he named Capitan. The El Paso and Northeastern Railroad built a line through the town to get to the Dodge coal mines 1 mile to the west. An aerial view of Capitan around the 1930s is shown above and another from 1946 below. (Both courtesy Virginia Watson-Jones.)

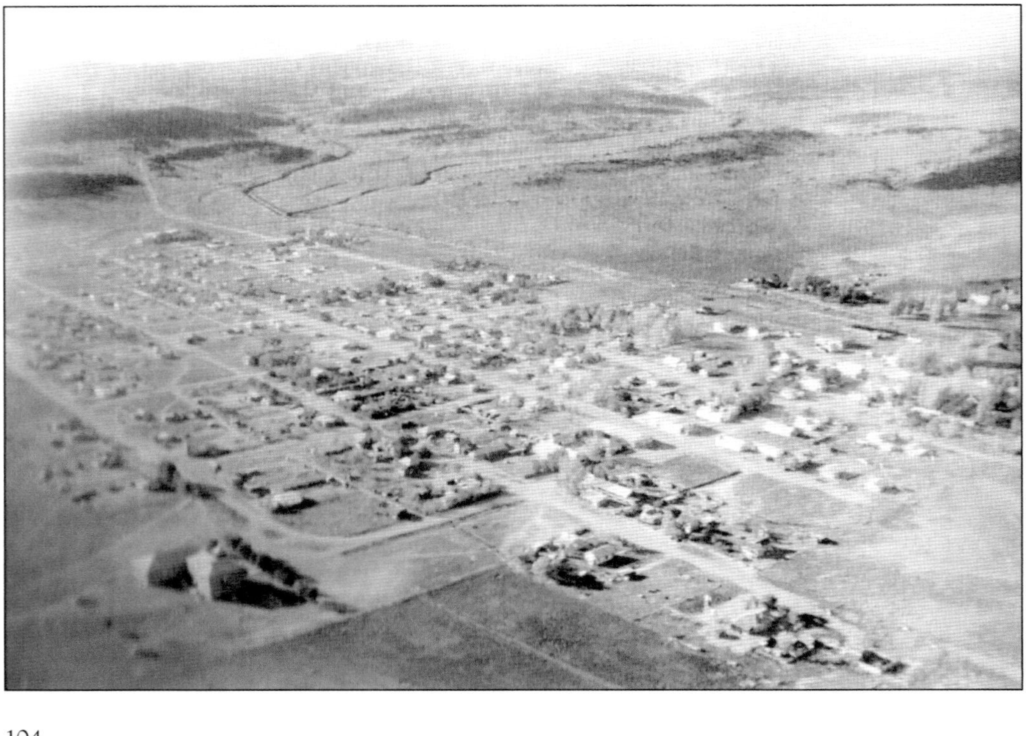

Capitan's claim to fame today is as the home of the real Smokey Bear (it is not Smokey the Bear, contrary to popular belief there is no "the" in the name). On May 19, 1950, a burned baby black bear was found in the nearby Capitan Mountains in the aftermath of a major fire. The cub was nursed successfully back to health and became the real Smokey Bear. Pictured right, Smokey Bear grabs Lyle F. Watts's forest ranger hat while the bear is inducted into the National Zoo in Washington, D.C., around June 1950. Smokey Bear was taken back to Capitan and buried there in 1976 after his death. Today Capitan has the Smokey Bear Historical Park and the Smokey Bear Museum where two unidentified boys pose in front of Smokey's likeness below. (Right, courtesy Virginia Watson-Jones; below, courtesy Linde Newman.)

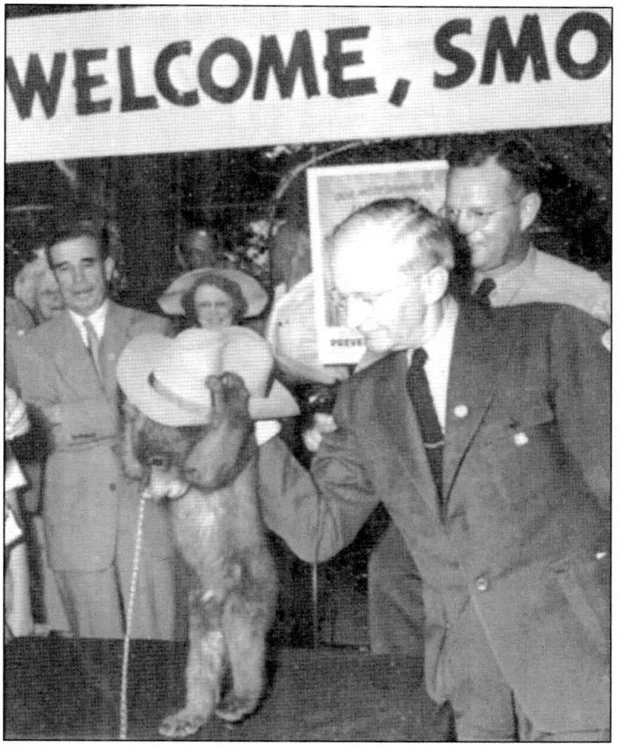

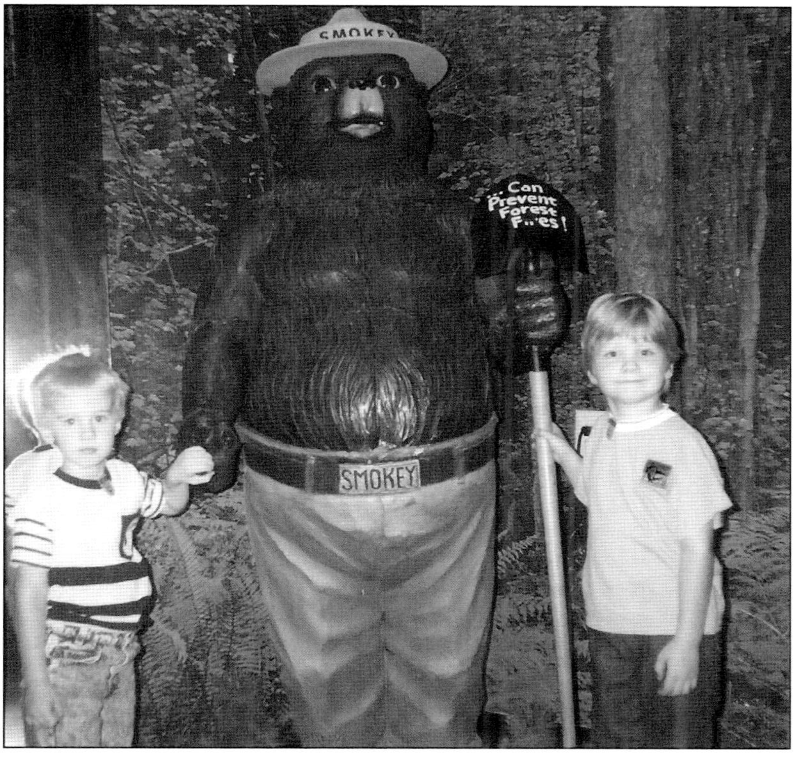

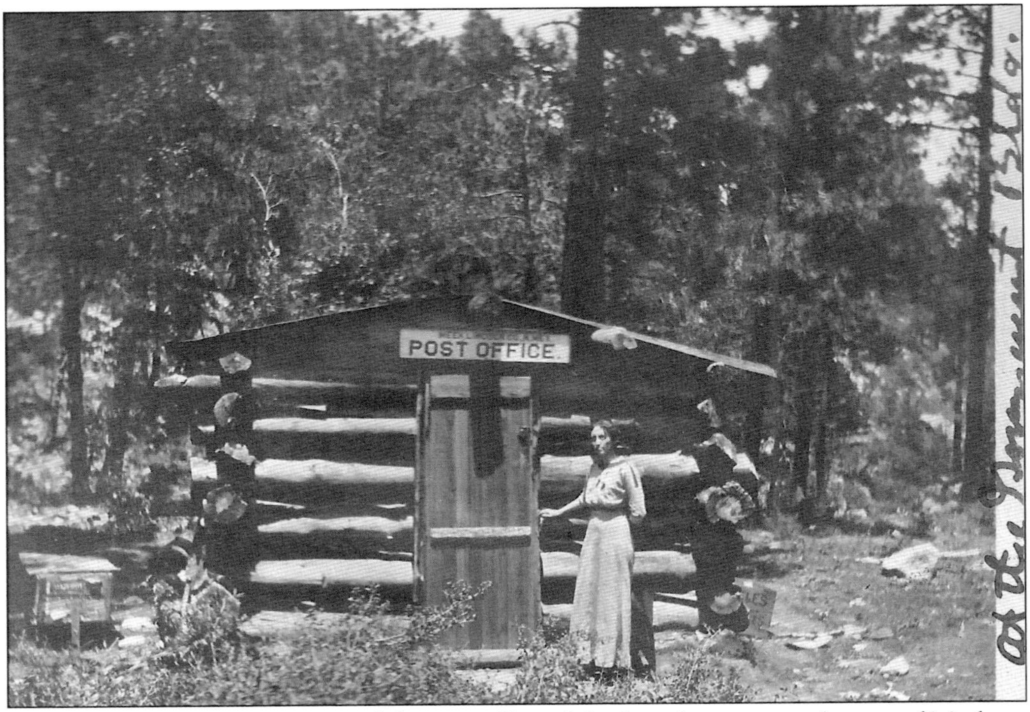

Above and below are two views of the post office of the long forgotten settlement of Meek, so named for the last name of its first postmaster, Thomas B. Meek. The post office at Meek lasted from only 1904 to 1922 according to Robert Julyan's *The Place Names of New Mexico*. Although they are both log cabins, the building above and the one below are actually different structures if one looks closely, but which one was the original building and which is the newer is unknown, as is the identity of the woman above. (Above, courtesy HSSNM #3090; below, courtesy New Mexico State University Library, Archives and Special Collections.)

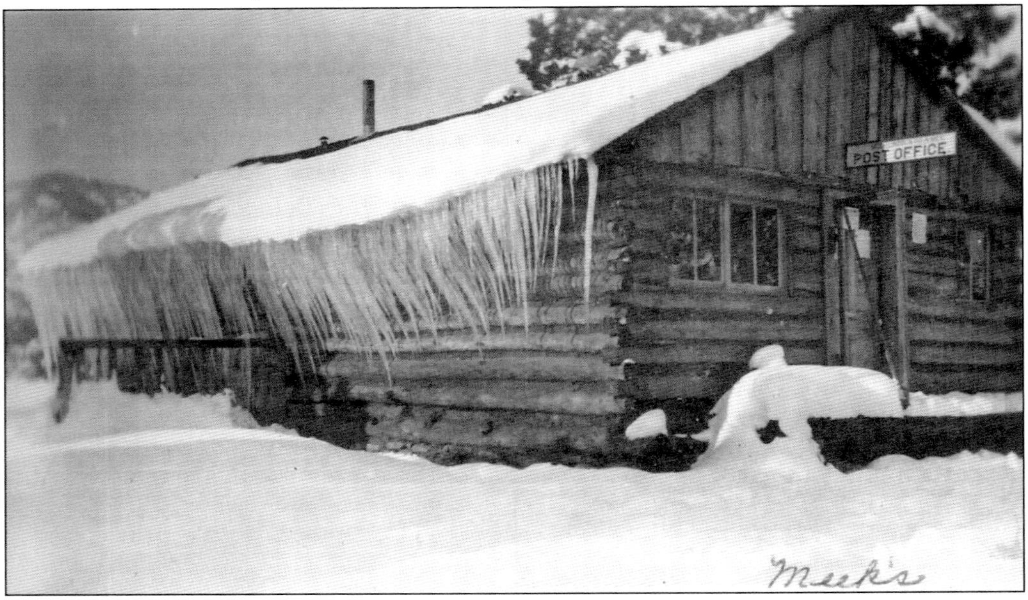

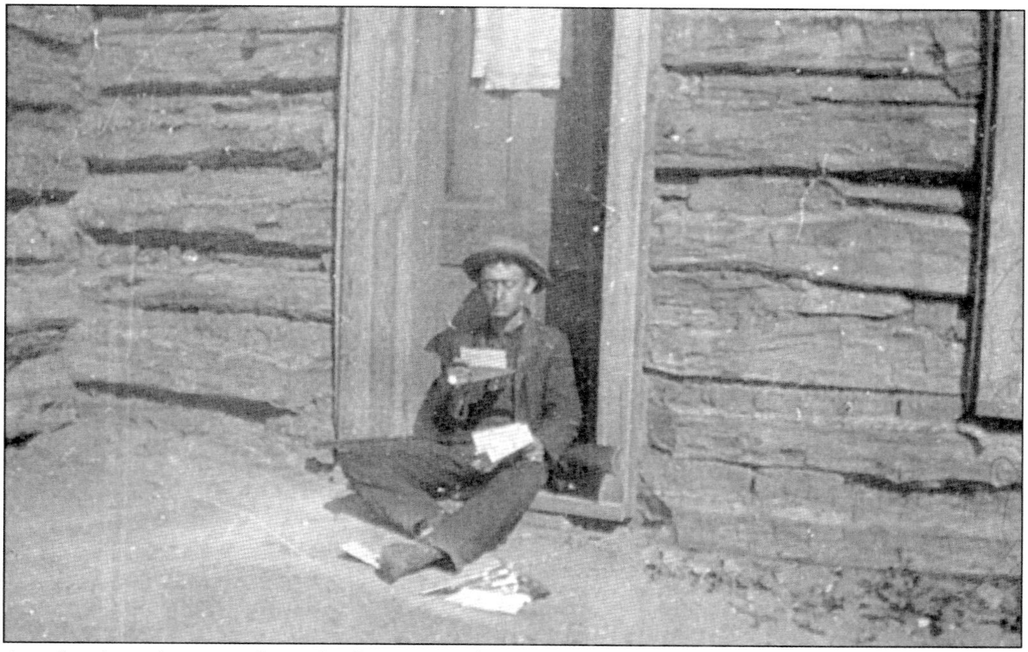

Another long forgotten Lincoln County settlement is that of Jicarilla, a mining community that came into being in the 1880s, even though mining had occurred in the Jicarilla Mountains since the 1850s. Jicarilla died out sometime after the Great Depression, though the post office, which began in 1892, managed to survive until 1942. Jicarilla gets its name from the Jicarilla Mountains nearby, which in turn were named for the Jicarilla Apaches. Pictured above, Charles Whiteman is outside of his Jicarilla store reading a letter, and below is the Little Joe Saloon, owned by Joe Long around 1902. The saloon appears to have a dirt floor if one looks closely. (Above, courtesy HSSNM #131E; below, courtesy HSSNM #4072.)

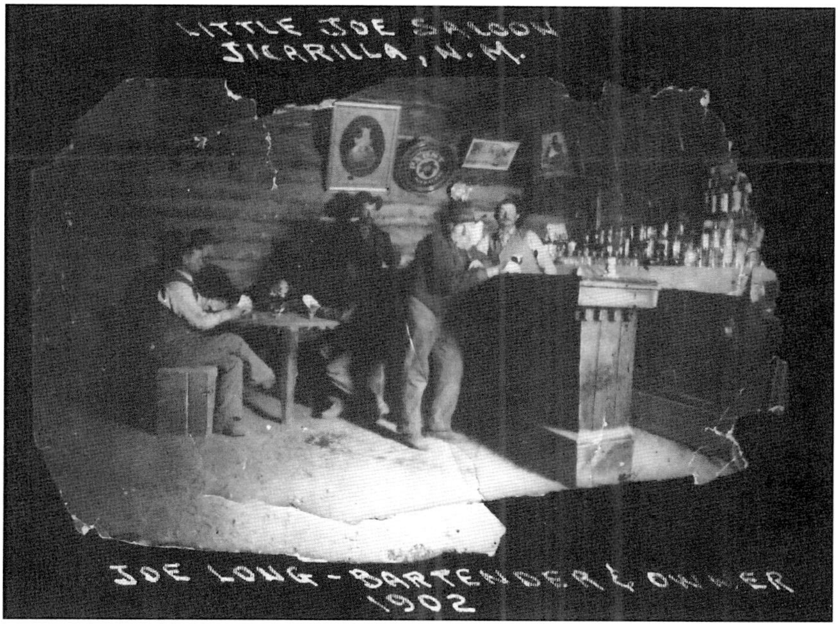

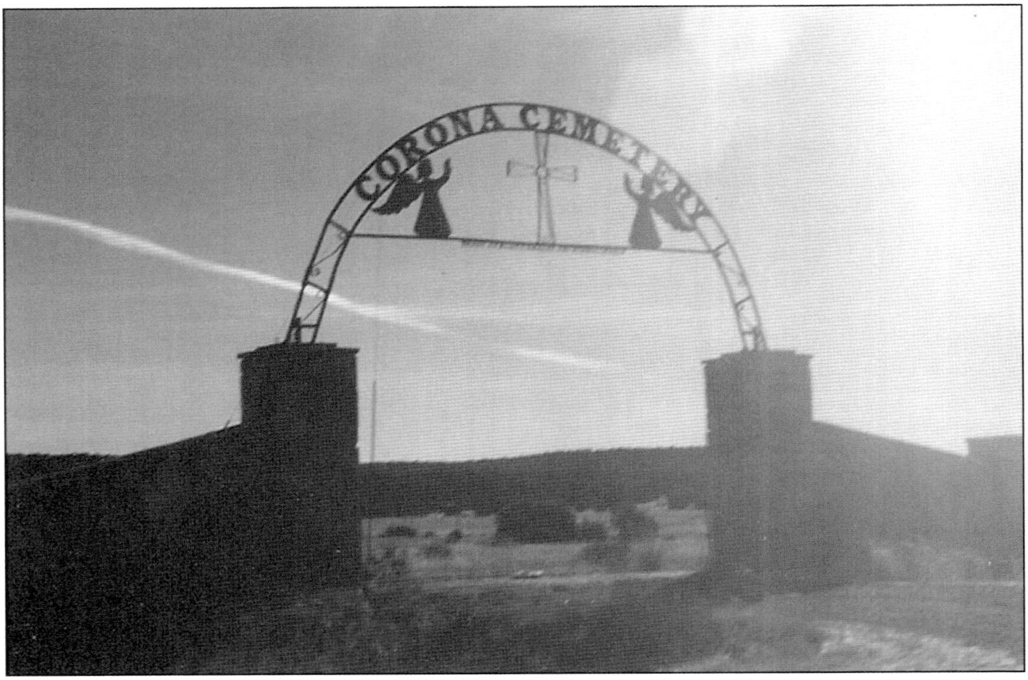

Corona is located in the far northern half of Lincoln County all to itself with no nearby neighbors. *Corona* is the Spanish name for "crown"; the town got that name from the El Paso and Northeastern Railroad when they put in a station there because it was at the highest elevation of their line in 1899. Today Corona is well known in UFO lore as the place an alleged spacecraft rained debris down on a sheep ranch before crashing closer to Roswell, 75 miles southeast. Two modern views of the Corona Cemetery, above, and the Corona Trading Company, below, are offered on this page. (Above, courtesy HSSNM #4192C; below, courtesy HSSNM #4192E.)

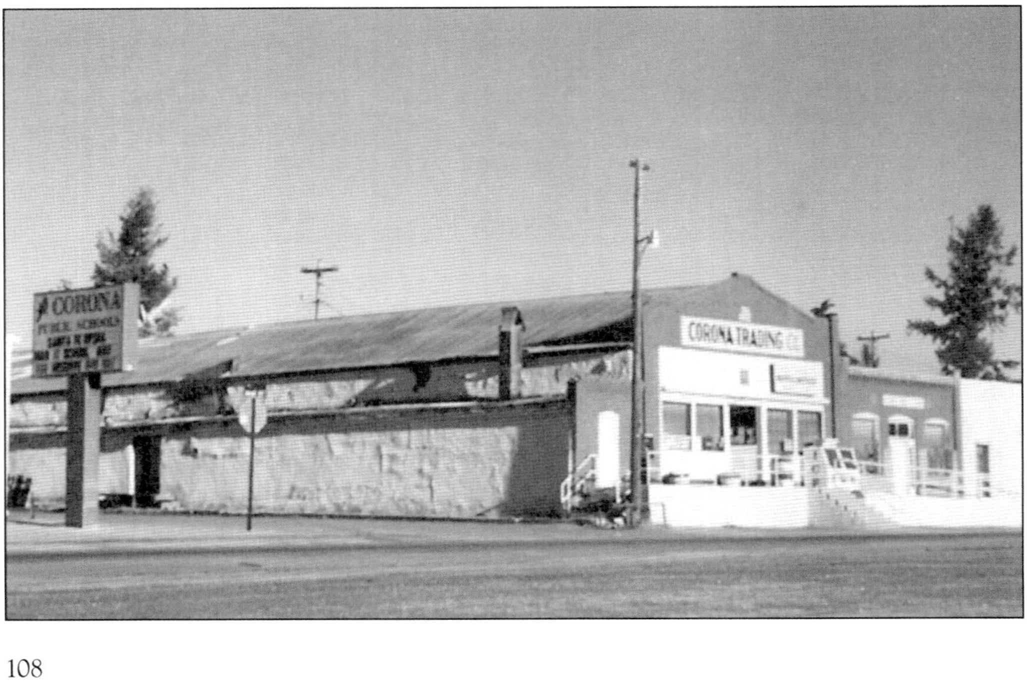

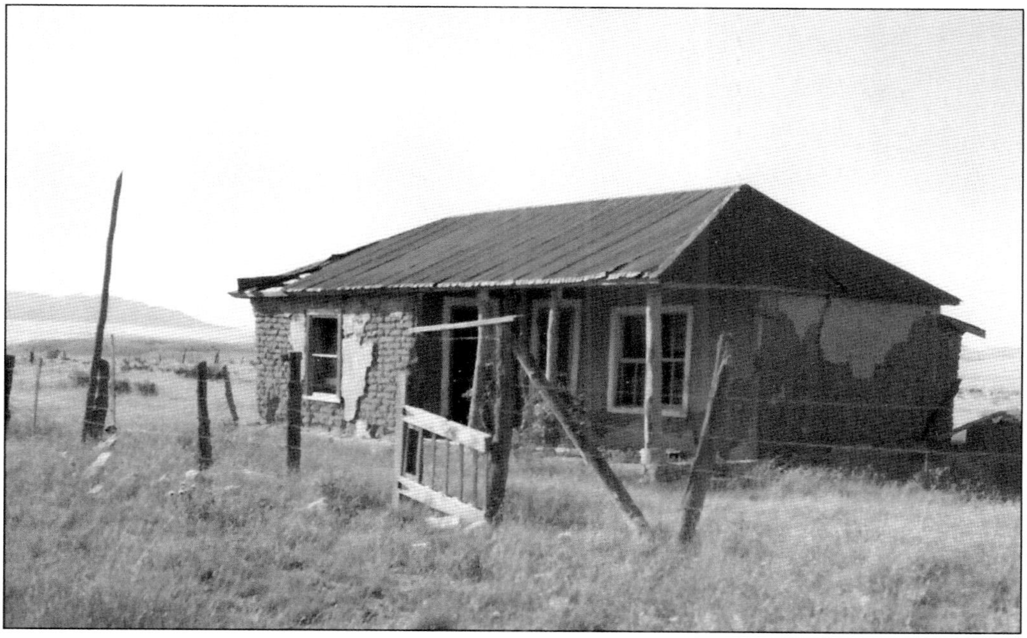

Little remains today of the tiny Hispanic settlement known as Escondido, in between White Oaks and Capitan, except for the building shown here. A tale about Escondido's old days, unearthed by Lynda Sanchez, involves a Mexican wedding *baile* that turned sour when several men began fighting over a young woman, and one of the men was stoned to death! (Courtesy HSSNM #6495D.)

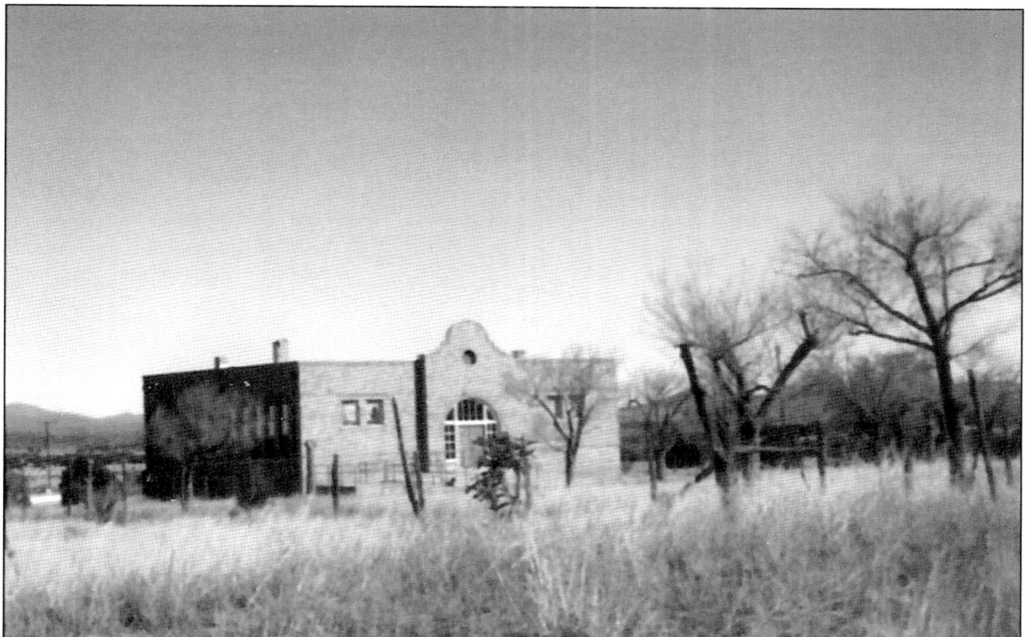

The remains of the old Ancho schoolhouse are pictured above. Ancho was born when the railroad created a station in the Ancho (meaning "wide" in Spanish) Valley in 1899. The community is sparsely populated today. (Courtesy HSSNM #4215.)

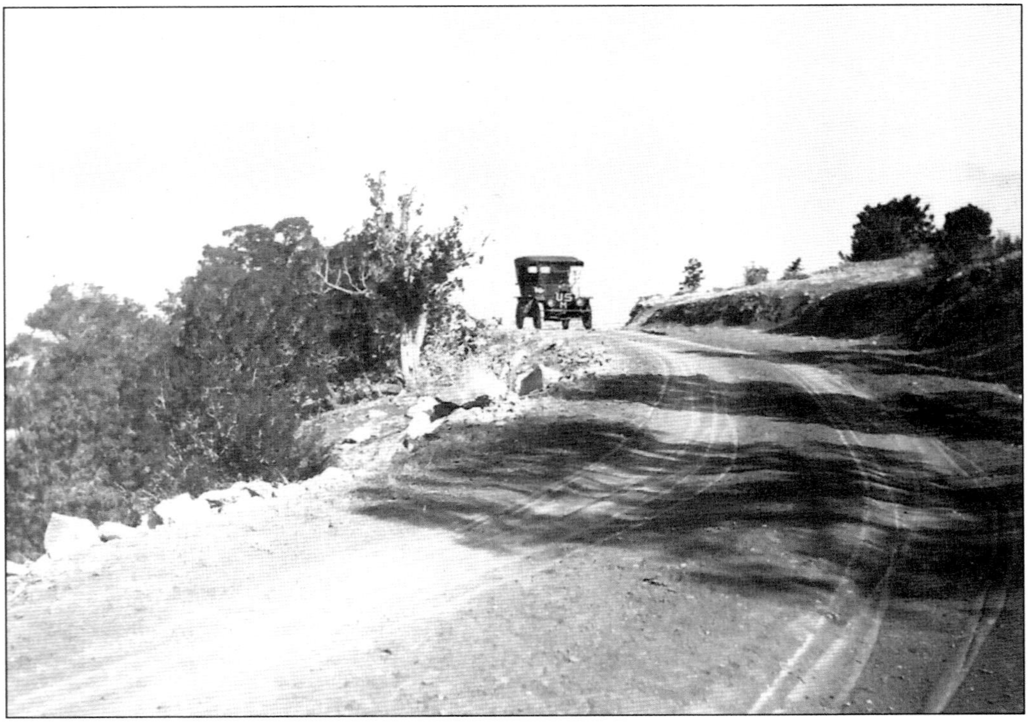

Another semi-forgotten Lincoln settlement, which still exists today, is Nogal. Nogal began life around the same time as White Oaks and for the same reasons in 1879, when gold was discovered there. Nogal Hill, above, was a popular spot on the mail route. Below is a postcard featuring the road to Nogal. (Above, courtesy HSSNM #2800F; below, courtesy HSSNM #5019A.)

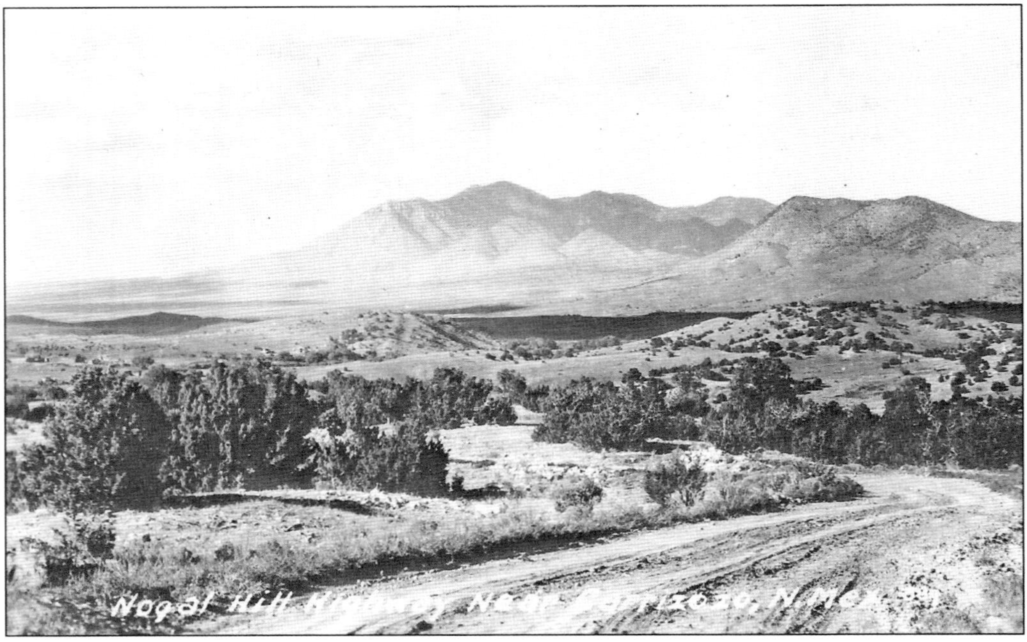

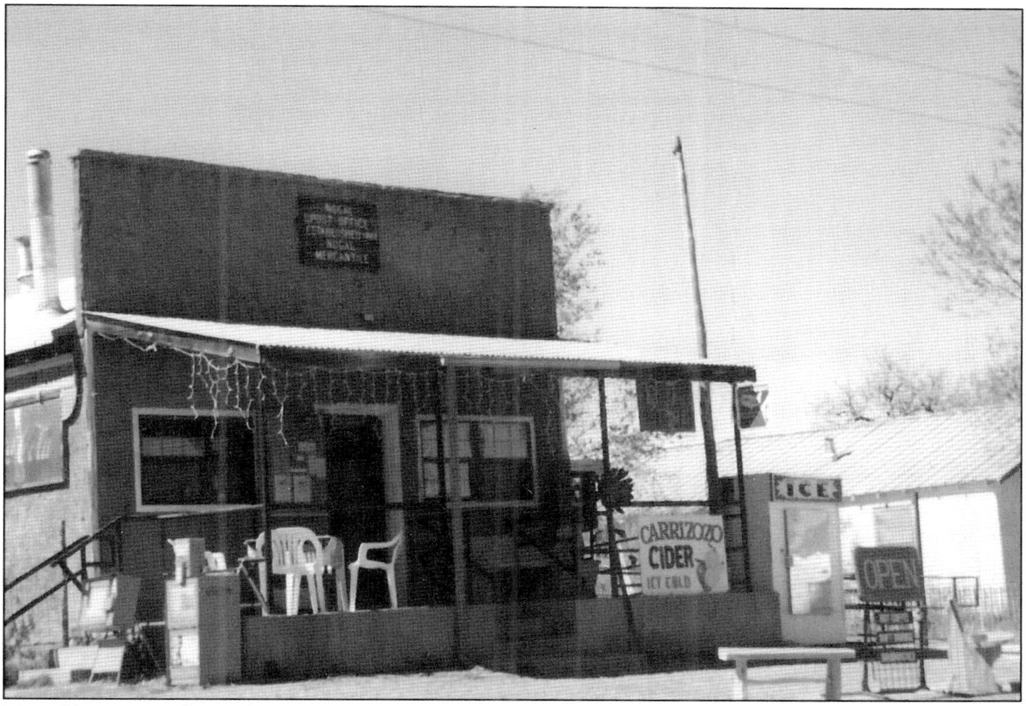

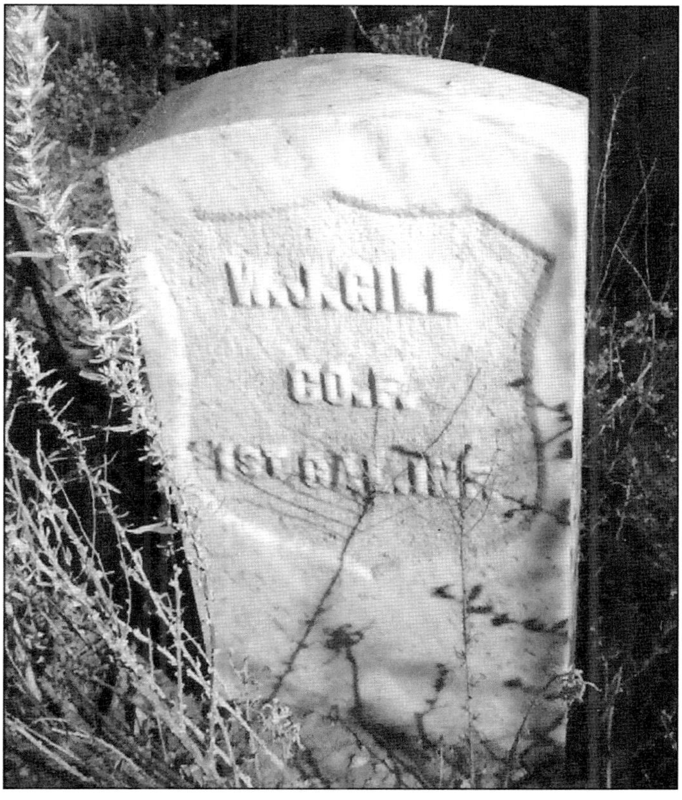

Nogal has gone through many different name changes; at first it was Dry Gulch, then Galena, Parsons, and finally Nogal, which means "walnut" in Spanish. Locals named it Nogal for the many walnut trees in the area, and coincidentally, there is a railroad watering station in the area named Walnut. Nogal's mines began to play out in the early 20th century, but the little community remarkably survives today. The Nogal Post Office and Mercantile as it looks today is pictured above. Right is the grave of Billy Gill, the owner of the American Mine at Nogal, one of its most prominent mines. (Above, courtesy HSSNM #4242; right, courtesy HSSNM #6006.)

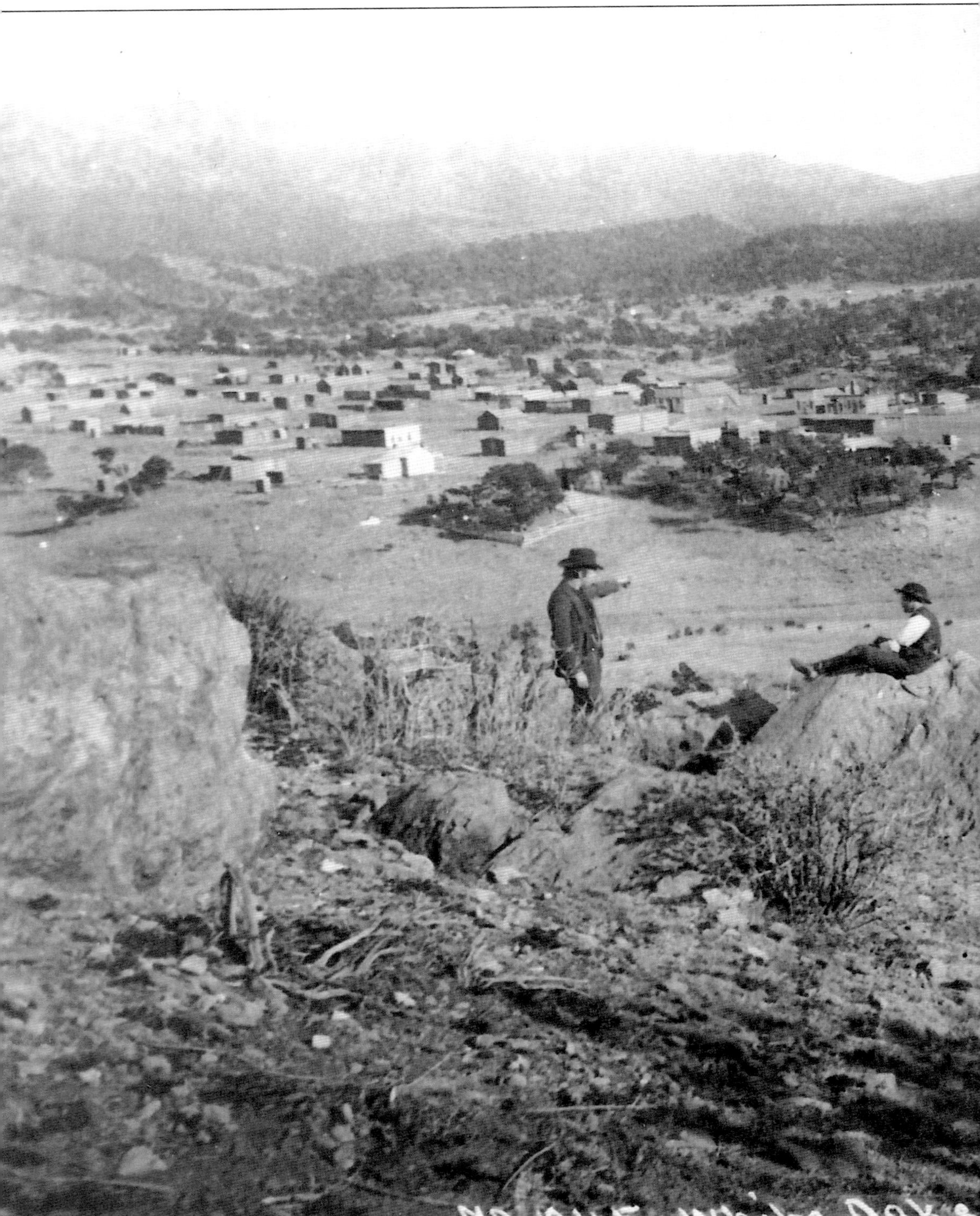
NO, 245 White Oaks

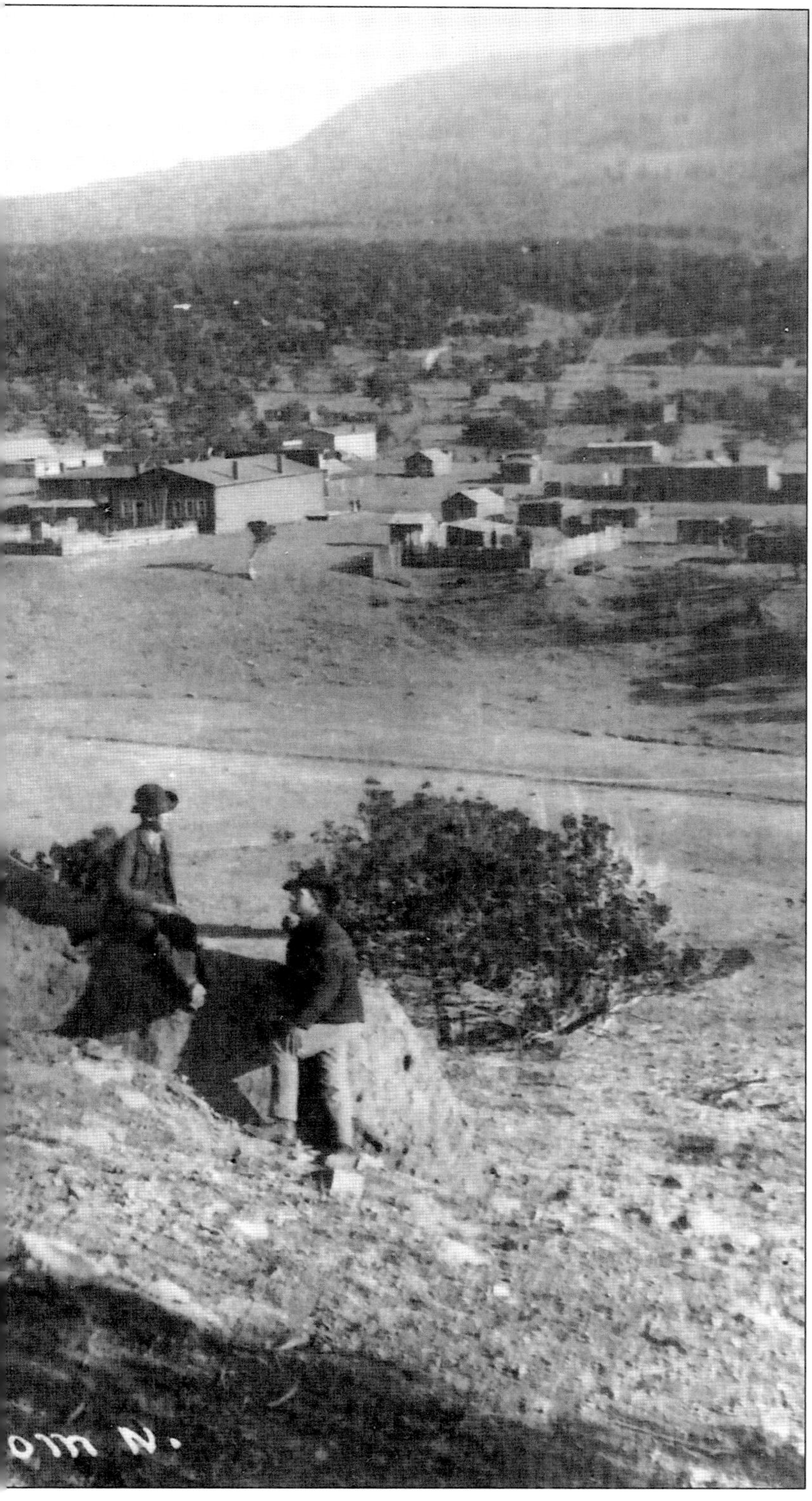

The legend of how the gold boom began in White Oaks has gone through several revisions with each telling the tale, but in short it goes that it was discovered by an El Paso prison escapee, John Wilson, who jokingly walked into the mountains to find a gold mine, only he actually did. Instead of developing his find himself, he sold his claim to John Baxter for $40 and a bottle of whiskey and went on his way. News spread quickly of the gold found on Baxter Mountain, enticing prospectors, and as more mines were discovered, more settlers came, and more homes and establishments were built. Thus White Oaks, the town these four men are looking at from atop this hill, was born. (Courtesy HSSMM Larkham Album 8 #2940.)

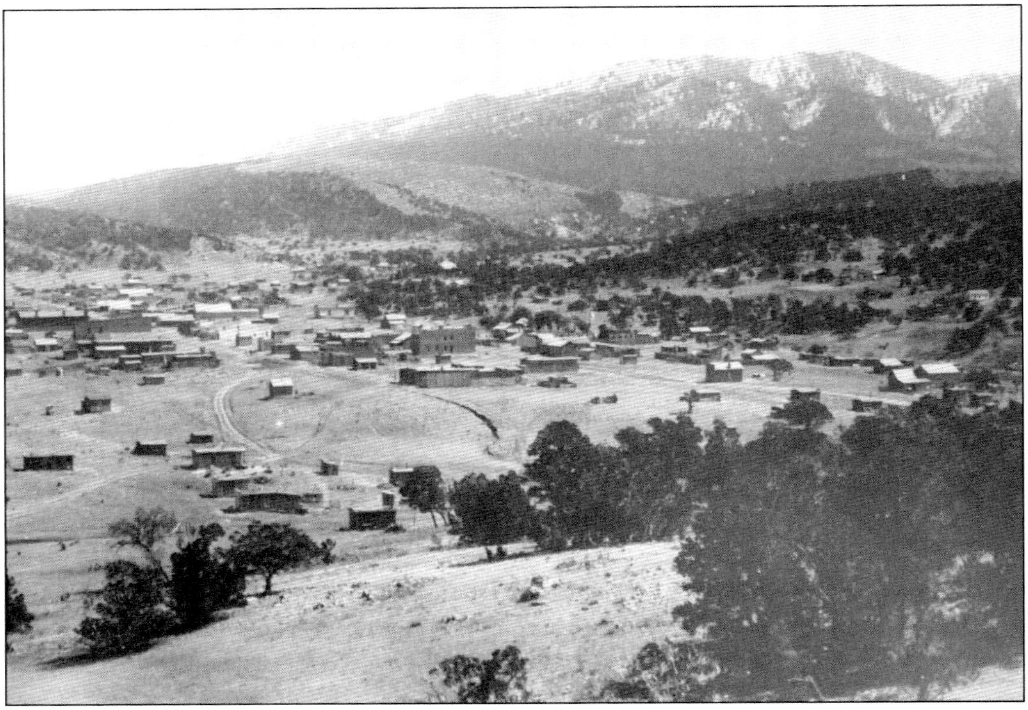

By 1880, White Oaks, named for nearby White Oaks Spring, was the hub of Lincoln County and the liveliest town in the whole territory. Nearly every Wild West cliché could be seen in White Oaks, with Billy the Kid often riding in with stolen horses to sell, Pat Garrett riding in after him on his trail, and prospectors gambling their gold away at the casino of a woman so slick she was known as Madam Varnish. All in all, White Oaks had two hotels, five general stores, seven saloons, three churches, a bank, a planing mill, a schoolhouse, an opera house, and the town published three newspapers. (Above, courtesy HSSNM #2160D; below, courtesy HSSNM #2160A.)

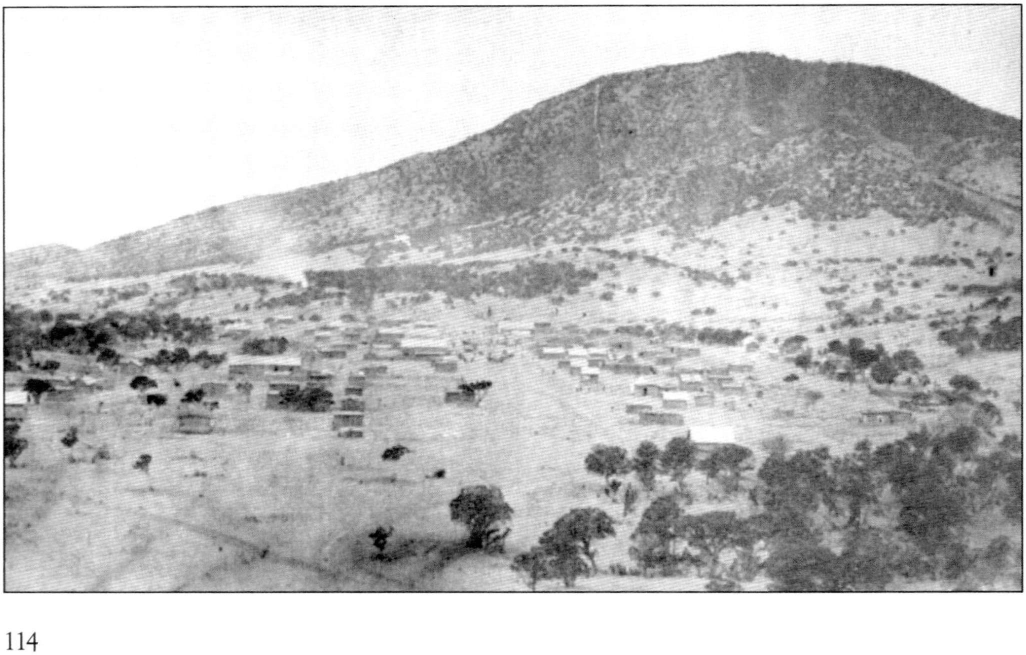

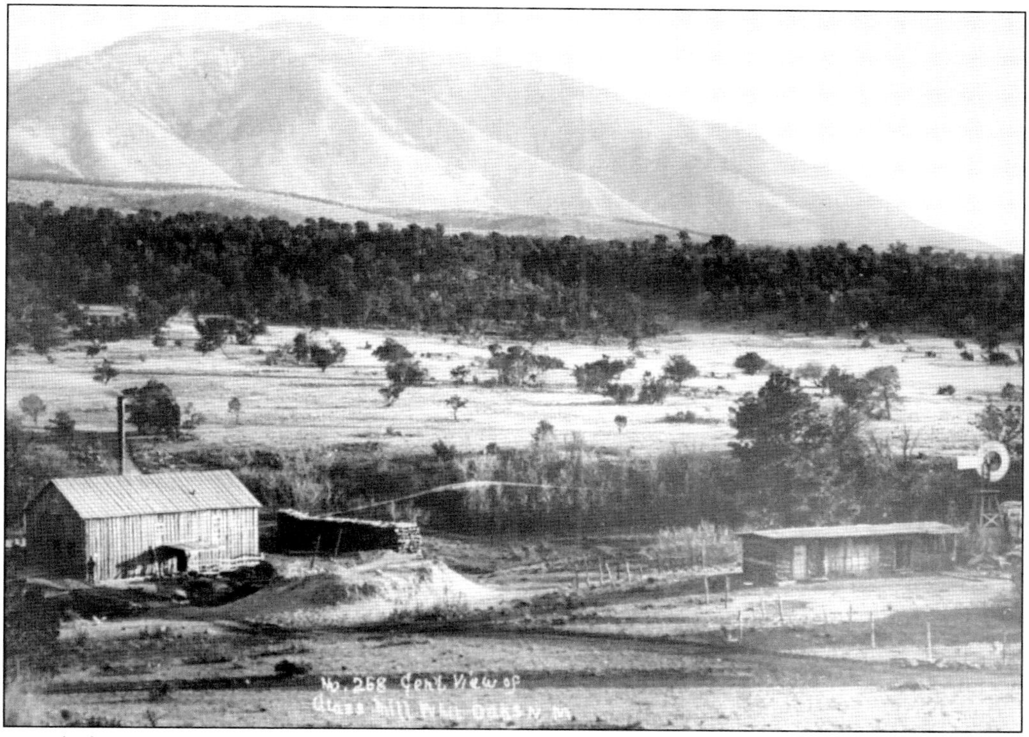

In only four short years, White Oaks accumulated 1,000 residents and even in later years was said to have as many as 4,000 people living in the area. But how did it almost become a ghost town? White Oaks boomed from about 1880 until 1900, when the railroad bypassed it for Carrizozo. With no railroad and with mines that would soon be depleted, people began to slowly drift away from White Oaks, though it was not officially dead until the post office shut down there in 1954. Below is the Cedarvale Cemetery, which houses people such as Susan McSween Barber, James Bell, and W. C. McDonald. (Above, courtesy HSSNM #2160C; below, courtesy HSSNM #2141A.)

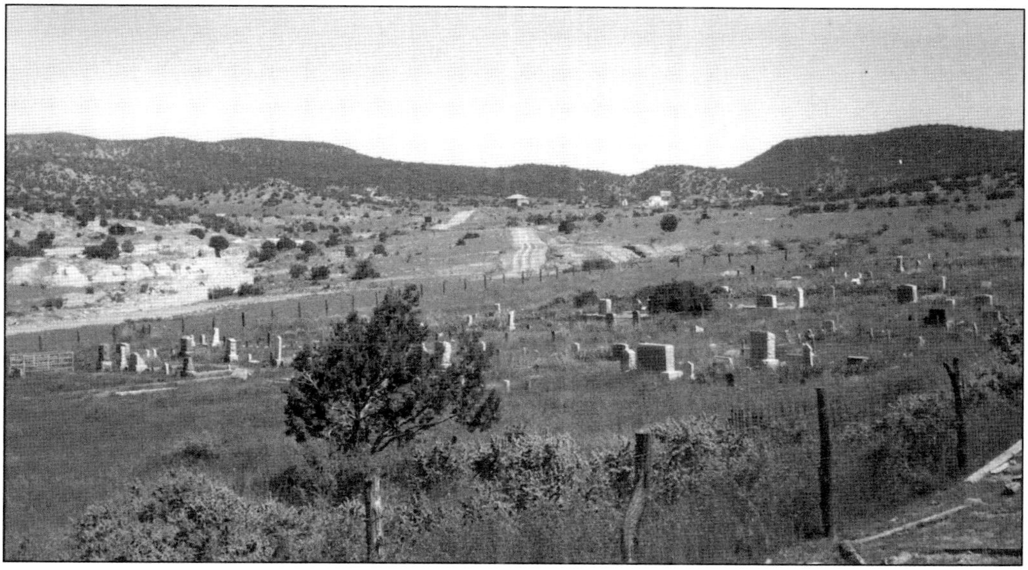

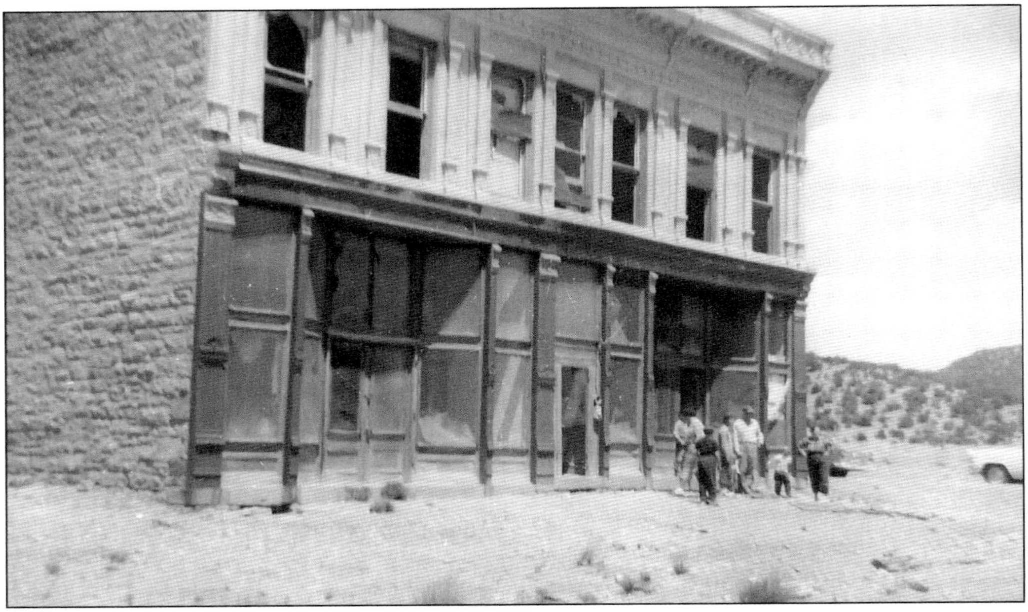

Today White Oaks is one of the finest and most well known "ghost towns" of the Old West. Artisans have begun restoring some of the older buildings, and some, such as the schoolhouse, are now open as museums. White Oaks also hosts various events, such as Gold Rush Days in the early summer. Travelers may also wish to stop at the No Scum Allowed Saloon, which still operates in the area. The White Oaks Exchange building is pictured above around 1956. Its second story housed the offices of W. C. McDonald, who would one day become the first governor of New Mexico when it became a state in 1912. An old White Oaks store is pictured below in April 1936. (Above, courtesy HSSNM #160; below, courtesy HSSNM #388.)

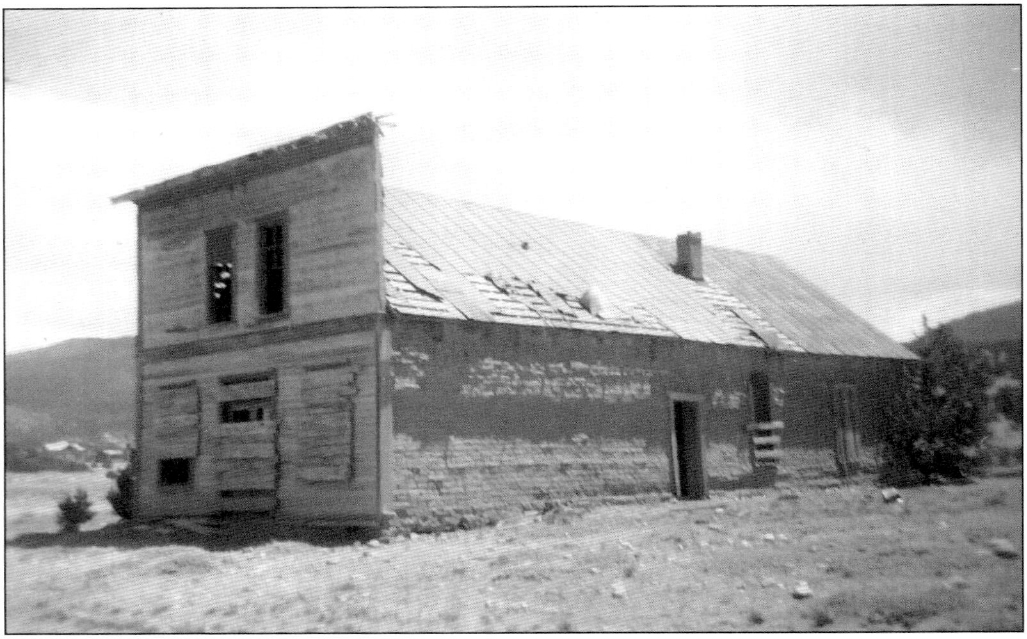

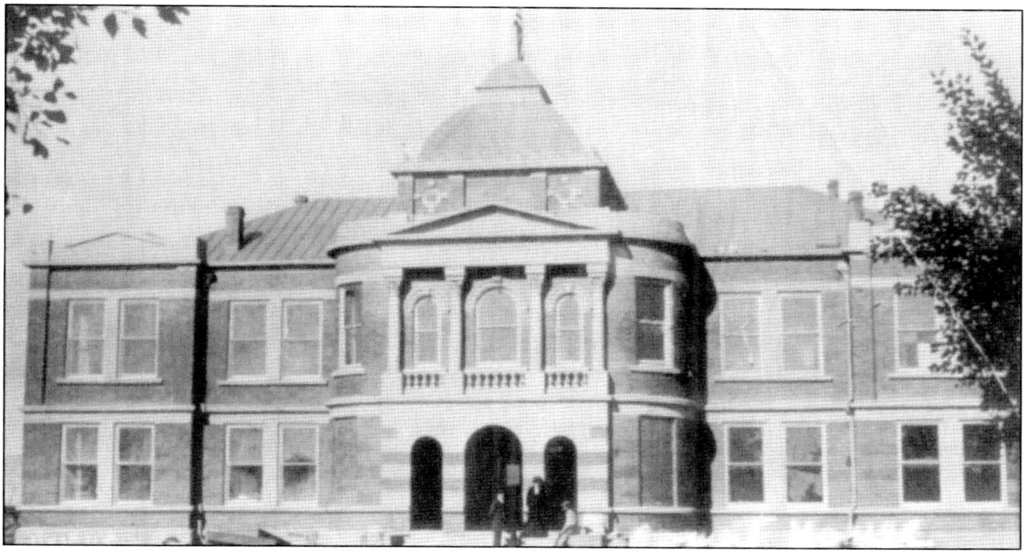

In 1913, the railroad town of Carrizozo became the new county seat of Lincoln County, although there was an initial protest by the Lincoln town residents where the county seat was originally located at the time. The vote to move the county seat to Carrizozo was actually carried out in 1909, but the U.S. Supreme Court would not legally settle the matter until 1913. On this page are two views of the original red-bricked Lincoln County Courthouse, although the bottom photograph incorrectly labels it as a Carrizozo public school. Unfortunately this beautiful structure was torn down in the 1960s to make way for a more modern facility for the courthouse. (Above, courtesy Johnson Stearns; below, courtesy HSSNM #1331.)

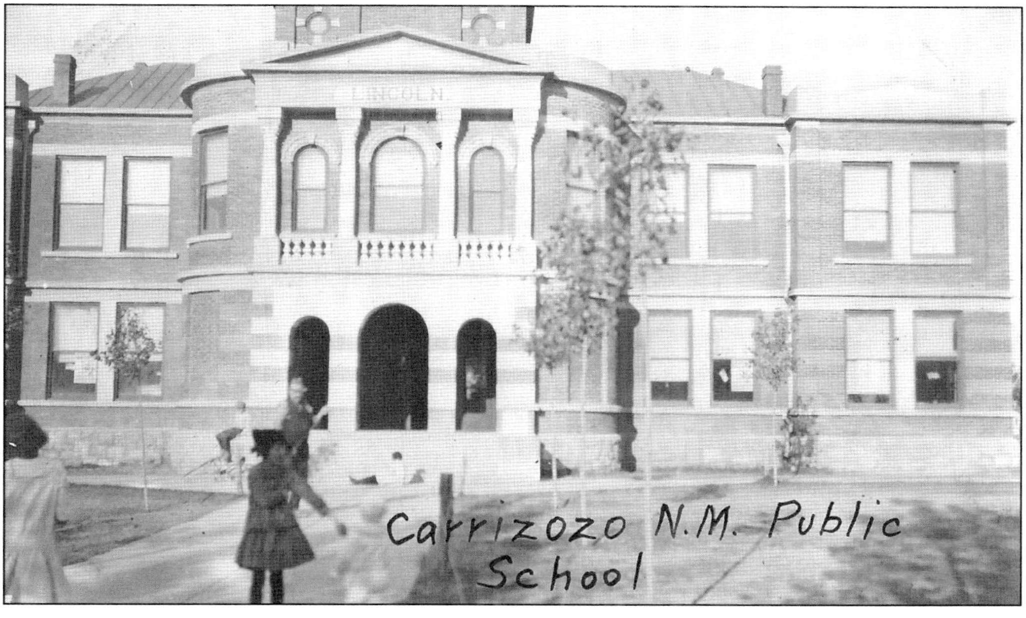

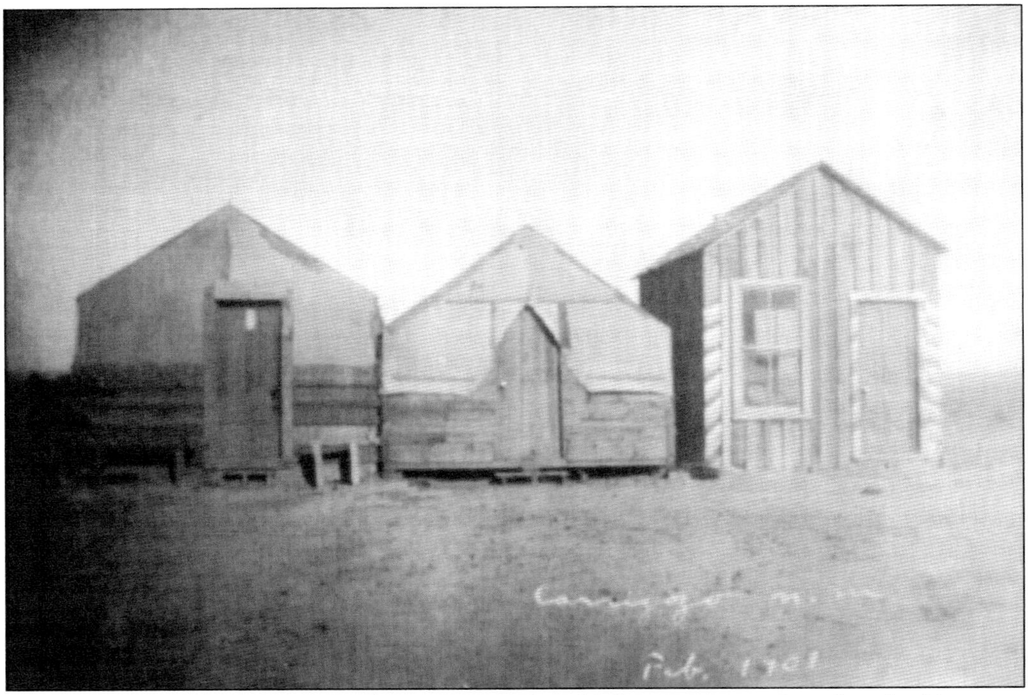

The photographs on this page display Carrizozo's humble beginnings; its first three buildings are above and its first café is below. Carrizozo had its birth in the railroad industry. Land promoter Charles B. Eddy, who also helped give birth to current day Carlsbad, and his brother, John, built a railroad line from El Paso to Santa Rosa, which had a branch line in Carrizozo and also extended through Capitan. Eddy's railroad line was called the El Paso and Northeastern but was renamed the El Paso and Southwestern when it was acquired by the Phelps Dodge Company. (Both courtesy Johnson Stearns.)

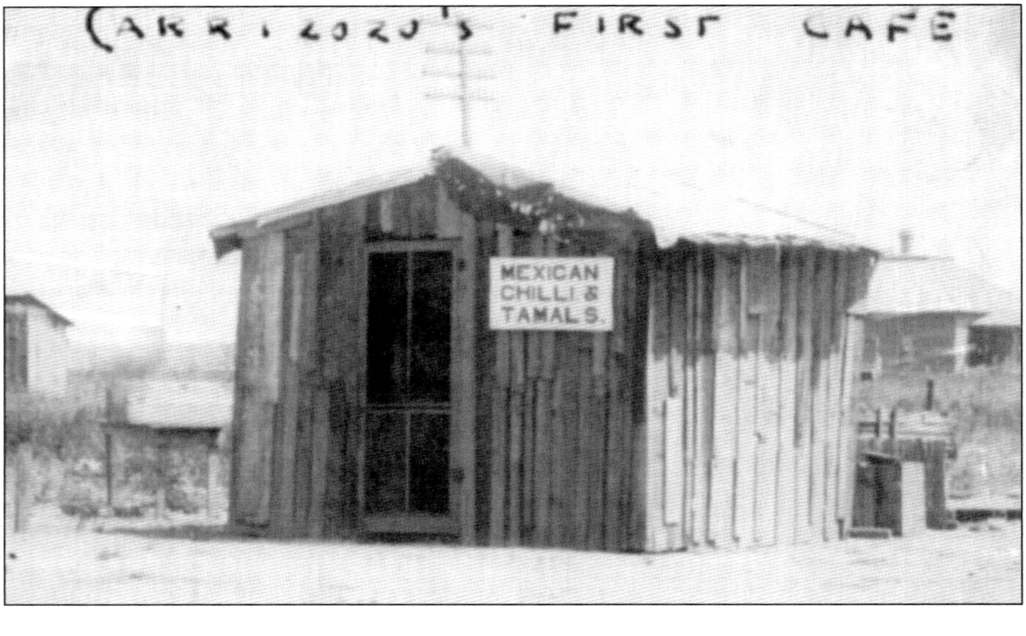

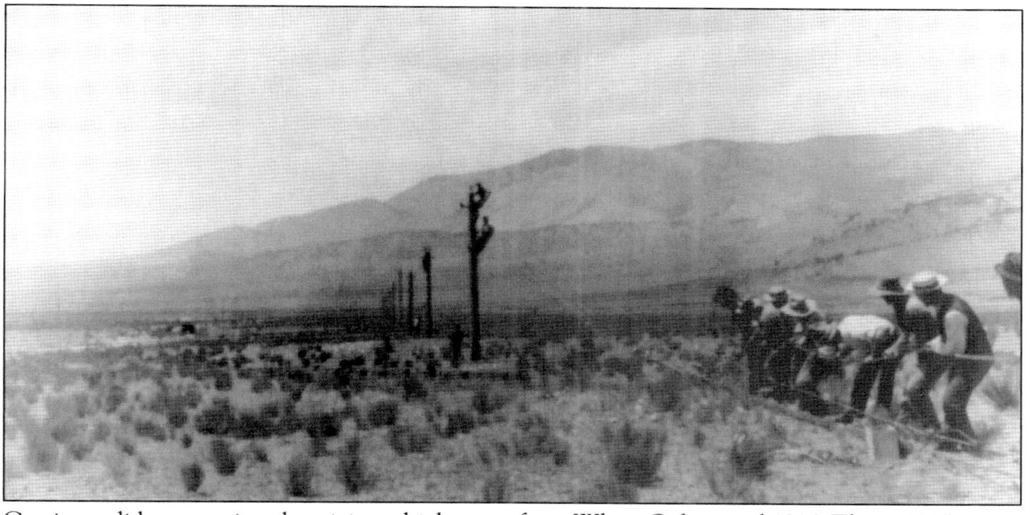

Carrizozo did not receive electricity, which came from White Oaks, until 1916. The *c.* 1915 image above shows electric lines from White Oaks being brought to the Parsons mine. Carrizozo used these same lines to get power. Eventually Carrizozo would outshine the booming mining town of White Oaks, which soon declined. (Courtesy Johnson Stearns.)

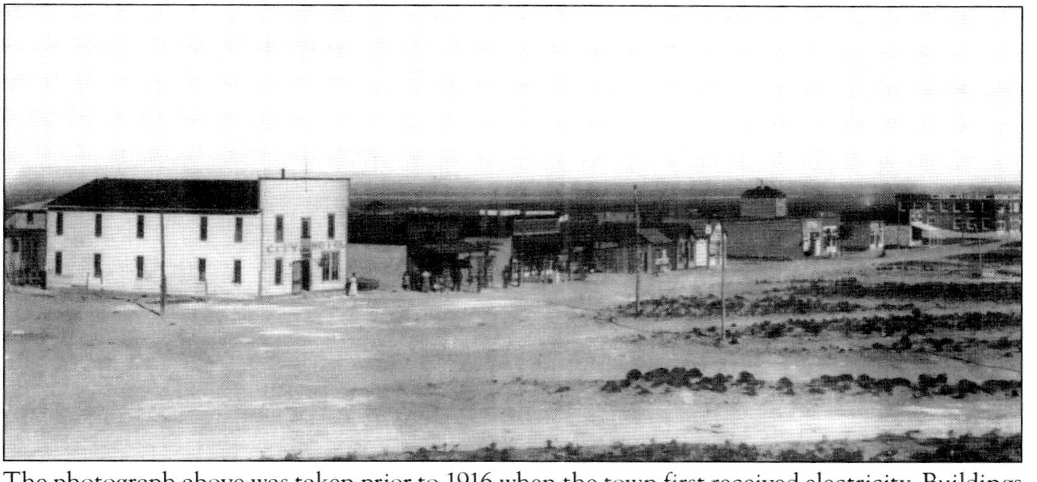

The photograph above was taken prior to 1916 when the town first received electricity. Buildings that can be seen in this view include the two-story city hotel, the Stag Saloon, Paden Drugstore, the Oriental Saloon, the town schoolhouse, and at the end of the street is the Exchange Bank. (Courtesy Johnson Stearns.)

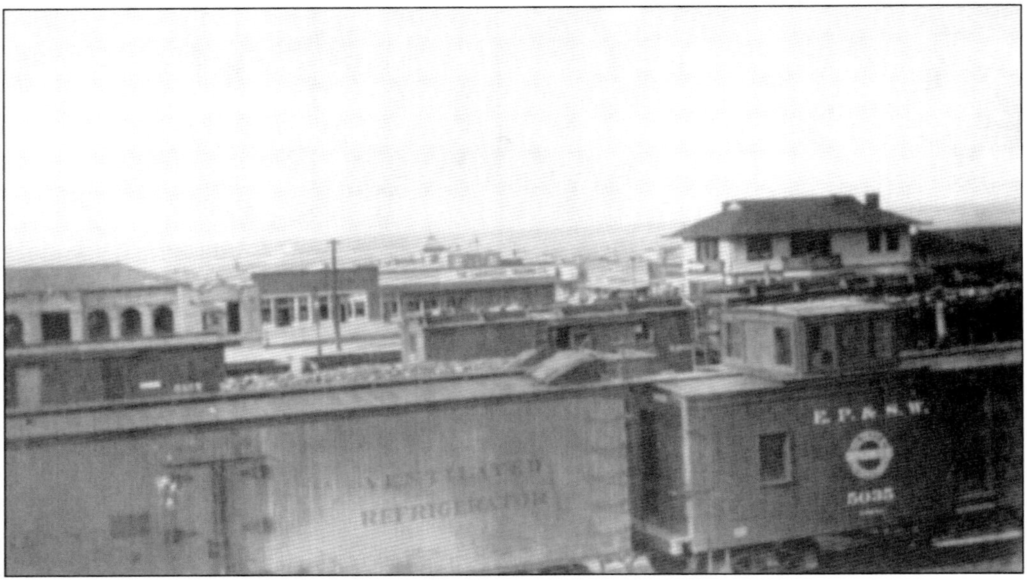

Carrizozo was named for the Spanish reed grass *carrizo*, which grows abundantly in the area, so abundantly that Carrizozo was named for them (the extra "zo" in Carrizozo emphasizes the abundance). At first the town was named Carrizo Flats when founded in 1899 and later Carrizo. James Allcook added the second "zo" in 1907 after the town had been platted. If one looks closely in these two images, they can spy the courthouse, unfinished in the left half of the photograph taken in 1912, and above, the courthouse dome can be seen in the background of the *c.* 1915 image. (Both courtesy Johnson Stearns.)

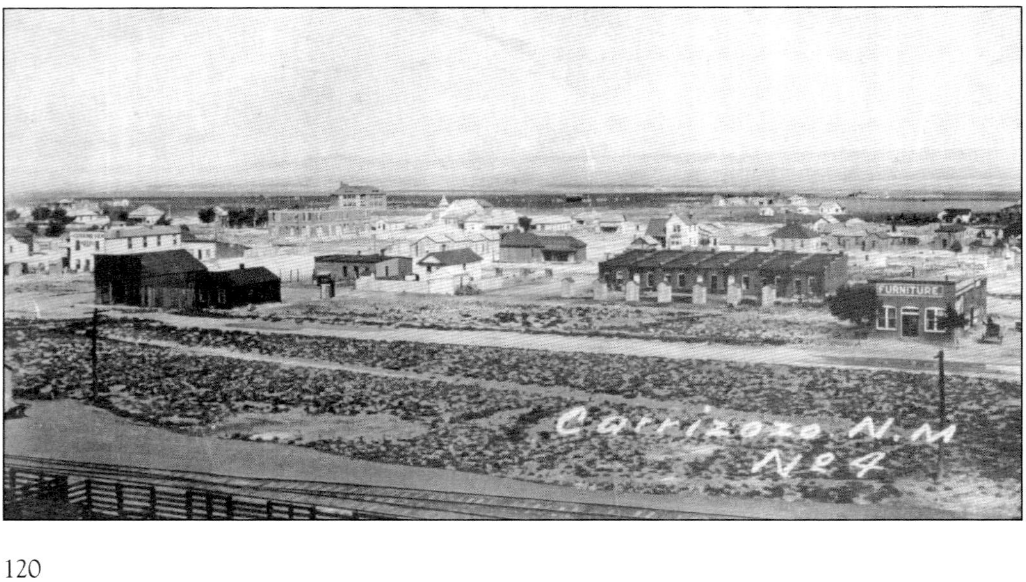

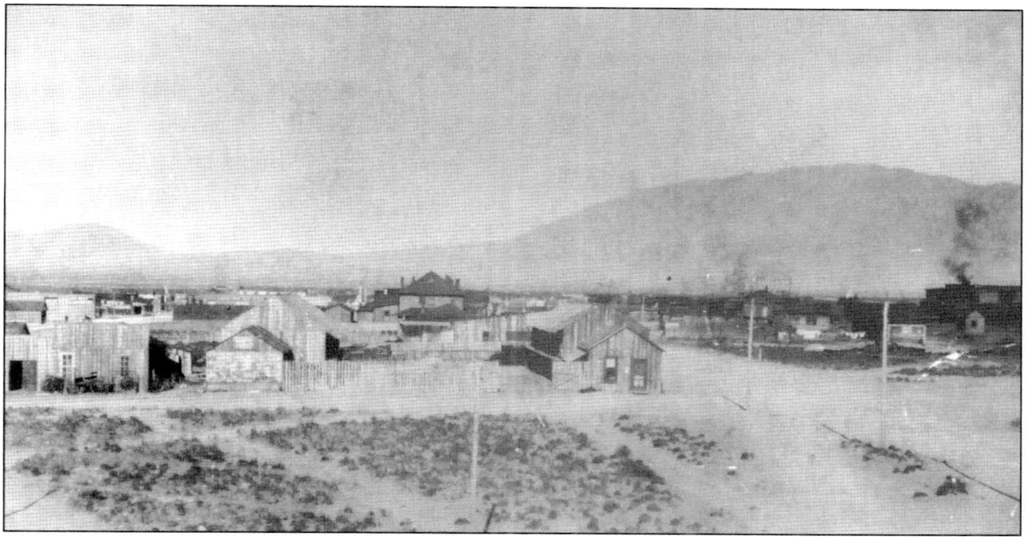

The grouping of buildings near the picket fence, pictured above, is Carrizozo's Western Lumberyard. To the far left in the foreground is the Robert Taylor Blacksmith Shop, and in the background behind it is the Ziegler Brothers Store. Toward the middle of the photograph is the El Paso and Southwestern Railroad Hotel, and to the far right in the distance is Carrizo Mountain. Below is the East edge of Carrizozo around 1915. It was in the decade between 1910 and 1920 that Carrizozo would grow from only 1,000 people to over 2,000. (Both courtesy Johnson Stearns.)

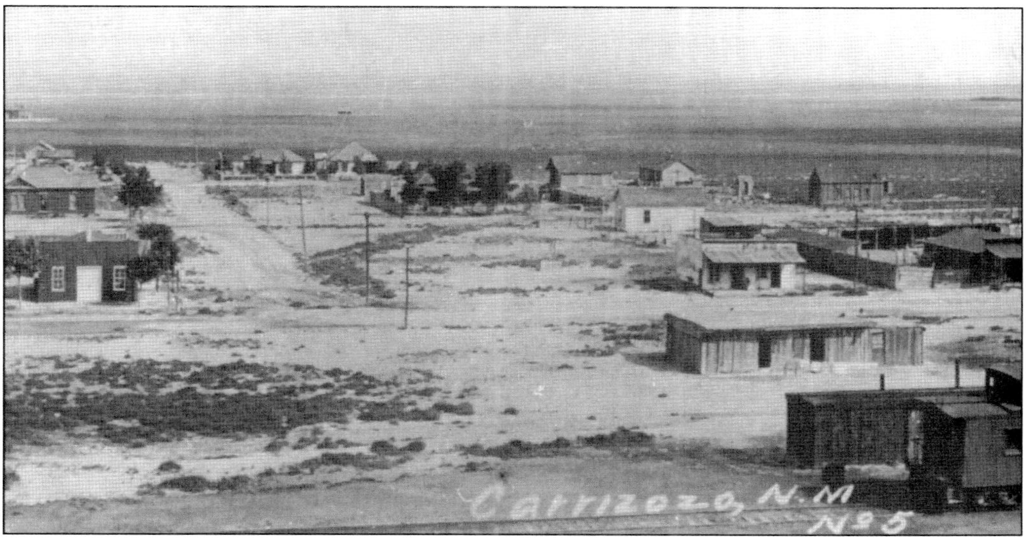

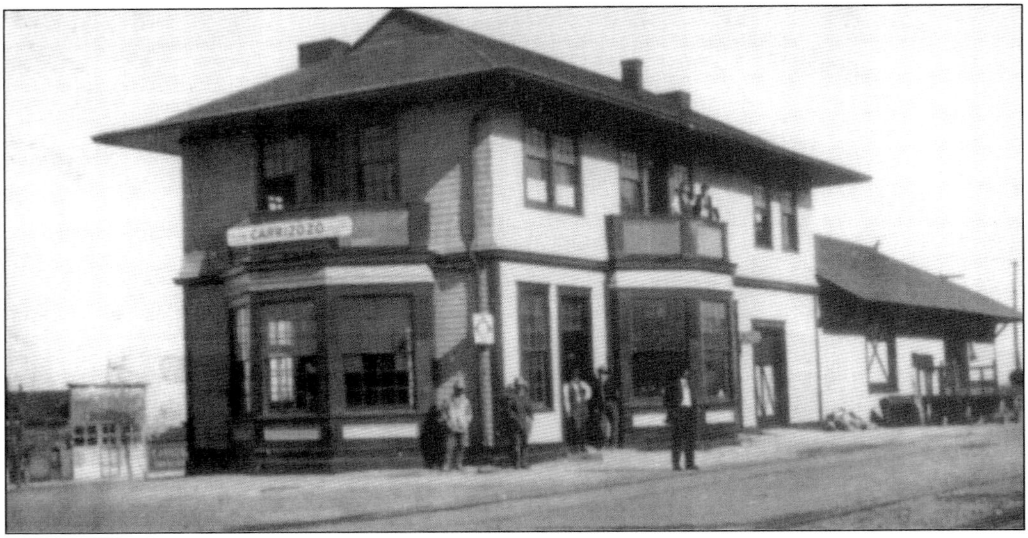

Shown on this page are two of Carrizozo's most important facets: its railroad depot (above) and the Carrizozo roundhouse (below), located directly across from the depot. The roundhouse came complete with a turntable, which can be seen in the photograph below. The Carrizozo roundhouse also had 12 stalls for the engines; however, later the engines were so large that they could no longer fit on the turntable, rendering it out of date and no longer usable. (Both courtesy Johnson Stearns.)

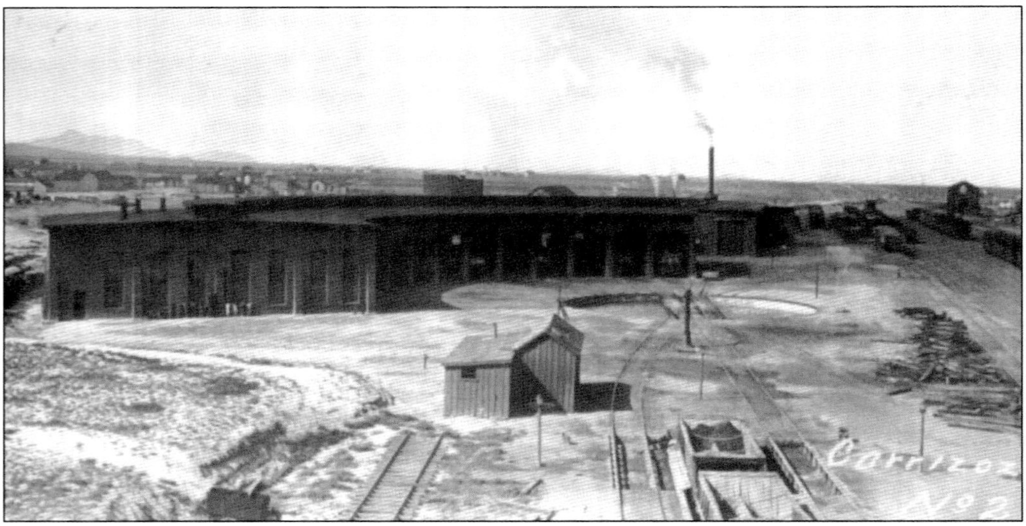

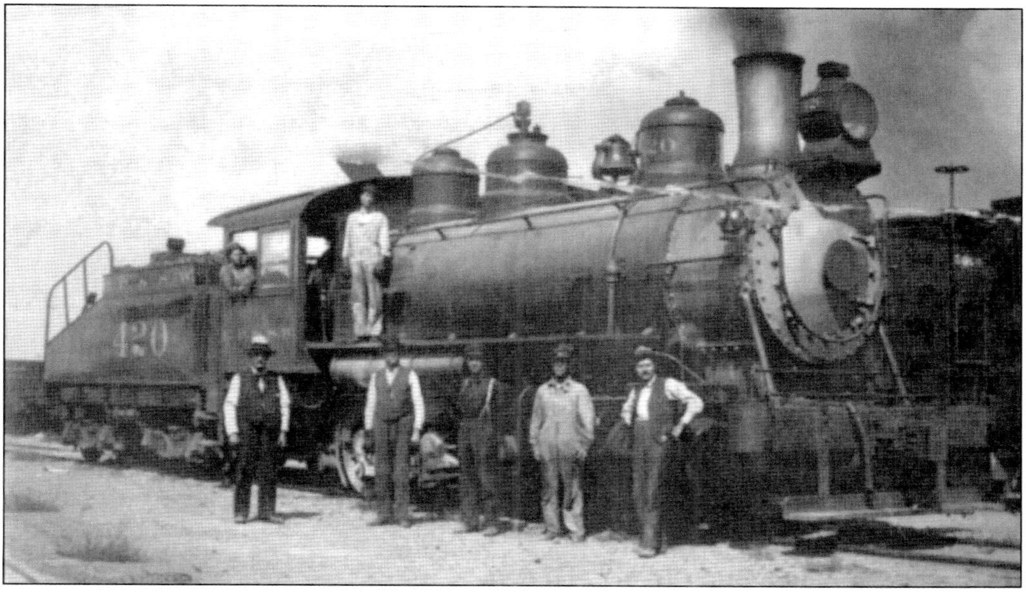

Most all of the Carrizozo photographs in this book came from the collection of Johnson Stearns. Stearns has lived in Carrizozo now for more than 90 years, is an avid promoter of the town, and stays heavily involved in the community. His parents arrived in Carrizozo at the start of the 20th century to begin work on the new railroad there. In the c. 1914 image above, third from right, is O. S. Stearns, part of the switch engine crew. Below is the El Paso and Southwestern Railroad Clubhouse for the railroad men. (Both courtesy Johnson Stearns.)

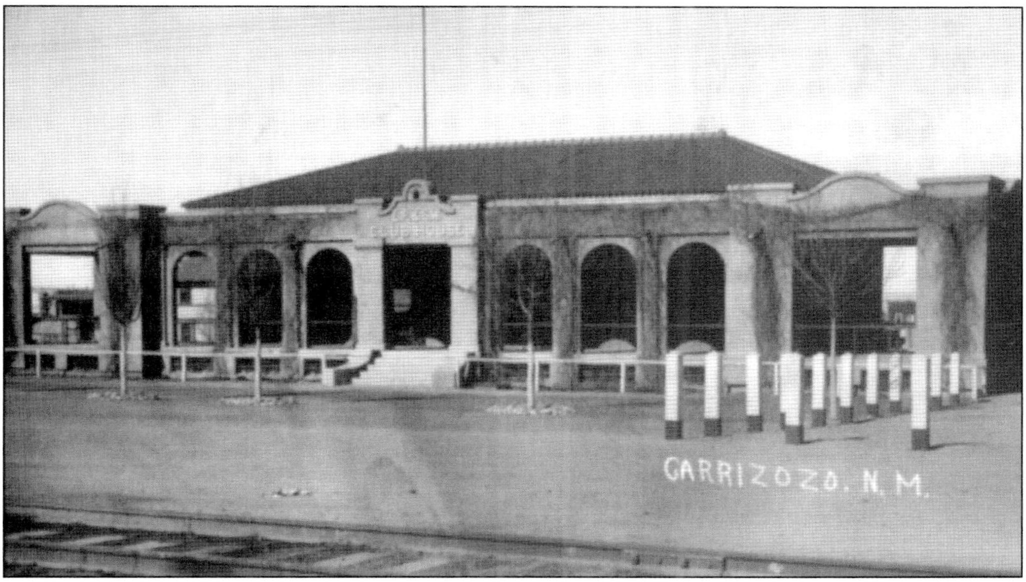

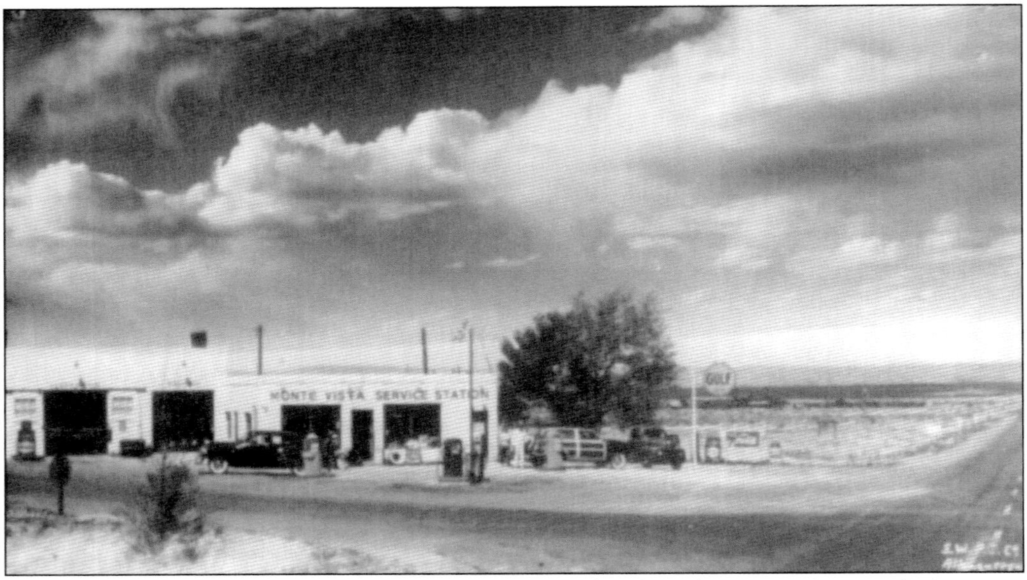

The Monte Vista Service Station, owned by Albert and Euda Roberts, was destroyed when a jet airplane crashed into it in 1947. The plane had made an emergency landing in Carrizozo the day before and crashed into the service station during a failed takeoff. The pilot and one other man were killed, and a young boy was seriously burned. (Courtesy Johnson Stearns.)

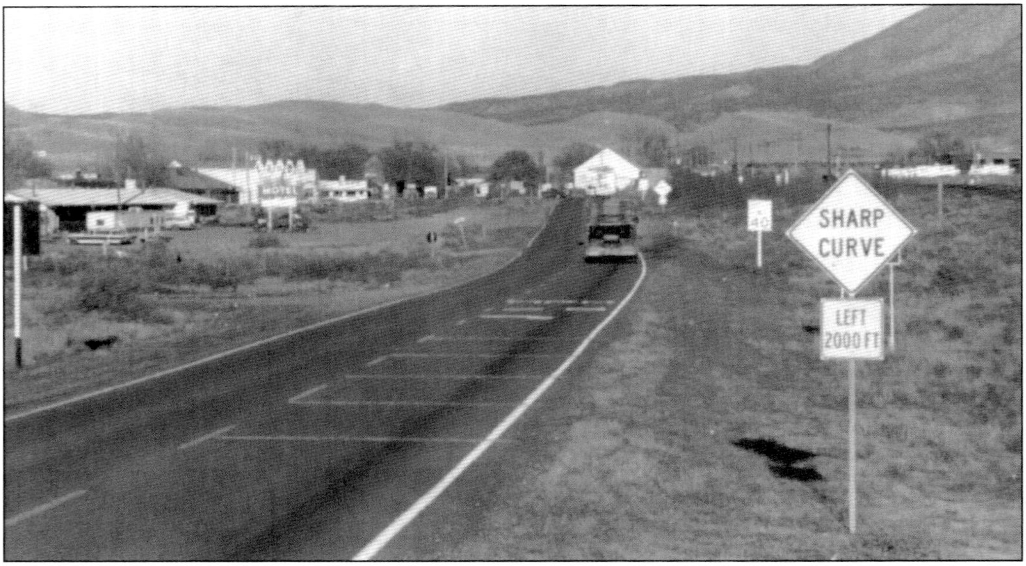

Carrizozo managed to outlive many of the towns that preceded it in birth, such as White Oaks, and remains the county seat today even though Ruidoso now has the highest population count of any village in Lincoln County. You can find Carrizozo at the crossroads of U.S. Highway 380 and U.S. 54. A more recent picture from the 1970s showcases Carrizozo as it is today. (Courtesy Johnson Stearns.)

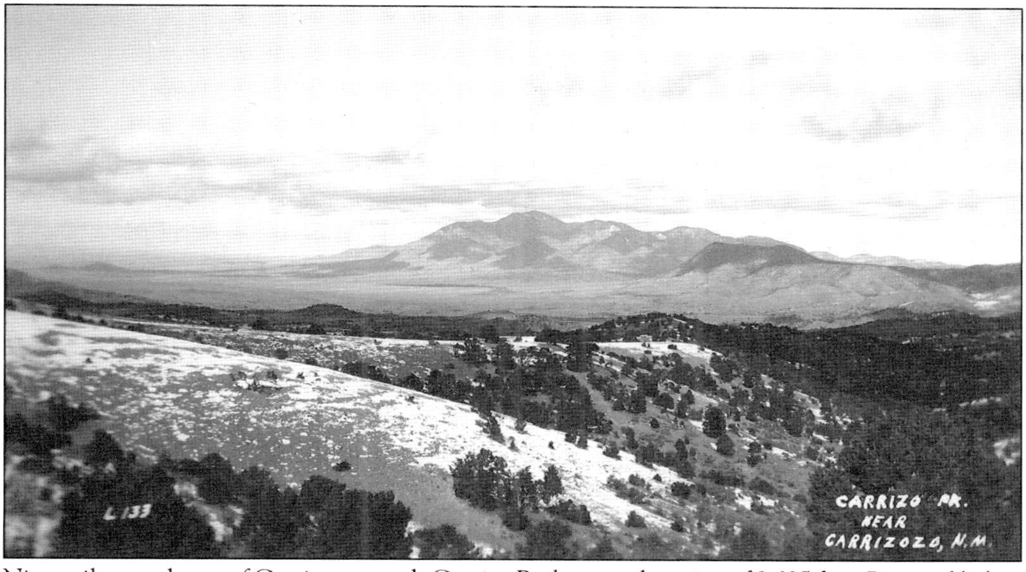

Nine miles northeast of Carrizozo stands Carrizo Peak at an elevation of 9,605 feet. Pictured below is the famous Valley of Fires State Park, a jagged landscape of black molten lava that spewed from Little Black Peak about 2,000 years ago. Valley of Fires, also known as the Carrizozo Malpais, was established in 1966 and is one of the most remarkable and best-preserved lava beds in the United States. It is located only 3 miles west of Carrizozo. From the town of Lincoln, a monument to the Wild West, to the quaint villages of the Hondo Valley, to mountain towns such as Capitan and Ruidoso, there is much to see and do in Lincoln County. Come and visit soon. (Above, courtesy HSSNM Larkham Album 3 #473; below, courtesy HSSNM Larkham Album 3 #6281.)

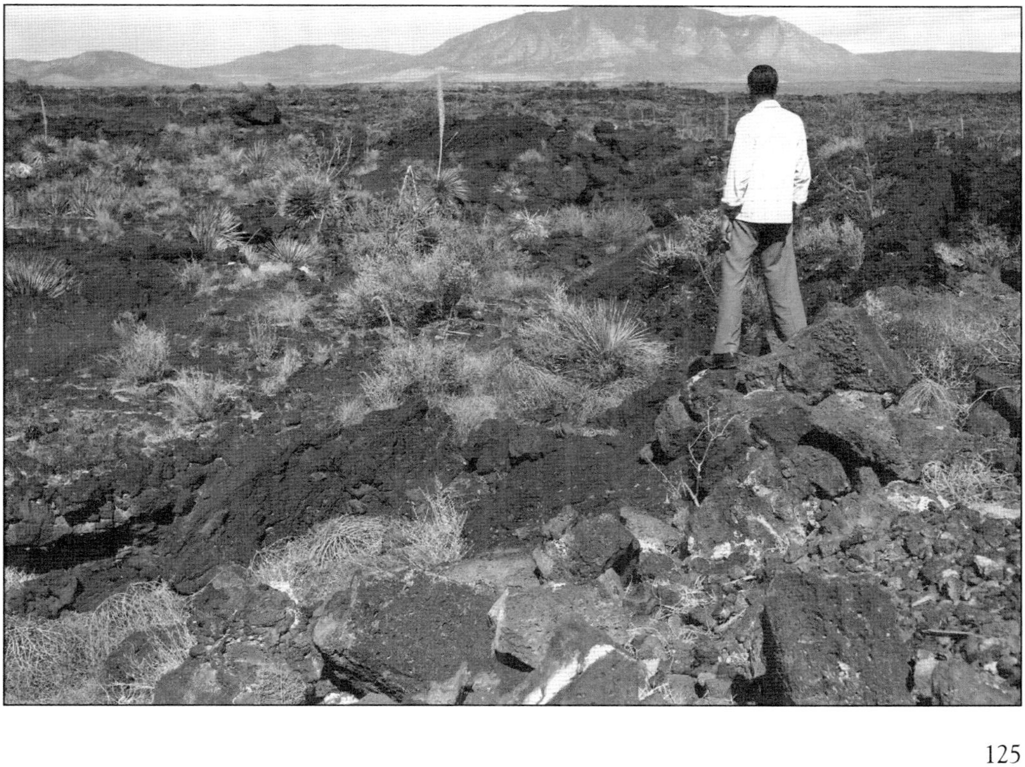

Bibliography

Banks, Phyllis Eileen. *Roaming Southern New Mexico.* Roswell, NM: By the Author, 2003.

Bell, Bob Boze. *The Illustrated Life and Times of Billy the Kid.* Phoenix, AZ: Tri Star Boze Publications, 1996.

Bonney, Cecil. *Looking Over My Shoulder: Seventy-five Years in the Pecos Valley.* Roswell, NM: By the author, 1971.

Fleming, Elvis E. and Ernestine Chesser Williams. *Treasures of History II: Chaves County Vignettes.* Roswell, NM: Historical Society for Southeast New Mexico, 1991.

Fugate, Francis L. and Roberta B. *Roadside History of New Mexico.* Missoula, MT: Mountain Press Publishing Co., 1989.

Henn, Walter R. *A Stroll Thru Old Lincoln Town.* Lincoln, NM: Lincoln County Historical Society Publications, 1996.

Julyan, Robert. *The Place Names of New Mexico.* Albuquerque, NM: University of New Mexico Press, 1996.

Kidder, Lyn and Herb Brunell. *Images of America: Ruidoso and Ruidoso Downs.* Charleston, SC: Arcadia Publishing, 2009.

Lincoln County Historical Society. *A Walking Tour of Old Lincoln Town.* Lincoln, NM: Lincoln County Historical Society, 2007.

Lippmann, Lionel W. and Virginia Watson-Jones. *Capitan, New Mexico 1900-2000: Home of Smokey Bear, the Living Symbol.* Capitan, NM: Friends of Smokey-Capitan, Inc., 2000.

Mullin, Robert N., ed. *Maurice G. Fulton's History of the Lincoln County War.* Tucson, AZ: University of Arizona Press, 1968.

Roswell Museum and Art Center. *Peter Hurd: The Roswell Museum and Art Center Collection.* Roswell, NM: Roswell Museum and Art Center, 1999.

Shinkle, James D. *Reminiscences of Roswell Pioneers.* Roswell, NM: By the Author, 1966.

Stearns, Johnson. *The Carrizozo Story.* Carrizozo, NM: self-published, 1987.

Wiggins, Walt. *Lincoln, New Mexico as it Was One Day.* Roswell, NM: Western Heritage Press, 1975.

INDEX